SACRED RELATIONSHIPS

*The Psychospiritual Path to Love,
Intimacy and Happiness*

Also By

DONNA BOONE & MICHAEL MCDONALD

SACRED RELATIONSHIPS WORKBOOK
(ISBN 0-9658841-1-2)

INJUSTICE FOR ALL
(ISBN 0-9658841-2-0)

SACRED RELATIONSHIPS

*The Psychospiritual Path to Love,
Intimacy and Happiness*

Donna L. Boone, Ed.D.
R. Michael McDonald, Ed.D.

BHP

BENTHALL
HALL
PUBLISHERS
Richmond, Virginia

SACRED RELATIONSHIPS
The Psychospiritual Path to Love, Intimacy and Happiness

A Benthall Hall Publishers paperback edition

Copyright © 1997 by Donna L. Boone, Ed.D.
and R. Michael McDonald, Ed.D.

Cover art and design © by The Creative Source Group
Kansas City Missouri

For information address: Benthall Hall Publishers

The personal stories in this book are composites of several actual cases. The names and identifying information have been changed to protect client confidentiality. The situations described are fairly represented, but are not descriptive of any one individual.

Benthall Hall Publishers, 10507 Mountainbrook Court
Richmond, Va. 23233-2629

PRINTED IN THE UNITED STATES OF AMERICA

First printing: July 1997

10   9   8   7   6   5   4   3   2

Library of Congress Cataloging-in-Publication Data
Boone, Donna L. (Donna Lynn)
McDonald, R. Michael (Richard Michael)

Sacred Relationships: the psychospiritual path to love, intimacy, and happiness

1. Psychospiritual therapy. 2. Codependency.
3. Soul mates. I. Title.

ISBN 0-9658841-0-4

This book is dedicated to
Patrick, Kelly, Dana, and David

God bless you on your journey to truth,
empowerment, and sacred relationships

Acknowledgments

The inspiration for this book came from true life experiences -- from our experiences and from the lives of our clients, our family and our friends. Many who know us will recognize a story that hits close to home, however, the names and identities have been disguised to protect the confidentiality of family, friends and clients. While the situations described in the book are fairly represented, they are not actual descriptions of any one individual.

Many we'd like to thank personally we cannot because of the confidentiality criterion. Please consider yourselves appreciated and thanked for sharing your dreams, your life stories, and your struggles toward empowerment with us. Those strong enough to look at themselves honestly and push themselves through the emotional catharsis of *tunnel work* are very special and rare people indeed. You know who you are. God bless you in your journey to full empowerment.

We'd also like to thank family and friends who have heard us talk about this book for a couple of years now. Thank you for understanding when we were too busy to have fun with you. Thank you for standing by us when we needed support in our journey.

We love you.

Donna & Michael

1997

Contents

Acknowledgments i

Index ii

Introduction 1

Chapter 1: Awakening to Our Inner Truth 5

Donna's Story Masks of Conventionality*
Meaning Concealed in Life Patterns*The Inner
Drive toward Empowerment and Unity*Awakening
to the Call for Inner Growth and Truth*Michael's
Story*

Chapter 2: The Road to Empowerment 31

*Path to Self Empowerment and Empowered Love *
Awareness of Unity*Beginning the Individuation
Process*Detours into Codependency*Completion of
Individuation*Learning to Connect Interdependently*
Readiness for a Sacred Relationship*

Chapter 3: The Pull toward Unity 51

*The Road to Unity*Ingredients Needed for
Interpersonal Unity*Seeing the Difference
between True and False Unity *Human Unity
and Unconditional Love*Spiritual Unity*

Chapter 4: Beginning Individuation: Learning 75
to Define the Self

*Understanding the Interpersonal Dynamics
of Thwarted Individuation*Scrutiny of
Selfishness and Selflessness*Commitment to
Full Individuation and Empowerment*

Chapter 5: Codependency: The Parasitic 107
Connections We Call Love

*Characteristics of Codependency*Complementary
Control Dramas of Codependent Couples*The
Codependent Family*Summary: The Bridge
from Codependency to Empowerment*

Chapter 6: Individuation Completion: *149*
The Decision to Leave Codependency

Incentives for Staying Asleep* What Is
Individuation Completion*An Overview of
Tunnel Work*Therapy and Tunnel Work*
The Spiritual Wake-Up Call*The Struggle
between Eros and Thanatos*Shortcuts through
Tunnel Work that Don't Work

Chapter 7: Tunnel Work: The Path *183*
through Darkness into Light

Commitments of Tunnel Work* The
Outcome and Rewards of Tunnel Work

Chapter 8: Discernment: Seeing, ... *219*
Sifting and Separating

The Stages of Discernment * We Must See
What Empowerment Is*Seeing Maturational
Differences*Sifting Through Differences in
Essence*Essence of Evil: Disciples of Darkness*
Essence of Power: Power Mongers*Essence of Fear:
Disempowered Dependents*Essence of Truth:
Armored Awake*Essence of Love: Disciples of
Light*How Discernment is a Tool for Growth

Chapter 9: Interdependency: Reaching Out *265*
in Power and Love

The Need for Emotional and Intellectual
Integration * Choosing Other Graduate
Students to Connect With * Characteristics
of interdependent Relationships*Steps for
Achieving Interdependent Relationships

Chapter 10: Sacred Relationship: The Final Exam *299*

The Purposes of Sacred Relationships*Teach
Us to Connect Fully * Cleanse Us of Residual
Fears and Unhealed Wounds * Mirror, Integrate,
and Balance the Divine Feminine and Divine*
Masculine* Test Attainment of Self Actualization*
Teach Us about Divine Love

Epilogue *319*

References *325*

About the Authors *309*

Sacred Relationship Seminars & Retreats *311*

Sacred Relationship Workbook *313*

SACRED RELATIONSHIPS:

The Psychospiritual Path to Love, Intimacy and Happiness

Introduction

SACRED RELATIONSHIPS:

The Psychospiritual Path to Love, Intimacy, and Happiness

The dawning of the new millennium presents a paradox. We find our world shrinking as satellites and fiber-optics connect us instantly with virtually everyone else on the planet. Fax machines, cable television, cellular telephones, and the Internet -- they all make it easier to reach out. Yet, despite this, we grow further apart. The very technology that should facilitate our more direct and intimate connection with each other increasingly isolates us. The process of connecting has become more important than the purpose. The substance and meaning in our connections have diminished.

Confronted by the many pressures of life, the one-way communication provided by machines has become an escape and a drug that numbs us to emotional sensitivity. We come home and turn on the television or radio for diversion. We engulf ourselves in busy-ness to avoid thinking and feeling. It's uncomfortable talking with friends or family members about substantive matters - so we don't. Our lives become shallow rituals of doing. We avoid the discomfort of real, honest and intimate human connections. Some of us have forgotten and the rest of us have never learned how to connect meaningfully with others. We freeze in fear of exposing ourselves to the pain of rejection, disappointment or judgment. We entomb ourselves behind false social masks believing they will protect us, yet all they do is isolate and separate us from others. In the deepest part of our knowing is a voice telling us we're starving -- dying a little more each day. We're starving from the lack of truth, joy, love, and deep intimate connection.

Sacred Relationships is about the journey through and beyond human loneliness, isolation, and fear. It presents a road map to that place of true human bonding and intimate connectedness. It leads through the maze of anxiety and self-doubt, helping us to acknowledge and accept difficulties as valuable life lessons. Our

3

empowerment begins when we acknowledge that we're not victims or pawns in life's cruel drama. When we choose empowerment, we choose to grow through our fears and limitations and to move beyond them. We become free to shape our lives and be who we really are. Embracing self-love enables us to give our *real* selves to others. We are ready for honest, intimate, and satisfying connections.

Sacred Relationships is not a book of shallow rules and clichés. It presents a different way of looking at self-development and relationships. Instead of recipes for "doing and acting," *Sacred Relationships* encourages us to drop our acting and instead work on our "being." We are gently led to that place deep within where the real *us* lives. As we come to know ourselves fully, we are free to admit our fears and grow beyond them.

This message is not new. Psychotherapists have been preaching emotional catharsis for over one hundred years. Yet, psychotherapy only goes so far. After opening our hurts and fears, psychotherapy often stops, not knowing where to go next to help us to heal. After expunging the hurts and pains of a lifetime, we are often left hanging -- not wanting to return to the past, but having no positive model for the future. Expunging our darkness leaves a vacuum that must be filled with light and hope. If that vacuum remains unfilled, despair and hopelessness rush in, filling us with heaviness and depression.

Becoming empowered means committing to full emotional, intellectual, and spiritual integration and balance. It is through this process -- this journey into wholeness -- that we become able to give ourselves openly and honestly to others. It is here that we find and achieve true heart connections. *Sacred Relationships* describes the journey and the detours that distract and tempt us along the way. The journey to self-empowerment and sacred relationships is the most interesting, most difficult, and most important journey of your life. Are you ready to begin?

4

Chapter One

Awakening to Our Inner Truth

Awakening to Our Inner Truth

Donna's Story

The cafe was crowded and noisy as usual. As university colleagues, we often ate lunch together. Nothing was unusual about today, except the absence of others who routinely ate with us. But everyone else was busy and Michael and I ended up together for our lunch time meal. Perhaps it was the sense of solitude in the midst of blurred chatter that added to Michael's reflective mood. His brow creased in concentrated urgency. The energy of powerful emotions was evident before he spoke.

His moist eyes showed the accumulated hurts of a lifetime when he looked up and asked questions painful to voice, painful to admit even having. "Why can't people connect honestly and deeply with one another? Why can't we get rid of our defensive masks and be real with each other? Why do people have relationships that are just about game playing, control, and manipulation? Why are people so afraid of each other they have to hide who they really are?"

For that brief moment, he did exactly what he was asking others to do. He made himself vulnerable to another and revealed his inner self. This brilliant man who had answers for most questions was admitting his bewilderment about human relating. His emotional candor was uncharacteristic. He usually spoke from his head and not his heart. This time he risked revealing a deeper level as the pain of his emptiness pushed aside his self-protective demeanor.

My heart bridged the emotional distance between us, but my head signaled a warning to self-protect. The quaver in my voice betrayed my head-heart conflict. "What you're saying is true. People aren't honest with each other. They don't know how to connect. They don't know how to be real with others. I don't understand this either. Let me think about your questions."

How was I going to answer questions for him I had not yet answered for myself? His questions became the impetus for examining my own life and the emptiness lurking just below my conscious surface. My twenty years as a psychotherapist had prepared me to analyze psychological and emotional blocks to human health and development. I used proven strategies for increasing communication and resolving disagreements. But these techniques were far from adequate to answer the deeper questions Michael asked. Why couldn't people genuinely and fearlessly connect with others? Why do we continue to protect the emotional barriers that only separate us?

I recognized my professional answers were safe and glib. Psychotherapists routinely revert to an expert stance and hide from the painful work to become real ourselves. Only when we risk breaking through our own denial, and only when we dare walk the path of truth in addressing our own pain, will we find the answers needed to guide ourselves and help others. My education only provided hollow and false answers. The true answers could only come from the depth of my inner knowing -- and I hadn't done the work to get to my own truth.

Michael's questions were about becoming fully empowered to live in his truth. He was asking why people didn't do the work to know who they really were -- what they felt, what they thought, what was the deeper meaning of their life experience. His questions were also about sharing this truth and meaning with others and connecting on a deep level of human unity.

Unity is complete emotional, intellectual and spiritual connection. Most of us navigate through life in a semi- comatose state of denial. We fail to look at ourselves and the emotional impediments to our full empowerment. We stay at a surface level of understanding and never develop into the fully vitalized, powerful forces for creative change that could be our destiny. Our human relationships remain superficial and unsatisfying. We long for an end to our loneliness and insecurity. We dream of human connections free of defensive barriers. However, we fail to achieve true connection with others because we haven't first looked inside ourselves and become who we are -- fully empowered, lovable, and guiltless.

Many people search outside themselves for the answer. They search for the perfect soul mate to complete their incompleteness. They search for the friend who will allow them to reveal themselves completely. In the end, most are disappointed and disillusioned. They fail because they cannot fill up from the outside. They cannot *make* a deep soul connection with another. They can only commit to becoming fully actualized, complete in and of themselves, *and then* commit to joining with others who are able to connect in total fullness. They first have to clear themselves of all fears and neediness. They must see themselves clearly and the world clearly. They must cultivate the courage to live their truth while resisting the world's pressure to conform.

Masks of Conventionality

Instead of clearing ourselves of fears and neediness, we cover our imperfections and fears with social masks. These masks are invisible to most because self-protection seems normal and necessary. It is out of the ordinary to show vulnerability and honesty. Those who have faced their inner demons of fear and neediness are able to embrace their specialness, take off their social masks, and freely live in the truth of who they are. Removing their masks clears their vision and they're able to see the protective defenses -- the masks -- that shield and isolate others. By learning to see themselves and their own impediments to full empowerment, they learn to see others as they are.

In childhood and throughout adolescence, I had a repetitive dream. I saw myself as an actress in a play. There were about a dozen other actors on stage with me. I saw the glistening wooden floor of the long, but narrow stage. The glare and heat of intense

9

stage lights felt uncomfortable. I, like the other actors, wore a heavy robe fashioned of burlap sackcloth that was dingy and mud colored. Each of us wore large, papier-mache masks. These brightly colored masks reminded me of Mardi Gras costume faces with grotesque exaggerations reflecting comedy and tragedy. Tragedy was predominant: most actors wore masks of grief, rage, fear, despair, and sadness. We moved with mechanical precision and exaggerated gestures. Then we stopped moving and bowed our heads. The curtain lowered. When the applause faded, I eagerly took off my mask. I felt great relief without its weight and suffocating confinement. I was too warm in the heavy robe and now joyously shed it too. The semi-darkness behind the stage curtain provided privacy and security.

For a few minutes I stood on stage enjoying the breeze through my light clothing and in my hair. I felt free and appreciated the sensations so recently muted by the heavy mask and robe. Slowly, I became aware that the other actors were standing motionless and silent on stage, still fully garbed. I panicked! Had I done something wrong by taking off my mask and robe? I gradually noticed that something was abnormal about the others. They appeared to be automated mannequins that had wound down and collapsed. My heart beat in my throat as I walked close to the actor nearest me. Curiosity outweighed fear as I lifted his mask. The face of a robot stared back. One by one I lifted the masks only to find the same. I was the only real person on stage! An overwhelming sense of loneliness flooded me. I had foolishly believed the others were real and were connected to me in a common purpose. Now I knew I wasn't connected to them at all. They were programmed dummies who lacked free will and life force. I alone was acting from my own volition. They were props, illusions of reality.

The dream recurred often enough that I can still recall every detail.

During college, I joined a dance group and we collectively

participated in the Greek play, *Oedipus Rex*. It took until the dress rehearsal for me to recognize that reality and dream world had merged. We wore heavy robes of mud-colored, burlap sackcloth. Our head disguises were large papier-mache masks reflecting Greek tragedy. For several weeks the actors rehearsed, but I didn't get to know them and I didn't connect with them. At the end of the play they walked off stage without costume, while continuing to wear their socially approved, yet invisible masks. I never knew who they were and they didn't know me either.

On a literal interpretive level, the prophetic dream forecast an actual event in my life. On a symbolic level, the dream was a spiritual symbol of the world play we call reality. As time and experience in this world play increase, I've become more and more aware of my own and others' social masks hiding our fears and inadequacies. Afraid of rejection, we embrace the mask of perfection, hoping others won't see our darkness and incompleteness. Afraid of abandonment, we wear a mask of compliance, hoping to fit in and be accepted. We're afraid to reveal our deep emotional wounds, so we don a mask of stoic invulnerability.

The masks are many and varied, but the outcome of mask-wearing is the same -- we hide from the truth of who we are. We fail to fully own ourselves. We miss out on true connections with others. We just play a game, act in a play. We aren't courageous enough to take off our masks and robes. We don't become real and we don't own our full potential. We expend large amounts of energy protecting our false persona and have no energy left for finding our inner truths or connecting with others.

Most people hide behind masks all their lives. "Playing at life" and "playing at love" is the substitute for really living and truly loving. If we once dreamed of deep and honest relationships, we've given up hope. We rationalize that what we have is all there is. We falsely believe the awkward and self-protective relationship games are the closest we'll get to knowing others and being known.

The Inner Drive toward Empowerment and Unity

Can human unity really exist? Can we connect fully with another? What force propels some to seek the ideal of unity while most accept mediocrity? Is it a remembrance of a higher unity once known in a spiritual realm? Is it based on our recollection of unconditional love and acceptance from our mothers?

I wasn't sure why I believed in the possibility of human unity, but this ideal was the measuring stick I applied to all my relationships. Sadly, none of my human associations measured up to this ideal of honest and deep soul connection. The urge for truthful relationships became an irresistible force causing restlessness and frustration with the "near miss" connections in my life. Without true unity, I felt something important was missing. Michael mirrored the same frustration when he asked the painful and desperate questions.

Until the time Michael asked his questions, I was comfortably asleep in denial about my relationships. His questions awakened an urgent yearning within me to seek truth and love. I perceived this yearning to be ever present but silently awaiting my conscious recognition. I remembered telling Michael some years earlier that I hoped I didn't leave this world without knowing and being known by at least one person. It was obvious that deep and genuine connection was important to me.   At the time I spontaneously uttered the desire to know and be known, I wondered why I revealed such a strange and emotional intent to Michael. He was a friend, but a rather stiff and aloof one. It was years later that I understood why I shared this desire with him.

Meaning Concealed in Life Patterns

I began to see that seemingly unrelated choices and life

12

experiences formed an interwoven tapestry leading me to this point of introspective questioning. One part of my life pattern was the choice to be a therapist and later a university professor. My life mission of understanding myself and others, as well as the complex interactions we call relationships, guided me toward these occupations.

Twenty years after my baptism into the sacred field of psychotherapy, I had to admit the therapist's role was merely tampering around the edges, affecting only the superficial surface of relationships. Every trick in my bag was useless for those ready for a deeper soul connection. My many years of education and experience left me unprepared to answer questions about the journey to full empowerment and unity. To be sure, most clients weren't concerned with deeper connections. They were content to stay in parasitic relationships of mutual neediness. Their energies were directed toward protecting their fears and defenses. Their relationship scripts consisted of power games and control strategies. They followed the "shoulds" that glue people into stagnant and unsatisfying unions. They lacked courage to rebel against worldly dictates. Thus, they remained isolated and lonely.

I could readily see the codependent games of others, but I had much more difficulty admitting my own long-term relationship wasn't much different. My husband and I connected intellectually in a compatible business partnership. Control and manipulation weren't obvious to us. Because we were both good people who believed in honesty and fairness, the business partnership worked well. But neither of us knew how to reveal our real self to the other. Neither of us knew how to connect in a real marriage.

I felt lonely and isolated. The image of being on-stage with no one to relate to became my reality. I wore a mask and so did my husband. I became increasingly uncomfortable with playing the role of wife without connecting intimately and honestly. He, on the other hand, was content with our relationship and was unaware of any problems. I often despaired and told him of my

13

dissatisfaction with our inability to connect. He couldn't understand my discontent and chalked it up to PMS or some other form of idiocy. My dissatisfaction grew. My willingness to live in an anesthetized state of complacency, to conform and live a lie was about to end.

I was ready to take off my mask -- he didn't dare take off his. Now I remember his mask with much sadness. After his grandfather died, I challenged his stoicism and asked him why he couldn't let go and cry. He responded, "I don't know who I'd be if I let go!" So he stayed behind his mask and played a script others had written for him.

While my own metamorphosis was in its embryonic stage, Michael pushed toward answers for his own disquietude. He was determined his questions wouldn't evaporate into oblivion. About two weeks after our first lunch-time discussion about unity, he asked the questions again. This time, I admitted my ignorance.

"Michael, the best answer I can give is that people must be on different developmental levels. Some cannot connect with others at all. They're like two-year old children who believe the universe revolves around them. They're too self-centered to connect. Others connect in need. They'll give to you if you give to them. You have to please them and respond to their neediness if the relationship is to last. I guess some people are fully mature and move past their barriers and fears and are finally able to connect honestly and deeply with others. I'm not sure I've seen any unconditional love relationships among romantic partners, but I know a few couples in therapy who commit to deep and honest connections with their partners. In my experience, these couples are rare."

Michael looked puzzled when I gave him my feeble answer. "Are you are saying that some people are better than other people? That doesn't seem right. I'm not better than other people, and they aren't better than me. This reasoning seems judgmental and elitist."

"Michael, just because people are on different levels doesn't mean that one is better than another. A kindergarten child is not of lesser worth than a graduate student. One is just more advanced in understanding and experience. A graduate student is ready for certain experiences that are quite inappropriate for the kindergartner. And the graduate student would, no doubt, find a better intellectual and emotional match with one at his same level. Can you image how ill-matched he would be for a romantic relationship with a kindergarten-level person?"

This quest to understand relationships signaled a turning point for both of us. It was the beginning of a time of inner turmoil and traumatic change. We were to begin a spiritual journey that was beyond our ability to create or control. It was a journey that we initially resisted, but which eventually propelled us forward. It was the fulfillment of our joint mission to discover the path to human unity. Now it's our task to walk this path with others who also ask, "Why can't people honestly and deeply connect with others?"

Awakening to the Call for Inner Growth and Truth

A few weeks after our conversation, I had a dream. It was so vivid that I remember every detail -- the colors, feelings, expressions, and words are still fresh in my mind. I was standing in a magnificent hallway lined with tall windows. Warm, intense light was flowing from the windows and illuminating the hall. The floor shined with mirrored brilliance. The long room reminded me of the Hall of Mirrors at Versailles. The marble walls glowed with vibrant, sun-filled energy. I was about twenty years old and wore a flowing white dress. I pretended to be a ballerina and danced around the empty hall. Layers of chiffon floated around me as I twirled. I felt I was floating on air. I felt completely free and happy.

15

A movement drew my attention to the end of the hall. A young man was walking toward me. He wore a white shirt and white pants. His face glowed and his hair was tinged with radiant sunlight. I kept staring at his face, hoping to recognize him as he came closer. Just before he reached out to take my two hands, I realized it was Michael. There was none of the heaviness and despair that the earthly Michael carried around with him. This Michael was radiant, happy, and confident.

He looked into my eyes and said six words: "It is time. You are mine."

My feelings were intense and contradictory. I felt fear, then excitement. The high of excitement evaporated into uncertainty and depression. At last I felt resignation, acceptance and deep love.

When I awoke, the emotional conflict intensified. "Damn, this is my good friend -- and only a good friend! What is he doing invading my dreams? Well, this dream won't ever be admitted. It must stay in the dark recesses of forgotten dreams."

Yet the memory persisted. I wondered what the dream meant. Was my unconscious trying to destroy my well-ordered, comfortable life? I again pushed my questions and concerns as far down as possible. Repression would ensure my safety and control.

When I saw Michael again, nothing had changed. He was the obsessive-compulsive workaholic who irritated me. Yet, he had such a good heart and positive energy that drew others to him. He was one of the few at the university who were intellectually developed and able to converse on diverse topics. As a friend, he was also emotionally supportive and ready to hear my difficulties as I navigated the waters of university sharks. He was the old shoe that felt comfortable and familiar. I could be myself around him and never apologize or be self-conscious. I knew he just accepted me for what I was -- faults and all.

Then something started happening to Michael. He was

16

reading many strange books that were theological and spiritual. As he finished a book, he would hand it to me to read. This self-acknowledged "recovering Catholic" who professed to being an agnostic was curious enough to delve into the murky waters of the spiritual universe.

He explained his new fancy as interest in quantum physics. This interest led him to *The Holographic Universe*. This book was the springboard for his exploration of phenomena that defied scientific understanding. His focus rapidly shifted from science to spirituality. He began having vivid dreams and waking visions. Alarmed, he frantically asked me to assure him he wasn't going crazy. While he was able to maintain a high level of functioning in his professional world, he spent more and more of his private hours in spiritual experiences.

I was intrigued by this change in Michael. When I was a new professor, it was Michael who had asked during a faculty lunch how anyone with half a brain could believe in God. I was horrified to hear my voice announce, "Well, I do." The eyes of six male colleagues focused on me, the one brave enough or stupid enough to profess such a belief. Michael challenged me: "Why?"

I replied that I'd find it impossible to live in such a cruel world if I didn't believe in a divine plan and purpose for my life. Michael said my answer was the best he'd heard for believing in God, but I could tell he remained unconvinced. Now, years later, I was somewhat amused to watch his spiritual awakening and his growing faith in a power greater than himself.

I was not so amused when he came to me about two weeks after my Hall of Mirrors dream and said he had a vision he thought I could explain. "I saw a shining spirit form that I knew was me. Inside my spirit form was another smaller spirit form that I knew was you. In this vision we were one. What does this mean?"

My face burned with embarrassment as I heard his words. His eyes betrayed no understanding of the dream's significance. He stood before me, naive and curious, asking an innocent question that would explode my well-ordered world. Why was this happening to me? I could have remained safe by repressing the Hall of Mirrors dream, but now the universe seemed intent on making me testify to my knowing.

I felt trapped. I knew what the Hall of Mirrors dream meant and what his vision meant. I just didn't want to tell him. Yet, he asked for honesty in a relationship and I had promised to be an honest friend. I could tell him I didn't know the meaning and hope he'd forget the vision, but that was cowardly as well as dishonest. So with a rush of emotion, I told him about the Hall of Mirrors dream. Both the dream and vision signaled the time of spiritual awakening. As soul mates, Michael and I had work to do. I didn't know then that our work would turn both our lives upside down. If I had known at this point how difficult the journey toward unity would be, I would have run in the opposite direction.

The journey has taken many years now, and there has been much resistance on both our parts to stay on the path. Now we've finally arrived at a point of peace and true heart connection. Our journey confirms that what is supposed to be will be, regardless of human efforts to control and manipulate.

Union requires two souls, two hearts, two minds. I, Donna, have given you a glimpse of the initial phase of my journey toward unity with Michael. Now it's his turn to give you his rendition.

Michael's Story

While my path and Donna's have led to the same place, the roads we have traveled have passed through markedly different terrain. When I met her, little did I know that she would be the answer to my lifelong prayer for a love that was deep and real. *Real* for me has always meant based in truth, that unequivocal inner truth you get when you read or hear something that resonates with absolute certainty through every level of your being: mind, emotions, and spirit. Donna is my affirmation that God exists and that humanity is more, much more, than a mere species of animal that can reason. Our work together is to learn what love is and what it isn't, and to impart this knowledge to others.

The world's definition of love is based mostly on rules, neediness and obligation. My former definition of love left me empty, cold and disappointed. I didn't know where to begin to find love or truth in a world of manipulation and lies. In human history, several great teachers have told us we come into this world to learn love, to give love, to receive love. At some deep level I knew this all my life. It was only after age forty that the sum of my life experiences began to make sense. Love, true love, is possible! Learning how to love is not only our birthright as human beings, it is our responsibility.

My understanding of what love is, and is not, has come from several rather painful life lessons. I was one of those sensitive children -- an odd blend of curiosity and seriousness, who examined everything. I loved to build things with my mind; a constant barrage of thought pictures and questions ran continuously through my consciousness. The most important ideas were attached to a deep emotional yearning or passion. Love was foremost among them. Yet, the real world surrounding me was never as perfect as those thought images.

As a child (and still as an adult), I constantly asked "Why?" Nothing taken for granted by the adult world escaped my attention. I critically observed everything that seemed important. I quietly watched and questioned. It felt like I was waiting for something truly remarkable and satisfying to come along. It never did. Life seemed an endless blur of disappointing, gray dullness.

The most important thing I noticed about people was their

sense of hopelessness and unhappiness. Apart from the occasional moments when they acted happy, as when their son's swing connected with the ball or when their daughter succeeded in staying up on her new bike, I saw little true happiness. People talked about love, but I didn't see it on their faces or in their behavior. It was as if people were living inside some sort of shell. They pretended and played at being happy, but they were lying to themselves. You could see it on their faces if you looked closely. There was a fear of being exposed. They hid from truth and protected their lies.

Something was seriously wrong with the world around me. I couldn't identify exactly *what* was wrong, but the emptiness in people's lives was clear. Where were the joy, the happiness, and the loving kindness that my young mind and heart imagined and yearned for? Everyone around me seemed to feel trapped and alone. Some functioned in an anesthetized robot state, while others displayed an unconscious defiance against their hidden realities of fear and loneliness. I wanted to understand and help them in some way. But, the adults could not, or would not, see what was happening. They had stopped asking "Why?" Worse yet, their hope had eroded into desperation, and their desperation into a great number of dependencies.

Many, like my father, were dependent on alcohol to numb the lie they felt within themselves. Most were dependent on someone or something external to themselves. From a young age, I intuitively knew and felt peoples' fear and desperation. Yet, this knowing was never verified by the outside world. No one spoke the truth or gave empowering advice. All I saw and heard were those who pretended to know, but who were themselves as scared as anyone else. Everyone was looking outside him or her self for answers. They wanted someone to tell them what to do to assuage the tedium and lack of purpose in their lives.

On Sundays, our church was full of people listening to the priest's definition of love and happiness. I wanted to believe the words were real, and longed to live in a place where they were manifest. Yet, the beautiful words - love, truth, and kindness - weren't demonstrated. The priests and parishioners all wore masks so well perfected through lethargy and stoicism that they could utter the beautiful words and stay blind to the unloving, untruthful, and uncaring reality of the world. They voiced these powerful words in church and then promptly ignored their relevance to everyday life. They were asleep. They were helpless and hopeless. They had given up and were cycling endlessly in routines where truth wasn't acknowledged. The world I so desperately wanted to live in was just an illusion.

Experience taught me why the world was in denial. I was one of five children born into a family with a strong, caretaker mother and a weak, alcoholic father. I say weak, because he never mustered the courage or commitment to confront his disease. His neediness and irresponsibility held the rest of us captive. I remember becoming hopeful once when my father was in residential treatment and a white jacketed psychiatrist proclaimed that about seventy percent of his patients remained sober. I, like others around me, was desperately looking to an external authority to give me hope and to assure me that everything would ultimately be OK. Unfortunately, Dad's sobriety lasted no longer following this treatment than it had any other time. Neither Dad nor I understood that while external help is sometimes needed, the growth that takes us out of pain and human desperation is our own individual work. No one else can do it for us.

Later, during a subsequent bout of Dad's drinking, my mother, older brother, and I talked about packing up the younger kids and moving away. We were disgusted with Dad's disease and desperately wanted to go to a nearby city and start over. Mom suggested she might go to the community college and get a nursing degree. My brother and I, both adolescents at the time, discussed ways we could supplement the family's income by working after school. But the pressures were too great for Mom and her two

21

prematurely adult sons. We never did it. My mother had all she could do to keep the family intact, which she did with never a whimper or complaint. Years later, I asked Mom why we didn't just leave. After all the years, I still regretted our inability to extricate ourselves from Dad's toxic presence. Sadly, Mom told me that she too had anguished over the decision, but in the early 1960s a single woman with five children had little chance making it on her own. There were no social services to help and the stigma of a broken home would weigh heavily on the three younger siblings. So, we toughed it out.

But that one occasion of planning and hoping for a new and better future made an indelible imprint. I had taken a first step toward self-empowerment. For a few short weeks, I had succeeded in stepping beyond the fear that kept my family frozen and had dared dream and plan a new life. When I had to give up the dream, it was a major setback. I, too, then turned to denial and repression in order to survive. Now I recognize that the setback was only temporary. I never really gave up dreaming and hoping for a better life. I never allowed myself to become totally blinded by the world's illusion. Somewhere, down deep inside me, I held firm to the belief that happiness and true love do exist. But at that time, I was devastated. All I could think was -- surely there had to be more to life than "this."

My older brother and I had felt both responsibility and guilt for our family's plight. We wanted to make things right for our Mom and younger siblings. As a teenager, I didn't own the power to change the wrongs and make them right, so I prayed to God to help us. I prayed for countless hours on end and pleaded with God to show mercy and cure my Dad, but nothing happened. It was in this crucible of thwarted determination and despair that my ability to love took its early form. I learned that love meant repressing my own needs and feelings and being consumed by the neediness of others. I learned to define love as caretaking.

Donna likes to say there are two types of people -- the selfish and the selfless. The selfish have dense, impenetrable ego boundaries. They have a hard shell of self-absorption around them and fail to care about the needs and feelings of others. Their egos demand constant attention. My Dad was one of those. When he was sober he was affable and a good provider, but, like most alcoholics, he projected a false image to the world. He appeared caring and fair to others and most people liked him. They only knew his superficial mask. We lived with the tormented and self-absorbed person who drew all energy and attention toward himself. He couldn't connect and he didn't know how to love. Lacking the courage to go within and deal with his inner demons, he drank and ran away from any attempt to establish real heart connections with his family.

Just as the selfish take, the selfless give. My mother, brother, and I earned grades of A+ in being selfless. I desperately wanted the love and respect of my father, but I received only criticism and aloofness. The harder I tried to connect with Dad, the more he seemed to push me away. There was no softness in his heart to which I could connect. I compensated for his rejection by feeling guilty and responsible. I believed I could earn love by taking care of emotionally broken people who attached to me and required my help. Someone had to take responsibility to make the world right and I felt that someone had to be me.

The burden of caretaking weighed heavily on me. Then, the onset of juvenile diabetes added another burden. I felt flawed and unworthy of love. I found little in the world to look forward to. Observing and feeling everyone else's pain as well as my own was simply too much to bear so I, too, retreated into a world of stoic cynicism and went to sleep. I numbed myself and expected nothing from life.

With my flawed understanding of love, I connected the best I could. I jumped into a codependent marriage at age twenty and, with children coming shortly thereafter, the responsible caretaker part of me took over. My marriage revolved around children and their needs. Work took what time and energy was left. My wife and I were very different and we did not grow as a couple. Our relationship was anchored in our neediness, and ultimately proved not to be a true, mature, heart connection. We were two damaged children who had never learned how to give or receive real love. So, like the couples around us, we did the best we could for our children and for each other. We were asleep in denial. We were living the American dream - and it was a lie.

My first wake-up call came eleven years after I completed college. I had become cynical and had given up on emotions as being only vestigial carryovers from a more primitive time. As a university professor, I perceived that success hinged on my critical intellect and obsessive-compulsive work habits. I was sitting at my desk when the phone call came. My normally reserved mother was sobbing and barely audible. I knew that only a death in the family would draw such a reaction. I braced for what she was about to say.

"Janie, Justin and Brooke were just killed in a terrible car accident." As she said these words, my world fell apart. There I sat, a man who had given up praying out of frustration, who had given up crying for its uselessness, and who had walled himself off from his emotions as protection against a reality that was too hurtful. My little sister Janie, Justin, my six year old nephew, and Brooke, my four year old niece, were dead - lying lifeless, bruised, and broken in a funeral home a thousand miles away. I started to cry, then I started to sob - and I didn't stop for what seemed like weeks.

I traveled the thousand miles home, tortured with anger and disbelief. A worthless God had allowed yet another senseless act. I was angry with God and I was angry with all the people who I knew would try, with good intent, to assure me this violent tragedy was part of some unknowable divine plan. The very thought of this hypocrisy and denial of what had happened made the mere act of breathing unbearable. There was no love in the world, only sadness, corruption, and cruelty. Either the world or I had to change, or I wanted out. My mind kept yelling the question "WHY!?!?"

This time, I got an answer. At the funeral parlor, I held back from all the rest as they went before the open caskets to offer their last respects. I just couldn't do it. Finally, after being told several times the coffins must be closed, I overcame my grief and went forward. As I looked at my sister and her two children, the feeling inside me grew more powerful than any I had felt or imagined before. My rage and hurt were enormous, but they dimmed in contrast to the deep love and connection I felt for my sister and her children. At last, after thirty-three years of yearning, I felt a love that was real, and deep, and true. But, at what price? Janie and her children had given me a very special gift -- the awareness that at our core, beneath the layers of responsibility, guilt, egoism, and all the rest, lies pure love. Her death awakened me to life. My journey within to find truth and love had finally begun.

Carl Jung once commented that coping in this reality really is not very difficult. Given reasonable intelligence and opportunity to master those skills and activities needed to live comfortably, most peoples' attention naturally turns to the question, "Why am I here?" I reached the magical age of forty and this question began to weigh heavily upon me. Age forty had been imprinted on me by my childhood physicians who cautioned and threatened of the seriousness of my diabetic condition. Their horror stories left me with the impression that I would not live past forty. If I did, I could expect to loose my eyesight, and possibly my feet or legs due to circulatory and nerve damage. But now at forty I also carried Janie's gift -- the knowing that a very powerful love lies at the core of each of us. The battle lines were drawn: it was my decision to accomplish my life quest for a deep, truthful love, or resign myself to the dire predictions of physicians who had warned me that at forty I had little time left.

I think many people wake up at some point in life finding

themselves confronted with a similar decision. Waking up to life and personal empowerment is not an easy thing to do. The world's definitions of love, success, and happiness are externally based. They contradict our inner search for truth and peace. To learn the true meaning of love may require a break with virtually all the rules that are used as control mechanisms by those still asleep. Refusing to capitulate to the neediness or manipulations of a significant other, a child, a friend, or family member often places the person committed to truth in an adversarial role. Even worse, since dependent and codependent relationships are the norm in most work and family settings, those who attempt to break away are bombarded with guilt. Shaming and blaming tactics are used, labeling the rebellious seeker of truth a villain, an egocentric abuser, or a crazy person.

Tentatively at first, and then with growing conviction, I committed to pursue truth in my relationships with others, and to demand of myself that I learn how to love fully and completely. I looked around, but couldn't find a mentor who had achieved this goal. Even worse, few had tried. Most didn't even know that such a thing was possible.

The world continued to sleep in its denial. Men, women, and children continued to numb out with their addictions: sports, clothes, cars, TV, work. Others who did seem aware of the shallowness of their connections fell prey to religions or spiritual fads that promised help through some external source which required little serious self-reflection or real growth. The world was much the same as that I had observed as a child. People would deny, rationalize, pretend, defer, or do virtually anything rather than take personal responsibility to manifest the God thought of *love* within themselves. No one had the strength or courage to name the dishonesty of the world - or the conviction to create a truthful reality based in love.

This was a challenge I could sink not only my teeth into, but my heart as well. My path led me to a place where I not only knew that Divine Love was possible -- I demanded it. I was no longer a child wallowing in self-pity, praying to a distant, non-responsive God. God had given me the tools I needed to create Love: a mind, a heart, a body, and an entire world to work within. The rest was up to me -- and the rest was not easy. Following the process outlined in Chapter 7, *Tunnel Work - The Path Through Darkness into Light,* I had to confront and cleanse myself of all the old tapes that were playing in my head, controlling my thoughts, feelings, and behavior. These were the tapes of experience that shaped my view of reality. My task was to keep my true perceptions and positive attributes and release false perceptions and emotions based in fear and neediness. If the power of Janie's gift of helping me discover truth and love was to become integrated, I had much work to do and a long way to travel.

We've all heard people say, "Be careful what you pray for, you just might get it!" Well, I prayed that I learn to commit fully to at least one other human being in this lifetime. I prayed for a Divine love based in truth, total sharing, and complete honesty. I also prayed for the wisdom, strength, and courage to see and confront those things about myself that needed changing. In my heart I knew that humans weren't intended to be isolated, desperate souls trapped inside a body of flesh. We are created for much more than that. While free will gives us permission to live out our lives in any fashion, we have the tools to create what we most desperately need and want - true heart connections with our Creator and with each other. The choice is ours. All we need do is ask for guidance and help, and then take full responsibility for moving closer to our heart goals. We must acknowledge that the Divine will work within and through us, but will not treat us as dependent children and do our work for us. This is the paradox - you will receive all the help you need in your journey toward truth and love, but you must accept full responsibility for completing the journey.

With each successive year after my fortieth birthday, my understanding of what I needed to do became more tangible. My personal truth began to emerge in the form of deep knowings. These knowings all pressed the same message -- I had to reject "business as usual"; I had to reject fear; and I had to reject the interpersonal games and shielding defenses that were the old me. If I were to learn about love, I couldn't hold on to any security blankets or maintain any sacred cows. I had to let go and let God teach me what I needed to learn. I had to submit to painful growth lessons that required me to confront -- gently with truth and love -- everything that I believed and everything I once was. So I ventured out of the old me and confronted the falsities that had made up my safe, emotionally aloof, miserable life.

Like most men, I had walled myself off from my emotions. Those I knew best were anger, impatience, and frustration. I was chronically depressed most of my life, but I hid it and relied on raw stubbornness to keep me afloat. I had directed my attention outward focusing on status and material rewards. To the world, I looked and acted just like them. As the level-headed professional, I fit in and made my way in the world. Now it was time for me to change. As I opened to it, a profound inner truth began to pour out of me in systematic and purposeful patterns. I believe I was guided in that transformation. And, I needed all the guidance and help I could get. My journey to find happiness and real love was underway.

Intuitively, I knew that the answers I was looking for could only be found through my emotions, so I learned to trace them. As I came across each hurt or irritant in my life, I focused on naming, evaluating, and weighing it with my emotions. This was tough work for someone who had rejected feelings as nothing but a source of great pain. One by one, however, the emotions emerged. I would struggle with each one and try to feel its physical location within my body. I would then focus on tracing the emotion to its source. Each emotion was connected to my past life experiences as if tied by a small silver thread. With each lesson I would give the newly found emotion a name, and I learned how to get in touch with the intensity of how each one felt. What started slowly picked up speed as my emotional sensitivity increased. My repertoire of emotions grew rapidly. I began to feel good about myself for the first time -- ever. With the truth of my life and my despair now coming into focus, I began the tremendously difficult job of cutting the emotional strings that had welded me to unhealed wounds and many needy relationships. This process of shedding took several years and as I became more honest with myself, I found myself healing and becoming whole.

The answer to my prayers for a truthful relationship came all wrapped up in Donna. The saying "God works in mysterious ways" certainly held true for us. As I pursued my search for truth in human connections, she emerged in my life traveling on the same path. Coincidence? Definitely not! She is my *Sacred Mirror,* a soul that has chosen to work with me, and I with her, to reflect the truth we each need to see in ourselves. In this process we help each other see through our blind spots which are tied to our unresolved hurts and traumas. Donna, having lost her father early in childhood, still had abandonment fears that kept her from being totally open and vulnerable. She feared exposing her real self and loving completely because her beloved might leave and devastate her. She shielded herself from total commitment in love. She needed to trust love and open to the experience of a deep soul connection. I hadn't resolved my own feelings of inadequacy stemming from my father's rejection and my shame about being a diabetic. Our struggle toward a sacred relationship exposed our unhealed wounds and self-protective shields. We needed to scour out all fear before we were able to love each other completely. Not all *Sacred Mirrors* come as marriage partners. These deep connections may obviously take many forms, with some lasting a lifetime, and others lasting only briefly.

29

In this book, Donna and I merge the insights that we and our clients have gained in our struggles to achieve full self-empowerment and true heart connections. We're walking the path toward unity and sharing a sacred relationship. Our journey is far from complete, but we've learned a lot and it's now our responsibility to share our experiences with others who choose to travel the same path. In sharing our experiences, and the experiences of our clients, we hope to help others find *their* answers to "How can humans join completely and honestly with each another?" and, "How can I empower myself and become ready for a sacred love?"

Chapter Two

The Road to Empowerment

The Road to Empowerment

Where has my journey taken me? It seems the path has been twisted with many stopping points along the way. From my very earliest recollections of contemplating God, I've always felt strongly about His presence in my life, but not a strong direction for action. My ever-burning prayer has been, 'God show me the way to go. What do you want me to do?' Answers seem elusive. Can I live my whole life without the answer? Is the answer here, but I don't see it? If so, why am I not willing to open my eyes? The only fear I have of the answer is that it might be too mundane to be satisfying. And yet I honestly cannot believe that God has a mundane plan for my life. Is that egotistical? Perhaps - or truth.

What is the lesson to be learned? I must have the freedom to express my individuality and with that comes the responsibility to know my individuality. So, who am I? I am a seeker of knowledge and understanding. The understanding has always been the difficult part. Why can't I just accept things without question or explanation the way others seem to accept what authority figures tell them. But I have to find my own answers and know them as truth. I squirm when I don't have answers. That's not fair, God! You're supposed to give me answers not questions! You're supposed to be my rock, not make me feel shaky! I want answers! You promised me! Why is truth so hidden? It wasn't intended to be that way, was it? John 1:14 says, 'The Word became flesh and made his dwelling among us. We have seen his glory, the glory of the One and Only who came from the Father, full of grace and truth.' I also desire to be full of grace and truth. Is it possible to achieve that state here on earth or is it only attainable when we are joined with our creator in eternity? And what does eternity hold for us? The search is exciting, but attaining the goal is also exciting. Eternity cannot be just a series of life experiences, ever seeking but not attaining our goal. What happens when we attain our goal of coming home to 'Our Father in Heaven'? Heaven always sounded a little boring to me. Everything perfect, praising God forever. How many different ways can we do that?

For now I've decided to leave a marriage relationship that is false and unconnected. I leave this good man in search of true love. Where is love?

33

Love is from God and God is love. But for now, I feel unloved. Even worse, I feel incapable of finding love. I need someone who can love me without needing to control me. Love should be freeing. Love should be a joyous union of spirits and celebration of life. Love should be honest and without fear. God's love is constant and earth love should be too. Love knows no boundaries. No amount of dissension will cause it to cease. No amount of challenge will cause love to grow dim. Challenge is confronted with assurance of self. That's the reason that God's love makes me squirm. He is totally self-assured and is therefore totally capable of being loving. He will love me forever because He knows the truth of me and is not afraid of me.

-Journal entry by Jane, a seeker of unity

Jane's journal entry exemplifies the beginning of a journey toward full empowerment. Throughout her lifetime, Jane viewed herself as religious. Religion was defined by the dogma and traditions of her church. There was little emphasis on spiritual development and a personal relationship with God. Nevertheless, Jane was aware of the Divine spark within her and steadfastly looked for God's guidance in her life. She refused to accept that the church had to be an intermediary between her and God. As a Christian, she took personal responsibility for deciding the meaning of Christ's parables and life. She saw many around her who allowed themselves to be programmed by interpretations and beliefs of others. But Jane's independence would not allow that. She needed to find and to feel her own truth. It was this independence that kept alive her internal belief that true love really does exist. This belief simmered just below the surface of her consciousness for forty years.

Jane came from a home that prized conformity and image. She was expected to do well in school, go to church every Sunday, and be a good girl. She and her sister obeyed the unspoken, but obvious dictates of parental authority. They knew they must conform and obey or they would suffer the fate of their older, rebellious brother. Roger was ten years older than Jane and she adored him. She couldn't remember details about the almost continuous fights he had with their parents. She just remembered the knot in her stomach when they started yelling. She didn't know why they couldn't get along and love each other. In her mind, Roger was perfect. He spent time with her and treated her as special and important. Whenever she heard his car turn in to the driveway, she'd run to meet him. He never treated her like a bothersome little sister, but rather gave her the attention and affection she was starving for. He'd talk to her as an equal. The strong bond between them comforted her when she was alone. She remembered the last big fight between Roger and her parents. She heard the screaming. She heard his car door slam and the tires squeal as he sped away from the house. She didn't see Roger until five years later. Roger had to leave home to gain his independence and to claim his individuality.

Jane learned her family's law well -- *conform and obey or you will be rejected and must leave.* She took the safe road and conformed. Even when it came to choosing a marriage partner, she accepted the proposal of a man who had the approval of her parents, rejecting along the way a man who was more like her in personality and temperament, but who was judged by her parents as unacceptable. Now, after forty years of silence, the same need for independence and truth that had frightened her about Roger came bubbling up within her. At mid-life, Jane finally awoke to her desperate state of discontent and knew she could no longer play the game of pleasing others. It was finally time to attend to her own truth and please herself. She left her husband of twenty-three years and she left her church. But she didn't leave God. Her commitment to find God and to find her inner truth was resolute.

At the beginning of her journey she was dismayed to find that, instead of discovering answers, she became more and more confused with an overwhelming number of questions. The journey inward was not straight·and sure, but twisted and dangerously steep. Appeals from family and friends to abandon her search and return to her old way of being caused inner turmoil and self-doubt. When she persisted, the appeals turned into condemnation and shaming. But Jane refused to turn back. One thing she was sure about was that the accepted way of the world -- pleasing and conforming to external dictates -- had not led her to the place of truth and peace. She knew she didn't love her husband, but the belief that true love was possible fired her determination to seek a seamless bond with another.

As she continued her journey inward, her psychological and spiritual growth blossomed. She searched tirelessly for the meaning of her life -- and for her divine mission. As Jane veered away from the confines of religious and worldly dictates, she began to separate from the false illusions that had held her captive throughout her life. She became even more committed to finding her truth and accepted responsibility for completing the difficult task of individuation; of seeing and releasing the fears and dependencies we all learn as children. As she began to see and to acknowledge her own strengths and weaknesses, she was able to reach out and connect with others in ways previously impossible. Her new connections with others were grounded in truth -- and the intimacy of honest relationships felt great. She abandoned her mask of perfectionism and aloofness and allowed herself to be vulnerable and honestly express her true feelings. With growing experience connecting in honesty and truth, she now yearned -- even dared to expect -- an ultimate soul connection. She knew the person capable of joining with her would not be controlling, fearful, or judgmental. He would have accepted the challenge of self-growth and freed himself from defensive masks. The love of two self-sufficient and mature adults would be freeing. The hope for this type of love -- a sacred relationship -- was the motivating source behind Jane's journey inward.

Path to Self Empowerment and Empowered Love

Out of our own personal experiences, and the experiences of clients like Jane, a road map to empowerment and empowered love has emerged. Like Jane, many people know their relationships are superficial and not truly connected. They know they're merely playing out false roles scripted by a world that represses truthful emotions and intimate sharing -- a world that knows and teaches very little about love. What they don't know is how to move away from the world's lies to a place of truth and power. They yearn to feel good about themselves and share themselves honestly with another who also is ready for a deeply loving connection. The way to a true heart connection begins with the commitment to look inward and see ourselves honestly and objectively. We must also examine the relationships around us. Are they based in love or in neediness and obligation? The truth about our disconnection will either awaken us to a call for growth and unity or freeze us in fear, denial, and stagnation.

This chapter presents a visual road map and brief summaries of the stages that lead from false unity, loneliness and separation, to the state of true connection. Subsequent chapters flesh out details of the tasks and lessons we meet in our journey toward full human actualization and true unity in mind, heart, and spirit with ourselves and with others.

The road map begins with our remembrance of unity -- that state of complete connection and belongingness. Against that knowing of perfect unity, all human relationships are measured -- and come up short. For those who remember unity, the world's definitions of love, connection, and personal fulfillment are unsatisfactory. But many have forgotten unity, and stay in denial about the adequacy of worldly love and success. After breaking our denial that reality is satisfactory and consummate, we look beyond conventional reality for a higher level of purpose and meaningful. In moments of serious introspection, we confront the questions, "What is the purpose of my life? Why am I here?"

37

Those who refuse to engage the struggle of responding to questions of deeper life meaning give up and return to the jaded belief that humankind merely exists to serve itself: to give, to receive, to use, to manipulate, to control. But, for those who are brave enough to believe in a higher and purer meaning for their lives, seeing themselves clearly and learning to relate truthfully with others become imperative.

Awakening to the shallowness of our most intimate relationships can be the most frightening experience we ever face -- and, for the brave of heart, the most energizing. Those who refuse to accept these shallow connections as love now see that more is possible, and they begin to see how it can be achieved. The six steps toward self empowerment and empowered love include (1) awareness of unity; (2) beginning the individuation process; (3) detours into co-dependency; (4) completion of individuation; (5) learning to connect interdependently; and (6) readiness for a sacred relationship.

Awareness of Unity

In Jane's journal entry, she begins by asserting her belief that God is present and active in her life. Many, like Jane, embark on a journey to inner truth and an exploration of the meaning of God's plan for their life. This journey often leads us to a conscious awareness that we are from God and a part of God. This remembrance of true connection and belonging becomes the measuring stick for determining the significance of human relationships. When Jane examined her relationships with those who were supposed to be close -- husband, parents, siblings, and children -- she was dissatisfied. Everyone acted his or her role and conformed to expectation, but the authenticity of heart connections rang hollow. Jane felt disconnected and alone. She decided to take off her mask of conformity and find out who she was and what she really wanted. Her husband, children, and sister

38

The Path To Empowerment

I
UNITY
State of Oneness; Fully Empowered; Able to
Love Unconditionally; Able to Connect Completely

BEGINNING
VI SACRED RELATIONSHIP   INDIVIDUATION II
Two Whole Persons Merge As One;   Lonely & Isolated; Needy and Externally
Aware of Life Purpose and Joint   Oriented; Present False Social Mask to
Mission; Totally Open and Vulnerable   The World; Fearful and Immature;
to Each Other; Connect Emotionally,   Ego-Centered; Firmly Grounded in
Intellectually, Physically and Spiritually;   Selfishness or Selflessness
Each Partner a Balance of the Divine
Feminine & Divine Masculine; A Human
Reflection of Divine Love

V INTERDEPENDENCY
Fully Integrated Emotional &
Intellectual Self; Able to relate in
Mature Adult/Adult Connection;
Focused on "Being" and "Becoming,"
not "Doing"; Choose Relationships
Without Power/Control Games;
Empower Others Rather than
Enable Weaknesses; Share Equal
Responsibility for Continuous
Growth in Relationships; Connect
In Truth, Love, Want -- Not in Need

CO-DEPENDENCY III
Relationships Based on Neediness and
Fear; Connections Based on "Doing"
not "Being"; Reliance on "Rules,"
"Shoulds," & "Oughts"; Blaming,
Shaming & Guilt Used to Control
Parent/Child Transactions; Win/
Lose Mentality; Stagnant Growth
Superficial Connections with Others
Others who wear Fear-
Constructed Outer Masks

IV
INDIVIDUATION COMPLETION
Awaken to Need to Grow; Commit to Break Free of Co-Dependency;
Commit to Rigorous, Ongoing Self-Evaluation; Engage in Tunnel-
Work to Purge Deep Fears and Hurts; Complete Psychological/
Emotional/Spiritual Catharsis; Embrace/Heal DarkSide of;
Self; Drop Masks; Complete Grief Work; Discern
Developmental Level of Others

chose to remain asleep, cloaked in their socially acceptable facades. Like the robots in Donna's *Oedipus Rex* dream, Jane was surrounded by undeveloped and hollow people. They had not individuated enough to know who they really were. They were programmed by the world to act a certain way. When Jane's growing discomfort forced her to awaken from her own robot state, she was able to remove her heavy robe and mask. She committed to be free of the world's restraints and to follow the path inward -- into her inner being and inner truth. She learned the same lesson that Donna learned in the *Oedipus Rex* dream: connections with undeveloped people are mere illusions. Those who choose to live out scripts written by others often live an entire lifetime never achieving even one true and honest connection with another human being. Their relationships stagnate in the protocol of acting out worldly shoulds. Empty relationships are maintained out of personal neediness or some externally induced sense of responsibility. Authenticity is missing in relationships because the real person is hiding behind roles assigned by others.

Somewhere in the recesses of Jane's mind was the awareness that something more vital and essential is possible in human relationships. She knew that marriage was much more than a legal contract. She knew that family relationships meant nothing without mutual honesty and personal commitments grounded in love. She owned the falsity of her relationships and prayed for truth and genuineness to replace the counterfeit connections that surrounded her. She admitted her loneliness, depression, confusion and fear. Jane embarked on the greatest and most frightening journey of life -- the journey to find Truth, and God, and Love.

Beginning the Individuation Process

Individuation is the process that leads us to a sense of our individuality -- our identify as separate and special persons. The question is how far along the road to completed individuation we choose to go. The process begins when we first become aware of being separate from our mother or other humans. It is that recognition of separation that evolves slowly into our awareness of individuality. As ego individuation advances, the demand for satisfaction of needs and wants increases. Ego gratification is the primary focus of immature individuals at this stage. The child who wants another's toy grabs it away and feels no guilt or shame. In this state of ego aggrandizement, he is the only person in the universe who counts. He deserves to get what he wants. Unfortunately, many humans in adult bodies have not progressed beyond *Beginning Individuation.* They abuse others and have no sense of shame or any internal limiters to curb their harmful behavior.

In *Beginning Individuation* a dichotomy of responses develops. Those in more permissive or child-centered environments learn narcissism or self-love. They learn the world revolves around their needs and wants. Without a balanced emphasis on perceiving and respecting the needs and feeling of others, these children develop into egomaniacal beings. They only see their viewpoint and channel all energy and attention toward themselves. Ironically, children from emotionally or physically deprived environments also develop closed ego boundaries and become selfish like the overly-indulged children. Their closed ego boundaries protect them from an outer world they perceive as hostile and uncaring. They believe survival is dependent on their looking out for number one. These ego-centered or selfish personalities emerge from the extremes of over-indulgence or negligence. Many of today's children appear to grow up in one of these two types of family environments and emerge into adolescence and adulthood without adequate knowledge of the need and manner of

41

connecting and caring for others.

Jane's family wasn't permissive or child-centered, nor were they neglectful. Her parents were controlling and rigid. They imposed their own will on the children, robbing them of the opportunity to develop and learn about self. Like others coming from parent-centered environments, Jane learned to be self-effacing, conforming, and selfless. Selfless persons are easily programmed by others' wants and needs: they become caretakers. Selfless persons have been conditioned to focus externally: they are constantly scanning the reactions of others for cues about their needs and wants. Too busy trying to please others, selfless persons don't pay attention to their own needs and wants. Their identity is based on what others think of them so they spend inordinate amounts of time and energy trying to be and do what others want.

The major task we each face in *Beginning Individuation* is to develop an awareness of our separateness from others that is balanced with an understanding of our oneness with others. Going too far in one direction or another results in selfishness or selflessness. Balanced persons can attend to their own needs, wants and rights and be equally aware and considerate of the needs and rights of others. Jane was primarily selfless -- giving herself away to the demands and wishes of others. Jane's external focus on pleasing and meeting the expectations of others left little time for her to attend to her own needs.

When Jane reached forty her inner truth would be silenced no longer. The truth buried deep within told her she was living a lie. She had done what others wanted her to do and never did what she wanted. She pretended to connect in love, but true connection was missing. While she didn't know where to find it, or how to get it, she *knew* that more, much more, was possible. She maintained independence of thought and guarded her free will. At mid-life, she claimed her separateness and her right to individuate and establish the truth of her individuality. She gave

42

up her conforming, caretaker mask and committed to self-exploration and growth. She also committed to live her truth no matter what the cost.

Most people are affected by deficits in the *Beginning Individuation* stage that result in their being more selfish or selfless. The balanced self who owns free will and individuality, but also recognizes a oneness and need to connect with others is rare. Most move onward in life with a crippled sense of self, never balancing selfishness and selflessness. Incomplete individuation leaves us in a childish state of emptiness and fear, always depending on others to meet our unmet needs. The selfish need others to dominate and control so their unquenched hunger for power and attention is assuaged. The selfless define themselves by shaping their identities around those who need them. Their self-worth and security hinge on mutually dependent relationships. They need to feel needed and dote on the adulation and approval of others.

Unbalanced individuation characterizes most of the people in our world. They look after their own needs and the needs of those closely aligned with them. Their primary objective is to judge, to dominate, and to control. In a thousand ways and more, they connect in order to draw energy and attention their way. True understanding and compassion for others are absent. True connection is impossible. Proof of the vastness of retarded and unbalanced individuation is easy to find. Most of us can see it clearly in our families of origin. If we desire more proof, we need look no further than the daily newspaper that reports the unscrupulous actions of people in politics and business. Our world is populated by those who have not achieved the *balance* of fully individuated adults. We live in a world of users and those who allow themselves to be used. True heart connections are possible with neither, because neither is balanced or mature.

43

Detours into Co-Dependency

In early adult years, people become aware of their detachment and isolation from others. The world's answer to loneliness is to join in *codependent* relationships. *Codependency* is the joining of two incomplete humans, who wrongly believe that another person's strengths will complete their inadequacies. Generally, codependent relationships have selfish/selfless complements: one person expecting to be given to and the other giving. Sometimes the dependency is between likes -- two selfless or two selfish individuals. When insufficiently individuated people connect, they stay asleep to their fully actualized and empowered self. Instead, they play a role and end up existing in a state of fear, depression, and control. *Codependency* is false unity. Lacking unity within themselves, codependents are looking for answers and personal completion outside themselves -- in work, in relationships, in substances, in fulfilling the needs of others. Instead of connecting, codependents remain isolated and fearful. In an attempt to preserve codependent relationships, partners engage in power tactics aimed at controlling others. Their relationships are one-up/one-down or parent/child relationships. *Codependents* control others with power, shame, blame and guilt. Manipulative control reflects their ego-centered nature and reveals their disrespect of other peoples' free wills. Rules and shoulds maintain codependent relationships.

Codependents have superficial relations based on joining of external masks and projected images. There is no genuine connection because there is really nothing to connect with. The inner core of codependents is not developed. They have not individuated to the point they have developed a substantive self. Without self-knowledge of their inner truth, they have nothing to join to or with. Their hollow connections are based on "doing": what they have done for others; what others have done for them. They keep score of their giving lest the return on their investment be short changed. Love becomes a tally sheet and relationships

44

become obligations. To the codependents, you owe them and they owe you. Tragically, they haven't a clue about the mechanics of true connection. Mostly, they are unaware they aren't connecting. They buy the world's definition of love and deny that something is missing. Hiding from the possibility of true unity, they fool themselves into believing *this is as good as it gets*. Unfortunately, codependence is the core ingredient in the world's recipe for love and relationship, and any who would seek a true heart connection must demonstrate the will and courage to break free of its grasp.

Completion of Individuation

Some of us awaken and grow weary of the emptiness of codependency. We are then driven to seek truth and genuineness in our relationships. Propelled forward to complete individuation, our first task is to rid ourselves of the fears and defenses that comprise our false persona. We must scrape off the layers of worldly encrustation that form our masks and free the real persons buried within. Growth of self-knowledge requires the painstaking *tunnel work* of emotional, psychological, and spiritual catharsis. Catharsis may include purging of childhood traumas, such as parental death, substance abuse, sexual abuse, or emotional neglect. Tunnel work almost always includes grieving the lack of intimate bonding with friends and family members who weren't sufficiently empowered to connect in truth and love. The nagging voices of fear, hurt, shame and guilt that have shaped our identities must be quieted before the real self can emerge.

Some people believe there are short-cuts through this difficult phase. Some believe God will do their work for them -- all they need do is focus on the light and disregard the dark. Others numb out. In denial and fear they seek refuge in diversions such as alcohol, drugs, television, and work. Escape from tunnel work is impossible if one wants to emerge an integrated, mature adult. We must embrace the darkness within us before we can be freed

45

from fear.

Completion of individuation empowers the individual to own and love all parts of himself or herself. Individuals don't become empowered by expecting a parent figure (or God) to do the hard work for them. They don't become empowered by avoiding truth, numbing out, avoiding emotions, or freezing in lethargy and fear. They become empowered when, grounded in faith, they dive into the dark recesses of their inner being and clear away their barriers to full love and connection. This process of cleaning out ones' emotional, psychological, and spiritual *basement* is dominated by two powerful opposing forces: Eros and Thanatos. Eros, the life force, is in constant conflict with Thanatos, the death force. Eros urges us to take risks and move onward into uncharted regions of Truth. Thanatos, the death force, urges us to retreat into the known regions of dependency and escapism.

Only those committed to growth and truth at all costs continue through the tunnel of *Individuation Completion*. Those of us who persevere along this journey begin to see ourselves honestly and to integrate both our light and dark sides. Commitment to self-scrutiny brings us to a place we can see ourselves fully and objectively. Self-awareness and self-vigilance yield the additional benefit of being able to discern the motives and developmental levels of others. Discernment of emotional, intellectual, and spiritual maturation is a necessary ingredient in the completion of grief work. With increased understanding of our own and others' maturational levels, our defensive postures of hate and judgment give way to understanding and forgiveness.

Empowered individuals own the responsibility of free will and create a reality based on internal truth and personal strength rather than one based on meeting external expectations of others. Protectiveness and defensiveness drop as we own our power and refuse to accept worldly lies or be controlled by others. We drop our false masks and love ourselves fully. We accept the adult responsibility of free will and develop trust in a divine plan for our lives.   Faith expands and enables us to accept life events (even negative experiences) as opportunities and challenges for accelerated growth.   Attainment of *complete individuation* is rewarded with wholeness, self-sufficiency, self-love and the defeat of our inner fears.

Learning to Connect Interdependently

Completion of Individuation is the passport to the higher level of *Interdependency*.   Purging ourselves of fear and neediness releases us from the external focus of codependency.   We are now ready to turn inward to the task of building our self-esteem.   We grow most rapidly when surrounded by others who are also committed to wholeness and empowerment.   Interdependent relationships are starkly different from co-dependent relationships. People relate to each other in mature, adult/adult relationships that encourage strength, growth, and actualization of full human potential. There are no power games or control maneuvers between interdependent partners. There is complete freedom and acceptance of each other, even the unhealed and shadow parts. That is not to say that the blind spots or undeveloped parts are ignored. Rather, interdependent partners point out, softly and lovingly, the deficits within each other that impede growth in their relationship. The focus of these relationships is on "being and becoming." "Doing" and spreading goodwill is a natural by-product of being in this elevated state, but relationships are not based on doing.   We cannot earn or achieve this level of relationship by doing.

Readiness for *Interdependence* depends on one's ability to be his or her true self and to offer the gift of self to another empowered being.   Empowered adults in *Interdependent* relationships share equal responsibility for furthering the relationship. Unequal power and controlling manipulations found in codependent relationships don't exist. Partners in interdependent relationships empower each other rather than enable each others' weaknesses. Connections are based in truth, love and want rather than need and fear.

Readiness for a Sacred Relationship

Those who learn to join in *Interdependent* relationships grow in readiness for a true-heart connection or *Sacred Relationship.* The *Sacred Relationship* involves two whole individuals who are ready to fully and completely connect on all levels: emotional, physical, intellectual, and spiritual. They are totally open and vulnerable to each other. True unity means there are no hidden fears or hurts creating barriers between the two. There is only complete honesty, acceptance and belongingness.

A *Sacred Relationship* is the human reflection of spiritual unity. At this level, we have found our way to true love. Self-empowerment, now actualized, is multiplied as two lives merge. Such couples are true soul mates or twin flames. But, as Chapter Ten illustrates, a soul mate connection doesn't mean the couple has "arrived" and will have only a smooth journey thereafter. It is paradoxical that this profound level of connection and love will also bring up the greatest pain. Any unresolved fears will emerge as these person's take the greatest risk of their lives -- being fully open and emotionally vulnerable to another. Fears of rejection and abandonment surface as each partner struggles to find his or her path together. Individuality, while never diminished, melds into mutuality. The force of two empowered and whole adults is multiplied. Their example of empowered love becomes a template of change for a world dominated fear and darkness.

The *Sacred Relationship* is the only true marriage, and is rarely found on earth. Such couples are mutually aware of their joint purpose and are attuned to Divine Guidance. While aware of the uniqueness of their relationship, *Sacred Relationship* partners don't

48

give themselves credit for achieving the intimate bond they share. They know their relationship is a Divine gift, given when two are ready to receive sacred love and unity. *Sacred relationships* exist to serve as emissaries of love to a world that knows so little about love and how to achieve it.

Chapter Three

The Pull Toward Unity

The Pull toward Unity

I remember a Junior High Science experiment where a Dixie cup was filled to the brim with water. You had to carefully slide a needle from the cup's side so it would float on top of the water. The surface tension of the water held the needle afloat. But if you touched the needle in the slightest, it would sink to the bottom. That's what relationships are like. They're held together by the world's surface tension- the shoulds and oughts that dictate our lives and box us into convention. We're connected only by fragile threads. Family bonds, marital bonds, friendship bonds all disintegrate instantaneously when the surface tension is disturbed. I'm tired of surface relationships without substance. I want my Dixie cup filled with solid material so the needle doesn't sink. I want real connections that are deep and impervious to the storms of life. Where do you find such relationships?

-Susan, age 40

Susan's heart desire was for true depth and unity with at least one other human. She wanted to love and be loved fully. She wanted to be known in the fullness of her being and feel comfortable showing her dark and unhealed side as well as the light and loving side. But Susan had arrived at the ripe old age of forty and hadn't found such a relationship. Try as she might to get beneath the surface and really connect with another, she continually experienced tension and fear when she got too close. Would he like her if he knew her dark secrets? Would she be ridiculed if she said something stupid? Would she be rejected if she followed her own drummer rather than conform to the beliefs of others? Susan looked around and saw others paralyzed by the same fears and doubts. Their answer was to protect themselves with socially acceptable, self-protective masks. They learned social games, etiquette, and rules for relating to others.

53

Before long, the outer crusts and games were all there were between people. Their inner truths had been forgotten and neglected. The truths within and between people were gobbled up by the cancerous growth of fear. The drug of robotic acting quelled their genuineness.

The shallow and fragile nature of surface connections is all many of us ever know. Yet, for many there remains an innate knowledge of unity -- that state of complete and seamless connecting. While few know how to achieve unity, most of us recognize when it's absence in a relationship. We know it when we say our relationship is "not clicking" or that "something is missing." But ask a person to explain what is missing or what doesn't click and you'll get only nebulous and vague answers. People don't know how to specify this rare and valued commodity and they don't have a clue how it may be achieved.

It's rare for us ever to be truly open and vulnerable with another about our most intimate thoughts and feelings. Even with those closest to us, we maintain a self-protective mask. Occasionally, the superficiality of our connections is brought into focus when a trauma ripples through our lives. It is at such critical points, when we desperately need understanding, support, and connection, that we become aware of our loneliness.

We feel something is missing with our partners, with our family members, and with our friends. We say we love each other and we define the word *love* as an emotional verb that connotes deep caring, possessiveness, and belonging. We *love* a person who is dependent on us, as children are. We love those who are with us in our times of need. We know this love is real because we're willing to give our lives for those we really love. But is our definition of *love* the same as unity? Do we fully connect on the intellectual, emotional and spiritual levels with those we love? Do our loved ones really know who we are? Do we really know another person fully in his or her strengths and weaknesses? Do we love all of another person and does he or she love all of us? Most often the answer is no.

Real love requires substantive connection -- a true sharing and joining of our inner truths and deepest emotions with another. Love doesn't have self-protective barriers, for real love has no fear. Only those who have attained a high level of emotional, intellectual, and spiritual maturity seem able to love without fear. In most relationships there is ample fear between people as they "act right" and "do good" to preserve the slender threads connecting them. They fear being real. They fear expressing their true feelings and perceptions. And their fear destroys love, for fear is the antithesis of love. Fear destroys the connections between people, and ultimately fear destroys the people themselves.

Love, as we know it and practice it, is full of fear. When Susan asked her mother what love was, her mother replied that love was "being there when another was in need and knowing they'd be there for you in your time of need." This definition of love anticipates a state of neediness and sees love as the insurance policy that will meet those needs.

Need-based love assumes a possessive relationship -- he loves me and must help me because he's my husband, my son, my friend, my brother, or my father. The love object is an extension of ourselves and belongs to us. This type of love is conditional and has strings attached. If we're honest, we'll acknowledge that this is the type of love found in most families, marriages, and friendships. Unwritten expectations and possessive love are the norm. Subtle messages are, "I'll do this for you and I expect you to do likewise for me; I'll accept you and love you if you meet my expectations." Love is reduced to obligations, rules, expectations, and "doing."

A purer and deeper love is based on one's essence or state of being. Regardless of the overt "doing," unconditional love requires knowing, accepting, and loving the very core of the person. But, before we can join with the inner essence of another, we must first know, love, and join with our own inner essence. We need to love ourselves fully and unconditionally. We must see the dark regions of our souls, embrace them, and commit to their healing. We must acknowledge the special gifts and strengths we possess and use those strengths to lead us to truth and peace. When we have faced and quelled our own internal doubts and fears, when we have learned to love ourselves unconditionally, only then are we ready to find unity with others.

The Road to Unity: A Journey Inward Leading Us Out

Unity implies harmony and oneness in thought, purpose, or quality. Fundamental agreement of and synthesis of varied parts of a whole constitute unity. With the coming together of various elements, we think of unity *with* others in group situations. Unity can also refer to a state *within* a person. We believe the journey toward unity must begin with an inward focus. We must examine to see if we are equally balanced in intellectual, emotional, and spiritual maturity? Are we centered in the knowledge of our purpose and life's greater meaning? Or are we tossed around by life's twists and turns? Do external situations -- relationships, jobs, money, status, power -- dictate our view of ourselves and our understanding of the universe?

The journey inward requires us to look closely at ourselves to find the truth of who we are. What are our strengths and weaknesses? What are our unhealed wounds and blind spots? What are the fundamental beliefs and values guiding our lives? Most people avoid such concentrated introspection, but those committed to reaching full empowerment and unity demand it. Empowered love with another is possible only with one also traveling the road to full actualization. The world has many distractions and snares pulling us from the road to inner unity, but only when we reject external world activities and focus on our

56

inner growth and on *becoming* will we find the truth, hope, and peace for which we seek.

Ingredients Needed for Interpersonal Unity

The belief in unity within ourselves and with others gives us hope. We long for the inexplicable joy we find in the moment we're fully understood and fully accepted. It's the hope of finding a safe harbor amidst the storms of life and knowing that we truly belong. Before the hope of unity is realized, we must scrape off our layers of self-protection. We must subject our inner darkness to the light of full scrutiny. It's a difficult life task to acknowledge and heal our hurts, defenses and fears. When we accept this difficult challenge, we commit to the journey of self-empowerment. We stand unashamed in the light of truth. Unfortunately, many of us would rather hide our flaws and insecurities and join with others who will cushion our weaknesses. Our relationships become "needles floating on surface tension."

We recently had dinner with a close friend, Donnie, who was going through a divorce. Donnie is a therapist and eagerly shared his pain and his understanding of the problems leading to the separation. In just a few words, he defined the primary ingredients of true heart connections. He said his partner "was not his friend and was satisfied with getting a C in life." Donnie wasn't satisfied with "good enough." He wanted the intimacy of true friendship. He wanted interpersonal depth and meaning that superseded ritualized game playing -- and his partner didn't. Superficial relationships seem fine until one partner decides to grow and change. The fragile balance of acting out stale, shallow scripts is easily shattered when one partner rejects the status quo and seeks more. Seeking more than a "C" in life is a requisite step in the journey to personal empowerment, happiness, and true love.

The other quality Donnie was looking for was true friendship.

Friendship is a word commonly used with little thought about its true meaning. The deep friendships we've observed have four commonalties: (1) friends trust each other to safeguard their well being; (2) they share basic personality similarities and values; (3) they're open and vulnerable in sharing their inner truths and feelings; and (4) they're committed to growth and wholeness. We believe these characteristics of true friendships give clues to the nature and process of achieving unity in friendships and in primary, intimate relationships.

(1) Friends trust each other to safeguard their mutual well being

Trust is an abstract -- you can't see it, package it or put it under your arm and tote it around. But you can emotionally feel trust, or the absence of it, in a relationship. People assume they know the meaning of trust, but when relationships are objectively examined, trust is frequently missing.

Two clients come to mind who recognized they had difficulty trusting others. When asked what were the necessary ingredients of trust, Janet responded "trust requires mutual respect, acceptance, and freedom from any threat of being manipulated or controlled." She was part of a large, tightly knit family that held conservative religious, political, and social beliefs. Janet remembered several times that she was ridiculed and embarrassed by family members for her more liberal views. The family culture was permeated with subtle and suffocating pressures to conform. Conditional acceptance and love were the payoffs for conforming. But Janet's voice wouldn't be silenced. She spoke her truth and ruffled the family's comfort zone. The one rule she dared not transgress was her mother's censure of gays. Her mother once told the family that a close friend's son had died of AIDS. She then added her belief that the disease was God's way of getting rid of "junk." Janet was numb with anger and pain at her mother's statement. While none of the other family members verbally supported their mother's hate-filled judgment, they shrank back

58

from confronting her about it. How could Janet trust any family member enough to tell them she was gay? Her conditions for trust -- respect, acceptance and absence of power games -- were all violated. She decided never to trust and share who she was with anyone within her family. It's sad they missed knowing the very beautiful and loving soul who lived among them in secrecy and fear.

Carl offered a different perspective on trust. He said trust exists on two levels: internal and external. Internal trust is our ability to trust ourselves. Internal trust is different from the false bravado that stems from our ego. Much that comes from our ego is contaminated by the deceptive facade we present to the world and the superficial roles we play when connecting with others. The process of building internal trust can be very threatening to our ego for it leads us to challenge each and every one of our defensive, self-protective responses. The process begins with continuous, ongoing scrutiny of our own motivations and intentions. It is through this rigorous self-monitoring and self-examination that we are able to finally know and understand who we truly are and to take control of our own lives. As a result of our questioning, we begin to see our unconscious psychological triggers. We become empowered to choose our feelings, thoughts and actions rather than being controlled by hurtful and disempowering tapes recorded deep within our subconscious. Internal trust involves owning and acting on our personal strength and power. Once we truly know and trust ourselves, we become empowered in truth. We feel secure enough to reach out, to open, and to connect with others.

External trust is an extension of our internal trust. The accomplishment of knowing and trusting oneself allows us to share our inner selves with others and establish connections based on truth, candor, and respect. External trust is possible with those who have done the same hard work of self-scrutiny as we. Trustworthy others are past self-absorption and ego-security needs. They are able to join with us in mutual support and understanding. Without manipulation, we can speak openly and honestly with one another of our needs, wants, and feelings. They extend to us -- and we extend to them -- in genuine caring.

Carl was having some difficulty with both internal and external trust. He wasn't sure if his perceptions were correct. He scrutinized his motives and the motives of others from every angle. When asked about the root of his distrust, he related a childhood memory. His father had a job that required weekday travel and he was home only on weekends. Tired and unable to cope with the demands of four children, Carl's father yelled and physically punished them for being noisy and rambunctious. Each Sunday he would exercise his paternal duty and gather the children for church. If one child was running late, he or she was threatened or slapped. Carl remembers many Sundays when he sulked behind the others as they walked into church. He was red-eyed from crying and full of rage at the unwarranted beating he had just endured. During the church service, he watched his father fervently pray and serve as a deacon. Even as a child, Carl seethed in resentment at his father's hypocrisy. Soon his distrust and anger spread to other adults who seemed to be only veneer. He believed adults were merely pretense and image without truth or substance.

As years passed, Carl had other negative experiences with selfish and power-hungry people. His distrust spread each time another person tried to use or control him. In adulthood, he's had several bosses who were like his Dad -- determined to control Carl and make him submit to their power. Carl isn't even sure he can trust his wife Mary, who often seems emotionally distant and unconcerned about his problems. In actuality, she's tired of Carl's paranoid behavior and wishes he would just "lighten up." Mary chooses to remain naive and believe those around her are all good, while Carl chooses to suspect others of being hypocritical users and abusers. Each had refused to go within to critically evaluate the source and substance of the old tapes that were controlling them. Now, they are each finding that real truth lies somewhere between her naivete and his self-protective cynicism. Carl is painfully and slowly working on internal and external trust as he owns his self-worth and lets down his self-protective barriers.

When we trust others, we know they won't hurt us or lie to us. We don't have to put on our social masks because they accept us for who we are -- light and dark, negative and positive. They know and respect the real us. Internal trust requires the same -- we must truly know ourselves, value our specialness, and accept the godliness at our core. The darker sides of who we are must be accepted, healed, and transformed. We trust true friends when they know themselves and will share their *real* selves with us. We extend our trust and caring to them, and we know they will reciprocate.

(2) Friends share basic similarities and values

Likes repel, but only in electricity and magnetism. Most people feel more connected with those like them in personality, values, perceptions and beliefs. We all know people who are very different from us whom we call friends. If we look closely, we'll probably admit they're only surface acquaintances. They don't share sufficient similarities with us to establish the deep, meaningful connection of friendship. While personality style and similar interests are bonding ingredients, we believe the most important components of meaningful connections are similar levels of intellectual, emotional and spiritual development. Those committed to continued growth and full empowerment are attracted to others of similar persuasion. True connecting is *not* something that forms on the surface, but rather, occurs deep within, down beneath the layers of veneer that we present to the outside world. It's the place we call resonance: where we either fit into and resonate with the thought patterns and beliefs of another, or we don't. Much like electrical or sound frequencies that don't match, human relationships that don't match become perturbed or dissonant. We want them to be genuine and real, but our disparate internal truths keep bubbling to the surface creating emotional distance, frustration, and even conflict.

The similarity between friends increases understanding, communication, and trust. When Michael first asked why people didn't genuinely and deeply connect with each other, Donna replied that people were on different developmental levels. Some people are stunted in emotional, intellectual or spiritual development and either fail to connect or connect only in codependent neediness. Other people have moved past their emotional barriers and connect honestly and deeply with others who are equally developed. Similar levels of maturity are of primary importance to sustained and impassioned friendships.

(3) Friends show vulnerability and openly share their inner truths and feelings

Sharing of inner truth and emotional vulnerability is analogous to baring one's soul. People need to first discover who they are at their core. They need to scrutinize their own strengths and weaknesses and share their unvarnished selves with trusted friends. Instead, people go through their entire lives without engaging even one true connection. While they marry, have children, and engage in surface friendships, they spend their lives "together, but all alone."

For us, sharing is working with our partner to discover and reveal our deepest truths, wants, and needs. This is the only true sharing. Whether or not the partner is willing to do the same largely determines the level of resonance we spoke of earlier. Equality, resonance, and sharing go hand-in-hand. For, unless there is deep resonant similarity, and unless there is commitment by each partner to grow, true sharing cannot occur. Sharing must be honest and deep; sharing must be reciprocal; and sharing must be total. Unless we commit to grow past our fears and dependencies, our relationships remain shallow and false.

The sharing that most of us have come to know usually revolves around "safe" subjects: sports, the weather, happenings during the day, or our health. Sometimes, we even share our intellectual truths, our thoughts, ideas, and perceptions. Rarely, however, do we share our emotional truths. While we may express our surface feelings, we seldom dive into the deeper water holding the secret origins of our feelings. We are much more guarded about the assumptions and biases that really direct and control our lives.

Howard is a good example of a person who believed he was sharing, but who was actually closed and controlling. Howard came to our *Sacred Relationship* workshop with one thought in mind -- he wanted to fix his wife Claire so she would again share her feelings and thoughts with him as she did before they were married. During one of the activity sessions, Howard told Claire, "When you were going through your divorce, you'd lean on me and tell me everything. Now you say very little to me and I feel the distance increasing." The melancholy cry of a man losing his wife was heart wrenching, but as the weekend progressed, sympathies shifted to Claire. Throughout the weekend Howard made passive aggressive remarks about Claire's homemaking, cooking, and decision-making abilities. She escaped his barbs by taking walks by herself and refusing to respond to his jibes. During a workshop exercise, Howard completed the sentence stem, "I was very irritated when" by citing an example of a person failing to complete contracted work to Howard's satisfaction. As we role played emotional sharing using this cue, Howard was asked to explain how he felt.

"I was just irritated. People should do what they say they'll do," Howard replied.

"You get angry when people don't live up to their

63

responsibilities. By not carrying their load, they shift an undue burden on you," Donna countered in an attempt to draw Howard out.

"Yes, they make me angry. But I just tell them what I expect, and usually they follow up after they're told." Howard could control most people with his one-up, autocratic manner.

Donna pushed Howard to look deeper into the source of his irritation. "Do you remember other times when people have reneged on their responsibilities and assumed you would carry their load?"

"Yes, many times," Howard spit out with intensity and venom.

"Who were those people and what were the situations that irritated you?" Donna inquired.

"I don't want to talk about it. You just don't understand me. I said I was irritated. What don't you understand about the word irritation?" Howard shot back.

"Is Claire one of those people who disappoints you by not completing tasks to your satisfaction?" Donna dared voice what was obvious.

"Yes. And don't ask me any more questions. You are tricking me into saying things I don't want to say." Howard was stonewalling and attempting to turn the tables and blame Donna. He was unwilling to dive into his inner truth and look at his own emotional imprinting. He was unwilling to give up his one-up, judgmental style. Frozen in his fear of being vulnerable, he closed emotionally.

Howard is an example of someone willing to share his surface feelings, but unwilling to search for the deeper emotional meanings behind his behaviors. Did Howard's parents model the one-up, judging style of relating he has now adopted? Does Howard need control over others to feel comfortable and secure?

There are many unanswered questions, but Howard is too self-protective to seek the answers that would free him from his isolation and disconnection with Claire. Claire seems destined to live with a husband who has thick ego boundaries and refuses to truly share himself with her. The prognosis for their connecting on any meaningful level looks dim. Instead of being friends and sharing emotional truths, they freeze in parent-child transactions with Howard judging and Claire escaping.

Being vulnerable and sharing feelings -- particularly the risky emotions that we can be judged or rejected for -- are essential to true connecting. Doing otherwise is just acting out socially acceptable, stiff, and essentially untruthful roles. Our feelings reflect our inner truth. When we stuff our feelings, we're hiding who we are. When we hide our feelings, we are moving away from inner unity and even further from unity with another.

(4) Commitment to growth and wholeness

Friends encourage our continued growth toward wholeness and balanced intellectual, emotional and spiritual development. Intellectual, emotional, and spiritual balance doesn't necessarily mean absolute equality between partners, although symmetry within a person and between partners enhances the resonance and depth of the relationship.

Those who seek intellectual wisdom have a thirst for a special kind of knowledge. Their intent is not to earn advanced degrees or to hold prestigious appointments, for wisdom has little to do with those materialistic affectations. What they want is to learn as much as possible about life and what it means to be fully alive. In a relationship, this continual intellectual growth requires the person to be honest, energetic, and committed. The intent behind intellectual growth is universal understanding and putting the pieces of life's meaning into a coherent whole. This definition of intellectual development is far different from the fragmented and narrowly focused definitions of intellectual growth offered in our universities. The world defines intellectual growth as knowing things. The more pervasive definition of wisdom includes knowing how to think abstractly and search for meaning hidden in repetitive, but obscure, life patterns. Those who are intellectually wise tend to choose friends who think like they do -- in the abstract rather than the concrete; with curiousity rather than arrogant smugness; with openness to new ideas rather than defense of old and tired answers.

The emotionally mature understand and appropriately channel their feelings. They are both forgiving of their own humanness and empathic to others' weaknesses. The empathetic friend feels with us. Emotional empathy is a transaction between equals. Sympathy, however, is feeling "for" another. Sympathy is a one-up transaction of pitying a victim. When we're confronted with a troubling life event, friends grasp us by the hand as supportive equals. We want friends to lend their energy temporarily when our energy is depleted. We want them to walk by our side through the rough times -- but not carry us. We don't want a condescending and sympathetic pat on the hand that translates into, "I'm sorry you're down, and I'm glad I'm not."

Friends walk beside us and lend us courage and strength to transcend life's difficulties. They express confidence in our ability to transcend challenges. Friends believe we need to connect and help each other with the inevitable pot holes along life's journey. Friends don't take pleasure from our transient emotional imbalances, nor do they condemn them -- for they know these imbalances are a part of every human who feels, takes risks, makes mistakes, and is truly alive. Friends are the first to applaud our accomplishments and the first to let us know when we're not living up to our abilities. Their love and commitment to us help us regain a balanced perspective and emotional equilibrium.

We achieve emotional balance when we understand and control unconscious motivations underlying our behaviors and perceptions. Howard's story exemplifies the unbalanced emotional self. Self-protected and defensive, he was unwilling to examine the emotional motivations beneath his pattern of one-up control. When a person is developed emotionally, she or he can readily identify emotions and trace emotional imprinting back to its source.

Emotional wisdom empowers people to share inner feelings with another. Emotionally balanced people are unafraid to feel and express their true feelings with trustworthy friends. Emotional sharing creates true bonding. In their mutual commitment to growth, both partners are able to share themselves in an *active process of becoming.*

The quest for spiritual maturity begins with questions about the meaning of life. Ultimately, it's our belief in a power greater than ourselves that gives reason and purpose to our existence. The search for spiritual meaning ignites our quests to become our true and empowered selves. As we commit to our spiritual journey, we often find we're able to connect most closely with friends who are also growing spiritually.

When we're committed to our own growth and to the continued growth of our primary relationships, we pledge to live and voice our truth in a manner that stimulates the growth of our partner. Most of us connect and establish superficial acquaintances with many people for short periods. These relationships remain shallow because they lack the prerequisites for deep and genuine friendships -- trust, vulnerability, sharing, similarity, and commitment to continued growth and balance.

Seeing the Difference between True and False Unity

Unfortunately, most of us maintain long but ultimately shallow relationships with people we call friends. The triviality in these connections comes from each person's unwillingness to grow and pursue internal truth.

Michael tells the story of a long term relationship that looked deep and real, but lacked the commitment to complementary growth, truth, and emotional sharing:

"I've learned the hard way that it's not the length of time we know someone that defines true friendship, it's the quality of the interactions during that time. If we spend ten years enabling each other's weaknesses in a codependent friendship, we've wasted ten precious years that could have been used to strengthen and deepen true friendship. Reggie, my best friend in high school and college, provides a sad example.

Reggie and I met in our sophomore year. He'd been in a serious car accident that had left him physically impaired with periodic episodes of pain and depression. I'd arrived at that point in my life carrying an equal load of anger and depression from an alcoholic father and the "unfair" onset of insulin-dependent diabetes. Reggie and I became best friends and were constant companions throughout the rest of high school and college. We shared a long-term history of togetherness, but we didn't help each other grow. We only facilitated each other's fears and weaknesses.

Reggie's heavy drinking in college turned into alcoholism after graduation. In the years that followed, he liquidated and rapidly exhausted the money he had received from a sizable land inheritance. Reggie and I remained close friends and I spent many days with him, watching him drink himself into a stupor -- and doing nothing. When I moved several states away, I let Reggie and his difficulties drop from my mind. On my infrequent visits home, I noticed Reggie's disease was becoming worse, yet I said nothing as he fell deeper and deeper into financial trouble and emotional despair. Reggie needed help, and none of his friends took any action. I wasn't shocked when I learned Reggie had killed himself. He'd been running for over a year from federal officials for income tax evasion. As his alcoholic disease and financial situation worsened, I guess he saw no avenue of escape. I live with the guilt of not intervening when hope was still possible. I regret not having the strength to confront Reggie about his drinking. I regret not being a mirror of truth to this man who desperately needed to connect with someone. Reggie needed to share his fears and doubts. He needed a positive perspective and hope for a better tomorrow. I could have tried to give him "a light at the end of the tunnel," but I didn't.

Certainly, the primary responsibility for Reggie's drinking and despair was Reggie's. But I was his best friend. What can I say about the quality of my friendship, my commitment to Reggie's growth, and commitment to the health of our relationship? Did my friendship stand the test of honesty? I saw and I did nothing. Reggie taught me a very important lesson about commitment to truth and growth in a relationship."

These requirements for friendship may seem stiff, and you may ask, Don't I risk losing my friends if I demand honesty of not only myself but of them? Walking the path to inner truth and full self-empowerment is the single hardest thing any of us will ever do. If we choose to grow while our spouses, partners, or friends chose to maintain long-anchored patterns of stagnation and dependency, we must examine our consciences and make some difficult choices. We may have to decide if we want to settle for a C in this life, or if we want an A+. Anchoring ourselves in complacency and fear with those who find the status quo acceptable will only enable and maintain a disempowered and codependent world.

Human Unity and Unconditional Love

Why do some seem oblivious to the pull toward true unity while others refuse to accept anything less? Unity is the state of complete and unconditional love. While unconditional love is a popular term, it's seldom understood and even more rarely practiced. During a recent group therapy session, group members discussed the meaning of unconditional love. The group, all wise and mature women, were firmly committed to their own growth.

Susan piped up with an answer that reflected both her intellectual prowess and emotional maturity. "Unconditional love is accepting and loving a person totally, in their darkness and lightness, their problems and joys. It's connecting with the essence of another. It's based on who the person is rather than what the person does. You can't earn unconditional love. Only a few people are capable of giving unconditional love, in my opinion."

Cathy had been silent during most of the group meeting. She always sat back and took in what others were saying before she offered her own opinion. A gentle, loving and spiritual aura surrounded her. She appeared almost too sensitive to survive in a callous and cruel world. "Unconditional love is God's type of love. It's the model of love shown to us by Christ. Those who love unconditionally won't accept hurtful and dishonest behavior. However, they do accept people without judgment or condemnation. It's a love with expectation of excellence. Those people who love unconditionally have grown to the highest level of intellectual, emotional and spiritual development. They gently urge others to commit to growth and maturity. Unconditional love is learning to love as Christ loved."

"I accept that definition, Cathy, but I see so few examples of unconditional love in our world. Everyone seems too caught up in themselves to look outside and really care about others." Diane added with a sigh of despair.

We have traditionally defined unconditional love according to behavior -- accepting each other without judgment and without strings attached. An example of unconditional love is the constant love of a mother for a child, even when the child becomes unacceptable to others; i.e., when the child commits a heinous, criminal act. Parents may be capable of unconditional love for their children, but unconditional love generally doesn't extend beyond the parent-child relationship (if it's found there). Most of us would leave a spouse if his or her behavior was abusive or insensitive to our needs. Most of us would reject the friend who asked for loans and forgot to pay us back. Most of us have conditions attached to our love. People put on their masks of unconditional love, but in the long run, the conditions attached to their love become apparent.

Unconditional love is found within each person's essence rather than in his or her behavior. Is the person truly loving -- of self and others? Does the person readily embrace his or her humanness -- both the good *and* bad, the light *and* the dark sides? Does the person balance his or her own needs and feelings with the needs and feelings of others? Does the person scrutinize his or her own personal intentions before passing judgment on another? Does the person seek the hard path of inner truth or does he bend to self-interest and materialism?

Love, truth, and discernment are the interwoven characteristics of people capable of unconditional love. In unity, we accept others and are accepted without reservation. We are equal among equals. We don't have to be good or pleasing to be accepted. We're embraced in the fullness of our strengths and our weaknesses. We can be just who we are. Connecting in unconditional love is the zenith of human unity, but few people are advanced enough to offer and accept unconditional love.

Spiritual Unity

James Redfield, in the *Celestine Prophecy*, defines unity as *a connection with the energy of the Divine.* In a world that validates only what can be confirmed by human senses, what propels some to believe there is unity with the Divine? Some explain this belief in unity as the remembrance of a soul connection with the Creator. Others say that the spark of the Divine is always within us and we never lose the connection. Most humans are too consumed with the world's "busy-ness" to give time and energy to the search for the Divine spark within them. Most remain asleep in their denial, refusing to accept the possibility of a God and their individual

71

responsibility in a larger Divine plan. They choose to remain victims of despair and cynicism. They accept and perpetuate the world's evils with either silence or deed. But others do stop and wonder about God and about their lives. Their search for spiritual unity often leads to life transformations that separate them from the drudgery of life's worries and heaviness.

Some humans have extraordinary spiritual experiences that result in an understanding of unity. Near death experiences (NDEs) generally have the common theme of exiting earthly consciousness and entering a state of unconditional love. The general experience of being in the presence of an all-knowing and all-loving Divine Being is common in NDEs. Unconditional love is so pleasurable that most NDE survivors say they'd rather stay in the "death state" than return to human consciousness.

For most of us, an understanding of unity is something tucked back in the far corners of our unconsciousness. We're not sure if it is a remembrance of a spiritual state or the symbiotic state with our mother. It's the belief that unity is possible that urges us onward in our quest to connect with others. In the quiet of our minds and hearts, we hunger for relationships that are genuine and deep. We may long for the right person, a soul mate, who will fully understand and connect with us on all levels. The belief in unity becomes the standard against which all relationships are measured. In unity, we fully belong and are fully loved. In unity, there is an end to disillusionment and loneliness. Deep within us is the relentless pull toward unity. We need only listen to the inner voice of truth and love.

When we tire of shallowness in our lives and in our relationships and when we find the courage to demand more of ourselves and of others, then our paths become clear. Happiness and deep connections with others cannot be found if our lives are distorted and controlled by denial, repression, and codependency. We must first commit to our full empowerment and then we must seek out others who have made that same commitment. Only then will we individually, and collectively, move toward true unity.

Chapter Four

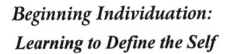

Beginning Individuation:
Learning to Define the Self

Beginning Individuation: Learning to Define the Self

In my dream, I was going to a Jimmy Buffet concert with four other women. We had to travel some distance by bus. We reached our destination and got out in front of an austere looking army barracks, where we spent the night. The next day we were in a buoyant mood as we dressed for the concert. We were in the lighthearted spirit of "parrot-head" party-goers. Although I wanted to look colorful and casual like the others, for some reason I put on an army uniform. We left the barracks and walked across a meadow to the concert arena. The person at the collection gate seemed odd to me. Her formal dress and stern, high-class bearing, contrasted with the flamboyant and rowdy parrot-heads surrounding the gate. My four friends handed her their tickets as I dug into my coat pockets looking for mine. I was embarrassed when I couldn't find my ticket and realized I must have left it in the barracks. I explained my predicament to the ticket taker. In that moment, I also realized I was inappropriately dressed. I asked the woman if I had time to go back to the barracks and get my ticket and change clothes. She gave me a cold, dispassionate look and said, "You will have to decide."

I spun around and started running across the field toward the barracks. When I reached my room, I dumped all the clothes from my suitcase and searched frantically for the ticket. Within a few minutes, I found the ticket. I then wondered if I had time to change my clothes. I decided not to change and started running back to the concert arena. As I ran, I wondered why my friends hadn't offered to go back to the barracks with me. I felt alone and angry. I reached the gate just as the last concert goers were filing into the arena. I handed the ticket to the woman and rushed in to find my friends.

- Susan, age 42

Susan looked perplexed as she finished reporting the dream during her therapy session. "What in the world do you think that dream means? It's just gibberish to me!"

With no surface meaning obvious, Donna concentrated on Susan's essence. The descriptive phrase that best describes Susan is "spark plug." Susan is energy plus. She's verbally quick and amazingly creative. She's a poet who combines words in idiosyncratic ways that challenge the mind to move beyond conventional understanding. Her apartment and clothing also echo her flair for the artistic, the unusual, the fun. She's a breath of fresh air. Susan is also a caretaker, which means some of her energetic and happy facade is a masquerade worn for the benefit of others. Her true feelings, wants, and needs remain buried. Susan shows only what is pleasant and acceptable to others. Like other caretakers, Susan believes she can buy love from others by pleasing and giving them what they want.

Susan barters for love -- pleasing and caretaking in trade for acceptance and belonging. To a world asleep, she seems the epitome of maturity, happiness and rationality. Susan expends much energy hiding her dark, brooding side. Buried beneath her masked depression are anger and grief over a lost childhood.

Susan had learned early that she must sacrifice her own freedom and individuality to the neediness of her rigid, fearful and controlling parents. Not able to function as fully empowered adults, her parents were more concerned with their issues than her growth. Her individuation process was stunted early in life as she molded herself into the daughter her parents wanted. The unique and exceptional person shrank as she repressed her feelings and her voice. Too young to rebel against suffocating parental dictates, she became the repository for the projected wishes and needs of others. The way she was with others -- her outer self-- was defined by the pleasing and caretaking game she had perfected through the years. Her inner self, that unparalleled person with special meaning and purpose, never developed.

Now, at age 40, she is finally beginning to grieve her lost inner-child. She grieves loss of the very special person who budded but never fully blossomed. She realizes the love she desperately wanted and sought to attain by subjugating her needs was not authentic love. Love with conditions attached is not real love; rescuing and caretaking are not synonyms for true love. Susan has learned what love *isn't* the hard way. She left two marriages after the pattern of non-reciprocal caretaking left her exhausted and bitter. Her undeveloped ex-partners expected a nurturing mother who would give to them without expectation of return. Both ex-husbands refused to grow and become Susan's equal partner. The weight of holding up these relationships alone had been too great. So Susan finally became resentful and left.

Susan also grieves the loss of meaningful family connections. Her mother, father and sister chose to live behind their masks. Like most people, they were conventional, conforming, and compulsive. They weren't real. None of them had undertaken the hard work of going within to find out who they really were. As a result, they had nothing of real substance to share. They lived together, but each was all alone. Superficial connecting was all Susan knew, so it seemed normal. Yet, a voice within her heart whispered that something much deeper was possible between people. Within her was a knowing of unity that kept her searching for the diamond among the rhinestones -- the true love among the counterfeit connections. Having reached a point in life where her inner truth was screaming to be freed, Susan was finally confronting the real source of her inner rage and depression. She was seeing the reason for all those lost years, lost relationships, and lost self -- and she was about ready to explode.

Tuning into Susan's essence helped Donna see her life pattern which had been so ingeniously presented in the dream. A wake-up call had reverberated from deep within her spirit warning Susan that unfinished business had been put off too long. It was time for Susan to reject her self-defeating pattern of buying love through self-sacrifice. In changing her pattern, Susan would need to take a serious look at how she defined love.

Donna offered an interpretation of Susan's dream: "Susan, I

believe your dream is giving you the signal that it's time to individuate and find your true self."

Trained as a therapist herself, Susan knew exactly what this meant, "The individuation process is one of separation from others and claiming the self. You believe I haven't done this yet?"

Donna nodded yes, "Pleasing others has been so ingrained into you that it permeates your every action and every thought. You're afraid to show the real you -- the unhealed and undeveloped parts you're embarrassed about. You will only show your "up side" -- strong, caring and cheerful. It's time to turn from being externally oriented and playing the role others want you to play. It's time to focus inward and find out who you are and what you want. Your dream seems to be telling you that. The Jimmy Buffet concert, with its promise of colorful fun, contrasted with the drab and stark image of army barracks. This dreary image is a reflection of how you view your restrained world. In the army world, everything is regimented and controlled. There is no room for individuality. People perform as a unit but never really connect with each other. I believe your family was like an army unit -- acting out roles instead of owning their individuality. They operated as a unit but they never connected."

On an unconscious level, I believe you're angry at those people who should have been close to you, but who remained too immature to have intimate relationships. I think you're depressed at the lost opportunities for real love and connection. All those people around you -- husbands, mother, father, and sister -- refused to look at themselves and grow beyond dependency, neediness and fear. They remained ensconced in their ego bubble of false security. Your dream draws attention to your gray and depressed inner self and challenges you to move forward into a more colorful and exciting world.

Donna continued, "Isn't it interesting that you didn't have the admission ticket and had to go back and search for it. And, you had to go back and search for it all alone. That's basically the story of individuation. People have a difficult time finding the path to true empowerment and self-actualization. Those who find the path -- and have their tickets -- open to a world that's much more exciting and colorful. You've been conforming and adapting to the rules of others for a long time now. It's time for you to find your own way -- your own truth. And Susan, as your dream has revealed, you must do this alone. That means no one can tell you what your inner truth is. I can walk the path toward inner truth beside you and be your sounding board and your support. But this journey is up to you. I've walked a similar path for myself and found it to be both exciting and painful. No one can force you to take the journey toward completed individuation and self-actualization. That's why the ticket taker told you, 'You have to decide.' Free will is always honored. You can choose to stay stuck in worldly shoulds and oughts, as did your family and two former husbands, or you can accept the responsibility to grow and become all you were meant to be."

After a few minutes of silence, Susan quietly added, "I'll think about what you said. We can talk about it during next week's therapy session." Susan was facing the challenge of self-scrutiny and the fear of removing her life-long, self-protective mask. She knew it meant the death of her old ego and her dependent identity. It meant taking risks that would be frightening and might be painful.

Donna got an urgent message from Susan the next day. She was crying and said she needed an emergency therapy session. "I want you to see me this way. I'm so low I don't think I can pull myself up anymore. I never let people see this side of me. You need to see the real me."

Susan was finally ready to travel through her shadow side and uncover her inner truth. And she was finally ready to share her real self with another.

81

"This isn't like me," Susan began. "I've always had faith in God and in the Divine spark of God within me. Never giving up, I was a master at making lemonade out of lemons. But now I'm so low I can't even believe in God anymore. Nothing works for me -- I've tried different therapists, I've tried the spiritual route. I'm still in the same place I was twenty-five years ago. I haven't found any peace and I'm thinking of giving up on therapy. I don't have any hope; I just can't try any more!"

Donna's joyful response shocked her, "Thank God you've hit rock bottom! You've spent your whole life playing by other peoples' rules. You've been acting a role written for someone else, and finally you're tired of walking the false road that only goes around in circles. You now see it gets you nowhere! And you're angry at God. Good for you, Susan. If you can get angry at God, humans won't be so formidable. I remember the time I hit rock bottom. I felt completely alone and I blamed God for all my misery. I screamed, cussed and played the 'poor me' child who criticized God for abandoning me. And you know what God did? Absolutely nothing. He let me wallow in my self-pity long enough until I got red hot burning mad. When I finally felt my rage, I felt my power. I got so angry that I became determined to fight. The world wasn't going to defeat me! I became righteously indignant with the world and with all the ignorant and cruel people who had tried to destroy me. It was during my worst hour that I made an oath to win. I knew I had the power to prevail. The real me had waited forty years to emerge and when it finally came out, there was no power strong enough to stop me from succeeding!"

As Donna's tirade slowed, a glimmer of optimism twinkled in Susan's eye. Susan's slight response convinced Donna to challenge her further: "Are you ready to give up the helpless child who expects God to save her? Are you ready to claim your adulthood and your full power? You'll have to strip off the worldly mask and let the real you shine! You will have to stop believing you are a victim. Gosh, Susan, what a diamond you are.

You are incredibly creative. Yet, your neediness and fear of rejection cause you to hide behind a socially acceptable, but false image. Stop being what others want you to be and start being you! You don't have to *do* anything to be loved. You only need to *be* the loving, exciting, and passionate person you already are."

Susan's natural vitality and joy were smothered by the draining influence of a severely depressed mother. Susan's mother was the ultimate "poor me" who existed in an ongoing state of self-absorbed misery. The family's energy swirled around the mother as they paid homage to her victim status by worrying and taking care of her. Susan's older sister, Claire, chose her mother's needy, poor me model. To the outside world, Claire projects the image of a helpless and fragile china doll, but within her family she rules with tyrannical force and ironclad control.

Susan recognized the same smothering web of neediness and fear in Claire's family that dominated her childhood. Claire steals the life energy from those around her, while Susan mimics her selfless, caretaker father. Like her dad, Susan became entangled in the caretaking game of trying to save others from themselves. There's no way to win this game -- the harder you try to make another person happy, healthy and whole, the deeper they sink into helplessness. Why should they change? They have your undivided attention as you unceasingly provide them with your energy and concern. Like psychic vampires, they suck the life force from others and never search to find the vitality within themselves. Susan and her father tried the impossible -- changing his wife, her mother -- but it never worked. They had searched frantically for "the ticket" -- the golden key leading them to connection, hope and happiness. Susan and her father never found that ticket and their caretaking efforts ended only when her mother died. Susan was left exhausted, confused, and loaded down with guilt for not doing more to save her mother.

Donna relayed a story that helped relieve Susan's guilt. "Susan, I remember receiving a frantic phone call from my mother during my freshman year of college. I still recall my mother's words -- 'Come home. You need to help your sister. Her girlfriend just drowned in a boating accident on the lake behind our house and Barbara blames herself. She's crying uncontrollably and I can't stop her.'

I rushed out of the dorm and took a bus to my home town. When I arrived, Barbara had taken a strong sedative and was asleep. The story tumbled from my mother in hurried and choppy sentences. Barbara was cutting grass when her two close friends arrived. They wanted to borrow her boat and go out on the lake. Barbara consented to joining them after she finished her lawn mowing job. A few minutes later, one girl came running back into the front yard yelling 'Michelle, is drowning.' With reckless abandon, Barbara sped to the lake and dived in, still fully clothed. She reached the boat and dived under the water. She felt Michelle grab her leg. Again and again, Barbara tried to pull Michelle to the surface, but Michelle's frantic struggle only pulled Barbara down. Barbara felt herself slipping from consciousness and emerged from the murky water to catch her breath. When she again dove down into the water, she couldn't find Michelle. Michelle's frantic struggle had ended, but Barbara kept diving and searching for her friend. Michelle's body was retrieved some hours later by scuba divers equipped to search the lake's bottom.

When Barbara awoke hours later, her crying resumed immediately. The burden of loss was too heavy for a fifteen year old who only understood life as a long and continuous journey lying ahead. Death was unanticipated and abnormal at her age. As we talked, Barbara slowly accepted the reasoning that she had no choice but to let go of Michelle and surface for air. Had she not broken free, Michelle's frantic struggle would have drowned both of them. The guilt slowly departed as Barbara recognized she wasn't responsible for the accident and that it was okay for her to save her own life."

Susan's lesson was much the same. She found herself being pulled down by her mother's depression and her sister's controlling fear. She kept trying to save them but they were too entangled within their victim/martyr script. Her life energy was consumed by their neediness until her potential to be full, creative, and empowered almost disappeared. After her mother's death, Susan chose two needy, alcoholic husbands who gave her further practice in disengaging from psychic vampires who robbed her of life force. Until she consciously recognized the toxicity in connecting to needy and selfish people, Susan would continue to repeat her self-defeating game of codependency.

The primary task of individuation is defining the self -- the unique and separate entity that is both different and like others. Individuation begins during the first year of life and continues throughout life. Unfortunately, there are many worldly snares along life's journey that impede full individuation. Susan's account tells of giving up self development and conforming to the needs and wants of others. Her predicament is common. She and the multitudes like her must decide whether they're willing to claim their empowered selves or not. The work of individuation requires us to (1) see and understand the interpersonal dynamics that have molded and thwarted our growth; (2) scrutinize selfishness and selflessness; and (3) commit to full individuation and empowerment.

(1) Understanding the Interpersonal Dynamics of Thwarted Individuation

Beginning Individuation is the stage of development that requires the person to admit and confirm his or her separateness -- the unparalleled and peerless "I." With adequate emotional, physical, and spiritual nourishment, the developing child learns to see himself or herself as unique and important. The child learns to value self and expects consideration and respect from others.

85

Autonomy and independence are necessary attainments of *Beginning Individuation*.

However, ego development is only part of individuation. In addition to owning our "separateness," we must also learn to connect with others in "oneness." We are not just singular entities, but a part of the larger "we." So the goal of individuation has two competing goals; separating from others and learning to join with others. It's recognition of our individuality that empowers us to develop our unique gifts, find our inner truths, and ultimately discover and fulfill the meanings and purposes of our lives. Individuation also requires that we learn to connect deeply with others, for our lives have little meaning if we've failed the final exam of knowing human love in its fullest sense.

Those who have reached full individuation are able to balance their separateness and oneness, but they are few. Most of us are stuck in *Beginning Individuation* and haven't come to this balance. We tilt too much in the direction of selfishness or selflessness. We develop a "mask" -- a false persona to hide our undeveloped selves. We attempt to act civilized and mature so we can fit in with the world. Most people concern themselves with their own needs and the needs of those closely aligned with them. Their actions reflect self-interest, security, and control over others. True understanding and compassion are absent. True connection is impossible.

From the moment of birth, we receive messages regarding our place and importance in the world. Some of us grow up in child-centered environments and are showered with care, attention, and love. We are the center of our parents' universe. Others grow up in parent-centered environments. The attention and energy in these homes revolve around the parents and children are expected to conform to their parents' expectations. Given most parents have not completed the *Individuation* process themselves, the direction of our parents' imbalance largely determines the type of childhood environment that molded us.

86

The Making of the Selfish Person: Parents who are more selfless tend to center their time, attention and energy on their children. They generally create more permissive home environments and their children learn to value themselves as separate and special. The energy of the family revolves around the children and their wants and needs.   Children of selfless parents come to see the universe as revolving around them. They learn to love themselves, but their view of themselves and their importance is often distorted.   Self-love becomes narcissism and myopic self-absorption. While owning free will, independence, and autonomy, children in these environments often fail to understand that others have the same needs for respect and freedom.   They often grow into selfish adults who invade others' boundaries and steal time, attention, and energy.   They inflate the importance of their perceptions and disregard the perspectives of others. Their truth is the only truth that's important to them.   They demand that all energy and attention center on them.   They do this by manipulation, intimidation, martyrdom and "poor me" neediness. Their need for attention remains childlike and immature -- they don't understand that others also have personal agendas.   They expect others to bend to their itinerary and they'll use and abuse others with utter disregard.   "Me" is number one.   As long as they get what they want, nothing else matters.

Ironically, the selfish person can also emerge from the opposite environment -- one that is devoid of parental nurturance and support.   In deprived environments, the child's primary needs -- physiological, safety and security needs -- aren't met.   Emotionally chaotic or abusive (substance abuse, emotional, physical or sexual abuse) households thwart the child's development and cause the child to withdraw into self for mere survival.   Antisocial personalities frequently emerge from the family cauldron of severe deprivation.   These warped personalities develop into adults without conscience who can kill, steal, and harm others.   Most from deprived environments don't resort to the extremes of an antisocial personality, yet they share a common trait: they don't have a desire to connect with others. They fear connection and generally seek one-up control over others or complete isolation from others. They go through life oblivious to the disastrous impact their selfishness has on the world.

The Making of the Selfless Person: In parent-centered environments, the child's needs and rights are subordinate to the needs and rights of the parents. Early on, children in these environments learn they have little voice in decisions affecting them. They're channeled in the direction of conformity and compliance. Energy, attention and time center on the parents' wishes. Children learn to be self-effacing, other-focused, and selfless. A selfless person is easily programmed by external influences and others' expectations of him. Like Susan, selfless people are robbed of opportunities to develop and learn about themselves.

When parents are particularly selfish or dysfunctional, they treat children in a dictatorial, rigid and judgmental manner. The more selfish the parent, the more selfless the child becomes. The parents may be image-conscious and view children merely as extensions of them. Accordingly, the child is not allowed to project anything but an acceptable facade. These children are conditioned to focus their time, energy and attention on the outer world since their major job in life is pleasing others. They're taught to do this by remaining hyper vigilant to the parents' needs, feelings, and beliefs, while ignoring their own. They become externally oriented -- always looking outside themselves for affirmation, acceptance and approval. The child's individuation process, while not overtly thwarted, is subtly discouraged.

Some parent-centered families are further complicated with one or two dysfunctional parents. Parents with compulsive disorders (such as workaholism, perfectionism, substance abuse or mental illness) pull the family members' energy toward them and their dysfunction. As Michael reported, the focus and energy in his family revolved around his alcoholic father. Susan's depressed mother drew the family's attention toward her. Children from parent-centered environments often learn to be caretakers and earn love by "doing" for or "fixing" others.

Selfish and Selfless Children Within the Same Family: For every rule of thumb there are exceptions. If family prototypes distort the individuation process and influence children to become either other-centered (selfless) or self-centered (selfish), children from the same family should be similar. While this is generally true, numerous examples abound of children from the same family who turn out quite different from one another.

One explanation for this variability is differing genetic influences; that is, some kids are just born with a certain personality and react differently to external influences. Some personalities are content to conform to external dictates, while other more rebellious and independent personalities stubbornly refuse to be molded by others. Another explanation is that kids are treated differently within the same family. Even in our liberated world, male and female family members are often treated differently. Some families elevate the status of boys, accepting and even encouraging their self-centeredness and aggressiveness. Meanwhile, those families insist female family members be passive, conforming and obedient. Sons become selfish and strong-willed while daughters are selfless and lack confidence.

Apart from gender discrimination, parents may show subtle or even overt favoritism. This is particularly likely if there is _covert incest_ among family members. Covert incest is not actual physical incest. Covert incest occurs when parents don't genuinely connect with each other and where a parent then turns to a child, usually an opposite sex child, to meet his or her emotional needs. The child who becomes the parent's confidant is then given more attention than other siblings. Although all the siblings may be selfless, the child who was party to the covertly incestuous relationship with the mother or father develops inflated self-worth

89

and may become selfish.

Selfless/selfish differences also may occur because of differential modeling. One child may choose to model the personality traits of his selfish mother, while his sister may choose to mimic the more selfless father. In Susan's family, her older sister chose to model her mother's self-absorbed, depressed, and controlling personality, while Susan adopted her father's selfless, caretaker pattern.

Where both parents are either selfless or selfish, you generally find the children taking the opposite. Diane and Ted are examples of two selfless parents. Both grew up with domineering parents who disallowed freedom of expression and independence. They were pressed into conformity by family, church, and school and never rebelled against the loss of self. They grew into selfless caretakers, always putting others before themselves. When their two children were born, all their energy and attention centered on the children. With the demands of work, graduate school, and family, the couple had little time for each other.

Selfless personalities can easily ignore themselves and, by extension, their spouses. Insufficiently individuated to know and give their children the gift of their inner truth, Diane and Ted primarily gave their children material gifts. Both children grew up to be selfish, greedy, and self-absorbed. The children expected Diane and Ted to meet their every need, but they didn't reciprocate with sensitivity and caring for their parents' needs and feelings. For example, they often forgot to acknowledge their parents' birthdays or Mother's and Father's Day.

When Diane tired of her selfless game, she begged Ted to go to counseling and grow with her. He refused to look at himself and balance the selflessness that perpetuated his "good boy image." His selflessness prevented his full empowerment as a man and a husband. When Diane separated from Ted, both teenage children decided to stay with their Dad who continued his selfless caretaking. Sadly, Diane learned the price of being selfless -- and the result of incomplete individuation: she had helped raise children who were selfish and unable to see beyond their own narcissistic viewpoints. Ted took no responsibility for Diane's decision to leave him and projected all the blame for ending their marriage onto her. Although Diane knew something was wrong with their relationship, and had pleaded with him for years to seek counseling, he chose to remain stuck in his selflessness.

Ted seems like a good person, but he isn't a real person. Ted says all the right things and looks like a loving family man, but in actuality he's an automaton -- a robot programmed to conform to the expectations of others. As long as others judge him to be "good," he's satisfied.

Ted and Diane's two children have reacted to their selflessness by swinging to the other extreme. They project blame onto others and fail to look critically at themselves. They don't put forth the energy to understand and empathize. They believe others should always come to them and understand them. Diane's lesson was bitter. She regretted the skewed self-perception she gave her children by centering her world around them. She regretted not teaching them about reciprocal love. Her children wanted to be given love and attention, but they didn't want to give the same. She regretted only giving them things and doing for them. If she could go back in time, she would have modeled balanced selfishness/selflessness.

The repetitious selfish or selfless treadmill ceases only when people commit to full individuation. Most people get stuck in the individuation process, having veered too far toward other-centeredness or self-centeredness. Rarely does a person emerge from childhood with a balanced selfless/selfish perspective.

(2) Self Scrutiny of Selfishness and Selflessness

Selfishness and selflessness seem to be opposite extremes, but actually they are two sides of the same coin. Selfless people really

91

don't give without expectation of return. They expect others to reward them for being good. Selfish people also expect others to reward them. Both selfless and selfish people must fill up with things from outside themselves -- power, status, money, job, or relationships. Both the selfless and the selfish are internally underdeveloped and both must rely on outside sources to define who they are. Generally, selfless people find it easier to admit their imbalances than do selfish people. The selfish often justify their actions by blaming others for victimizing *them*. Rarely do they admit to the numerous hurtful interactions they impose those around them.

The State of Selflessness: Selfless people give up energy, time, and attention to others, but strings are generally attached to the giving. The reward is in the "good guy" image and the power to control people through guilt and obligation. While appearing self-effacing, they actually expect others to be beholden to them. The whole identity of the selfless centers around the role of caretaker. They receive accolades for being so giving. Those involved with selfless people find themselves enmeshed in prisons of external expectation and control. Selfless people control by being in the one-up caretaker position, and they need the recipients of their caretaking to stay in the one-down child position. It is this positioning that assures their identity and self-worth.

Selfless people are in control -- they give what they want to give and exact a price with their giving. Often the price is an unspoken obligation to stay dependent on them. If their dependents become able to take care of their own needs, selfless people feel betrayed. Their whole identity is based on being needed. Selfless people haven't developed enough to give of themselves without expectation of return. They merely do for others and expect others to need them and be appreciative of their martyrdom. They fail to realize that giving can be hurtful when the implied message is that others are incompetent, immature, and

92

incapable.

The selfless are always giving themselves away and putting others' needs above their own. Their unspoken and unconscious motto is, "As long as I deal with other people's stuff, I don't have to deal with my own." Always worried about others' feelings, they are unperceiving of their own. In the codependent world we have constructed, selfless givers do not perceive any need to develop themselves. As long as they are viewed by others as the "poor victim," or the "good guy," they perceive everything as being fine.

There are some positives to being selfless. Selfless people do value connecting with others and are sensitive to the needs and feelings of those around them. For the most part, it's not likely they will intentionally harm or use others. On the contrary, they frequently bend over backwards to help others. Selfless people are generally self-effacing and tend to blame themselves when there's a problem. The main drawbacks with selflessness are: (1) not learning to love yourself enough to meet your own needs; (2) attracting selfish people who will ultimately drain you and leave you frustrated and resentful; (3) focusing on others' needs and problems and not on your own; (4) controlling others through guilt and obligation; and (5) not developing yourself fully, which prevents you from developing deep, truthful, intimate connections with others.

A dramatic depiction of the selfish/selfless dynamic comes from Cathy who saw a symbolic visualization of her selfless state during hypnosis. Cathy saw herself at age two or three standing before the looming figure of her mother. Her mother shook her finger at Cathy and told her she had been bad and asked her why she acted the way she did. Like *Alice in Wonderland*, Cathy saw her selfish mother grow larger and larger, while her own figure shrank smaller and smaller. Cathy shrank to the point of non-existence in the hypnosis visualization. In real life, Cathy also shrinks from standing up for herself. When others point a finger of blame at her, she absorbs the blame without question.

She continues to see herself as bad and unworthy of love. She continues to hold an intense fear of authority figures. Cathy hasn't learned to claim her power as an adult woman. At forty, she still sees herself as the little girl who has to please others to gain acceptance.

Cathy finally broke her cycle of selflessness when she garnered the courage to confront her parents about their negative judgments and controlling behavior. In a firm and loving manner, Cathy met with her parents and talked about their verbal and physical abuse during her childhood. Cathy told them about the devastating impact their behavior had on her self-esteem. Her mother acknowledged Cathy's assertions, apologized, and resolved to listen and get closer to her. Her father angrily condemned Cathy for confronting him late in life when he was about to die. The selfish lack eyes to see and ears to hear the truth. Even though Cathy's father didn't change, Cathy did. By standing in her truth and confronting her parents about their harmful abuse, she empowered herself to step outside of her conditioned pattern of selflessness.

Selfless people are conditioned to believe that pleasing others and conforming to their expectations will earn them love and acceptance. When they're finally able to see the futility of trying to earn love, it's not uncommon for them to become bitter and vindictive. Resentment builds as they admit the lack of commensurate return for their giving. Such rebellion can be very healthy if it represents a step toward balancing their selflessness with self-love. The selfless must validate their own needs and own their power to be sufficient and independent. They must look squarely at the devastating impact of their selfless caretaking on not only themselves, but on those they take care of.

Natural Resistance to Selfless Indoctrination: Donna has numerous clients who have rebelled against the conforming dictates of parents, spouses, or significant others who sought to render them selfless and dependent. One client describes herself as joyful, exuberant, curious, and full of life during her childhood. That all changed when she hit puberty. Her father became alarmed when the apple of his eye began to develop into a sexually attractive adult. He began criticizing her when her skirts were too short by saying she looked like a slut. She was accused of being too permissive with boys when she still saw boys only as playmates and friends. She was continually put on restriction for failing to follow her parents' unwritten rules. Both parents became so fearful of their daughter's budding adulthood they tried to freeze her in a state of childhood dependence. They squashed her power and independence with strict rules and critical admonitions.

At fifteen, she felt compelled to choose between becoming completely selfless or rebelling against the suffocating domination of her parents. She couldn't stand to relinquish her self completely. She couldn't stand getting all negative responses and no positive affirmation of her worth. Her parents were so fearful of losing their little girl, they tried to kill off the blossoming autonomy of an adult woman. She chose to fight back. She rebelled by running away from home, taking drugs, getting involved with the wrong type of guys, and engaging in minor criminal behavior. Now some twenty years later, she's feeling guilty about her adolescent rebellion and is harshly judging herself. Donna surprised her by telling her to "celebrate her shadow." The fight impulse within her saved her real self, the budding woman who now handles delinquents with courage and aplomb.

While some children rebel against selfish and controlling parents, others rebel against selfless parents. Tom epitomizes the self-preserving rebellion against his selfless father. Tom's parents were divorced when he was fourteen and he decided to live with his father. His mother couldn't adequately explain that she was drowning in the selfless prison of non-connection created by her husband's unwillingness to look at himself and grow in self-love. Finally, she balanced her own selflessness and focused on her needs.   She bravely and honestly confronted the lack of connection and the sham of a marriage. With much regret, she finally decided to leave her husband, but she stayed close to Tom. A couple of years after the divorce, Tom followed his mother and left his still selfless father. Now living with his mother, Tom explained that his father never talked to him. His father would sometimes silently stare at Danny and never confronted any conflict between them.

Tom felt the tension of unspoken judgment when he failed to meet his father's expectations to conform and present *a good image*. But Tom is not selfless and doesn't want to be. He is stubborn, independent, and largely self-sufficient. His father never discusses any real feelings, so Tom doesn't know the real person hiding behind his father's mask. Tom explained to his mother that the emptiness between he and his father created impenetrable anxiety and tension. He hated to see his father come home; he even hated hearing his father breathe. Words were few between them and, when spoken, were superficial and meaningless.

Tom and his mother talk and disagree at times, but they're open and real with each other. Tom can connect more honestly with his mother because she's developed enough to project who she is and accept him for who he is. She expects to be respected and, in turn, respects Tom for the young and independent adult he is.

The State of Selfishness: In contrast to the selfless do-gooders, selfish people look greedy, ill-mannered and inconsiderate. While many choose to distance from selfish people, few confront them about their abrasive behaviors. The world often praises selfish people, viewing them as powerful with political savvy. We accept their rudeness as signs of their importance. We view their unethical and uncaring tactics as "just the way the real world works." We empower selfish people to be abusive to others because we don't name them for what they are -- overgrown and undeveloped bullies with an adult body and a child's emotional

96

Selfish and Selfless Characteristics

Selfish	Selfless
* Primary focus on one's own wants, needs, and rights	* Primary focus on others' wants, needs, and rights
* Projects blame, shame & guilt	* Absorbs others' blame shame & guilt
* Attempts to gain love through power and control	* Attempts to gain love through serving & giving
* Prevalent focus on being secure	* Prevalent focus on obtaining love & belonging
* Projects Intimidator, Interrogator Aloof, or Poor Me Image	* Projects Martyr, Placator, or Caretaker Image
* Universe revolves around self	* Universe revolves around others
* Fragile and externally oriented self-esteem	* Fragile and externally oriented self-esteem
* Sees self as victim	* Often a resentful, passive-aggressive victim
* Often raised in child-centered homes	* Often raised in parent-centered homes
* Aggressively or passively steals energy or attention from others	* Gives energy, time, & attention to others
* Empty and fear driven	* Empty and fear driven
* Thick ego boundaries protect	* Ego boundaries not sufficient to protect them
* Has self-centered, novel view of reality	* Needs others to verify their view of reality

and spiritual understanding. Cultural judgments concerning selfish individuals contradict. Whereas religious and parental edicts generally condemn the ego-glorification of the selfish, our business and entertainment industries put selfish people on pedestals. Often ruthless and unethical, selfish people are rewarded with success and high positions. They don't have fairness and ethical behavior to limit them. They view life as an ongoing conquest of getting what they want at the expense of others.

Selfish people appear to have more internal focus because their actions are directed to their personal needs and wants, but they are actually externally focused. They need the goodies of the world -- power, status, money, and position to fill them up. Without internal maturity, they have no emotional or spiritual steering wheels to guide them. Selfish individuals are empty, and like their counterparts, the selfless, draw energy to them like vampires needing the lifeblood of others to survive. Without the ability to connect genuinely, selfish people wander aimlessly looking for someone or something outside themselves to fill them up.

Selfish people have problems in close interpersonal relationships. Unless they're in relationships with completely selfless individuals, they meet resistance. Often outwardly charming, selfish people know how to act to get what they want. It may take much time and many sour experiences with selfish people before we learn to see them accurately. But doing so represents a major step forward in our lessons on discernment.

Flow of Selfless and Selfish Styles: Selfishness and selflessness can be defined in terms of energy flow. Selfish people pull energy from others in either active and aggressive ways or in hidden and passive ways. Selfless people allow their energy, time and attention to flow from them to another person. While the selfish are parasites who survive on the energy of others, the selfless are willing donors of energy transfusions.

The flow of energy is readily detected when selfish people pull time, attention and energy from others in their attempts to control and be one-up. Aggressively selfish people openly shame, blame, bully and criticize in their attempts to steal energy from others. They want to deplete the power of others so they can dominate and control them. Adept at manipulation, selfish people can give the impression they care about others. In reality, they're just manipulating to get their way. They never do anything for others without expecting a return. While they project blame and shame on others, they never scrutinize their own shamefulness. Their self-centered perspective allows them to ignore the unfairness of using others for their advantage. They like their selfish game and see themselves as winning and being in the one-up control position.

Ego gratification is the primary focus of self-absorbed people. Like the child who wants another's toy and grabs it away, the selfish also steal what they want and feel no guilt for taking from another. In this state of ego aggrandizement, selfish people believe they deserve to get what they want. They are blind to their abuses, often painting themselves as the victim of others, when they are actually the victimizers.

Nan tells of a friend, Jill, who chastised her for forgetting her birthday. Nan felt guilty and immediately rushed out to buy her friend a gift, hoping for forgiveness for her oversight. On her throne of one-up superiority, Jill was always criticizing Nan. If Nan didn't call regularly, Jill told her she was angry and felt neglected. If Nan saw other friends, Jill became jealous and demanded equal time and attention. Nan was always doing the giving, and Jill was always intimidating Nan with her criticisms and complaints. Nan, a full-fledged selfless person, always absorbed the blame and tried even harder to meet Jill's demands. It didn't even occur to Nan that her relationship with Jill was a one-way street. Jill never did for Nan any of the things she expected Nan to do for her. Then Nan's birthday passed without a word, card, or gift from Jill. When Nan asked her about the birthday oversight, Jill nonchalantly denied knowing about Nan's birthday. Jill never apologized for her negligence nor did she buy a gift for Nan. Nan finally got it. She finally saw Jill's selfishness and she became resentful. As long as selfish people get attention they're happy. But, they don't reciprocate by giving attention to others. Nan could finally see that her selfless pattern was only reinforcing Jill's selfishness, so Nan has decided to distance from Jill and not fuel her selfishness any more.

Other selfish people are more subtle. They often play the victim role and pull others to rescue them. These are the passive-aggressive selfish people. Addicts are good examples of selfish *Poor Me* people who ensnare the time and attention of others. Addictions may range from overt compulsive patterns such as alcoholism, drug addiction, and gambling to the more invisible addictions of workaholism, shopaholism, perfectionism and relationship addiction.

The interpersonal dynamics of passive-aggressive selfish people involve playing the one-down or child position attracting the energies of a one-up parent. Their message is, "I'm not empowered to take care of myself, I need you to take care of me." When pulled into the web of a passive-aggressive selfish person, the unwitting caretaker gets drained of energy, time, and vitality. Selfish people are insatiable and they drain life energy from others in the way a leech drains its host of life blood.

Judy had a grown daughter, Ann, who was a passive-aggressive selfish person. Ann constantly drained Judy of time and energy by being the consummate victim. Ann was recurrently sick, always unhappy, and consistently overworked. Her world was dark and dreary and she wouldn't take responsibility for changing her life. Judy and her husband tried to be supportive and give Ann solutions to escape her misery, but Ann persisted in her quagmire of gloom and doom. Ann likes being stuck. She enjoys complaining because it gets her the attention she wants.

The apex of Ann's negativity was a suicide attempt by drug overdose. Years later, Ann uses her suicide attempt as a threat when others won't give her the time and attention she wants. "You don't care about me, you don't love me, I might as well die," have become idle threats that still worry Judy. The only way to break Ann's game is to name it for what it is -- an addictive game that enables her weaknesses and dependency. Judy's counselor advised her to forego rewarding Ann's selfishness. She was to ignore Ann when she complained and moaned, but give attention when Ann acted in a positive and empowered manner. Ann was given a list of positive actions -- volunteering at a nursing home, becoming a Big Sister to a needy child, serving food to the homeless. Each time Ann chose to engage in positive activities, she was rewarded with Judy's time and attention. When she withdrew into lethargy and childish whining, Judy ignored her. Although it was difficult for Judy to carry out this counter-conditioning, she recognized Ann's selfishness was an addiction and her reward of time and attention only fueled the negative power of the addiction. By breaking the selfish/selfless game, Judy was taking the hard road to tough love.

It was difficult to resist Ann's selfish manipulation and idle threats. It was more difficult for Judy to break her own selfless, caretaking game. Selfless people have much difficulty understanding and seeing selfish people. Blinded by the ego-aggrandizement of being needed, selfless people often fail to see that the selfless-selfish game they are playing is really harming both participants.

(3) Commitment to Full Individuation and Empowerment

Jenny is an example of a selfish person. Of course Jenny doesn't see herself as selfish, but almost everyone around her does -- except her husband James. While others are repelled by her self-centeredness, James feeds on it. His identity is so underdeveloped he would have little purpose in life if he could not play victim to Jenny's tyranny. James and Jenny attended a *Sacred Relationship Workshop* we conducted at our mountain retreat. It took only a few hours before Jenny's ego-centeredness began grating on other workshop participants. While sitting like a queen on a throne, she demanded that James get things for her and wait on her hand and foot. When her selfish demands extended to others, they became resentful and began ignoring her. In every conversation, Jenny pulled the attention to her. Several workshop participants threatened to leave the workshop rather than endure Jenny's irritating selfishness. Michael and Donna decided to separate the group so other participants wouldn't be subjected to Jenny's incessant need for attention.

During role playing exercises, Jenny continually attempted to draw the attention away from other participants and back to her. Finally her turn arrived. She painted a self-portrait of childhood neglect and abuse that softened others' attitudes toward her. Then she extended the scope of her childhood traumas and depicted herself as a victim in virtually all of her interpersonal interactions. She lambasted her husband for appearing so helpful and caring and accused him of actually being childish, irresponsible and passive-aggressive. She was angry that he received praise as the good-guy caretaker while she was criticized as the overbearing tyrant. She claimed to handle every responsibility for the couple, while he handled virtually nothing. When questioned, it became apparent that Jenny's perspective was very skewed. Even though all her children were grown and living on their own, Jenny didn't work outside the home. James worked a full-time job and came home to wait on her. Jenny's only responsibility was to pay the bills once a month. In Jenny's mind, the two hours a month job constituted her doing everything and her husband doing nothing.

Jenny also pulls energy toward her by being a sickness tyrant.

She has an endless array of aches, pains, and ailments that she uses to escape adult responsibility. Jenny is a selfish person who has no incentive for changing and becoming more considerate of the rights, feelings and needs of others. James is such a selfless caretaker, he seems satisfied living a life of constant emotional abuse. However, children, friends, and family members distance from Jenny to avoid her toxic intimidation and selfishness.

We told Jenny to confront the emotional pain of her deprived childhood, grieve the loss of nurturance and love, and grow past her neediness to become a whole and empowered adult. Only if she was willing to give up her victim/intimidator mind set would she be open to becoming truly empowered. Only when she could let go of the myopic focus on herself and focus on the rights, needs, and feelings of others would she acquire the balance that would draw others to her -- not push them away. But Jenny's reward for being selfish was too great. As long as James played foil to her manipulations, she wouldn't change. James decided to remain selfless and Jenny persisted in being selfish. Both are paying a high price -- missing out on love and connection with others and real love between themselves. In their isolated selfless/selfish cocoon, they've become the ultimate punishing pair.

Balancing Selfishness and Selflessness: Stunted individuation is a major stumbling block in the journey toward empowered self and empowered love. The selfish person cannot see beyond self to really connect with another. The rules of fairness and consideration that apply to others don't apply to them. They see themselves as special and above others. They expect others to recognize and bow to their needs and their superiority. Playing superior is how they fool others into giving up their energy and attention to them. They're empty and hollow, without developed heart or spirit. The dwindling number of people who will put up with their selfishness may give them a clue something's wrong. After a number of people leave, they may look at themselves and ask, "What's wrong with me?" But don't hold your breath waiting for the selfish person to see the light and reform. They usually resist change unless and until a serious trauma befalls them or until they find themselves completely alone and isolated.

The selfless person has an equally difficult time breaking from their identity as caretaker. The world heaps adulation upon the selfless person for being caring, giving, kind, and good. Even the Bible tells us it's more blessed to give than receive. Childhood admonitions further entrench and reinforce selfless tendencies with sayings such as "don't be selfish" and "don't brag about yourself." The selfless person has followed the rules and expects his adherence to pay off. Sometimes too late, the selfless person learns his payoff is being used as a doormat. In some cases, the selfless live an entire life giving themselves away until there's nothing left. They die lamenting the shallow connections surrounding them -- knowing they have given, but no one seems to have appreciated. It is a very sad end -- not fully knowing themselves, not being known by others, and not knowing or connecting with others.

Like many other sex abuse survivors, Wanda swung between the extremes of selflessness and selfishness. She was molested by her teenage cousin when she was five and raped by an older acquaintance at seventeen. Believing her reputation ruined when others learned of the rape, Wanda blamed herself and believed she was dirty, bad, and unlovable. She became promiscuous and convinced herself that sex was merely recreational and had no emotional meaning. She used men with reckless abandon, as they also used her. When she entered therapy, she appeared flippant as she nonchalantly described numerous sexual liaisons. On the surface, Wanda appeared selfish and uncaring about the damage to herself and others caused by her meaningless, short-lived flings. But, underneath her tough demeanor was a scarred and powerless child. Wanda's sense of self-esteem and power had been stolen by her child-molesting cousin and the adult rapist. Wanda committed to the painful process of uncovering and healing these deep emotional wounds.

Using hypnosis to retrieve deeply repressed memories of her traumas, Wanda struggled, explaining that the hypnosis was like reliving the situations. A less committed person would have recoiled and withdrawn, but Wanda recognized her need for emotional catharsis to free her from selfless/selfish extremism. She began grief work and felt her rage at the offending males who violated her and robbed her of dignity. As a child and teenager, she was too young to access her self-protective anger. Her abusers had accurately read her selflessness and power-lessness. Now, as an adult, her fury tumbled out in a mixture of crying, yelling, and beating the tackling dummy. As she expunged the toxins long locked within, she remembered the innocent and loving child she really was. Seeing through the eyes of an empowered adult, the innocent child within her was able to release the long carried and paralyzing guilt.

She could now place the blame squarely on her offenders. She could love herself at last. Wanda had no idea where to find the older acquaintance who had raped her. However, she wrote a long letter to her cousin telling him she hadn't forgotten his abuse. Wanda abandoned fear and stood up for herself. She committed to retrieving the lost parts of herself -- her integrity, her openness, her goodness, and her faith in love. For twenty-some years, Wanda maintained a thick, protective wall around her true self. Now she has found the courage to tear down her defensive walls. Currently, Wanda is in a committed and connected relationship with a man who loves her as an equal and empowered adult.

In completing individuation, selfless and selfish persons must learn to balance self-love with love for others. By coming to center, both the selfish and the selfless empower themselves by releasing others from their control. Our first step is to understand the dynamics of individuation. Then we must look honestly at ourselves and at those around us and see the selfless and selfish patterns underlying our interactions. We must commit to undoing the emotional havoc caused by our own incomplete individuation. It's the first step toward giving and receiving the honest, non-manipulative love we all really want and deserve.

Chapter Five

Codependency: The Parasitic
Connections We Call Love

CODEPENDENCY:
The parasitic connections we call love

I need to connect on all levels -- physical, mental, emotional and spiritual. That's what I want with my wife, but she has a wall around her that keeps me at arm's length. It wasn't that way when we first met. She told me everything about herself. She was in an abusive marriage and after divorcing, she was involved in a string of terrible relationships. She told me about all of them. I'm a fixer. I saw her neediness and I wanted to take care of her pain. We married within a few months. Almost immediately after the wedding, she closed up. What happened? We shared so much, and now it's dead. I tell her I need more from her and that our marriage isn't working. She cries a little at the time, but the next day, it's as if nothing has happened. She goes about cooking me meals, making preserves and planting a garden. But she does nothing to remove the shield around her.

She's truly a wonderful person. Everybody loves her. She's very giving to others. She's so good -- in fact, she's too good! Where is the real person--the one who gets angry, feels joy, gets excited, and feels depressed? Am I the only one who has a dark side? God, she's so perfect. I feel bad talking about her. She's always pleasing others. No one would understand if I left her. I'd get all the blame, particularly from my family. They think she's the best thing that's happened to me.

I don't want her to please me and earn my love. I want the real person -- the bad, the good, and the ugly. I want truth. I need passion. All I get is silence and a smile. I need a real, honest, human being to connect with. Maybe it's me. I've been in needy relationships before. I've had my share of women but I'm always looking for the one I can be myself with. I'm looking for connection. I want it with my wife, but I'm beginning to give up hope. Is it me or is it her? Should I settle or listen to the inner voice of discontent? Is there such a thing as true connection or am I just dreaming?

-Warren, age 49

109

Warren is describing a codependent relationship -- the common form of human connection that is stagnant, exhausting, and fear-based. Codependency is the result of imbalanced selfishness and selflessness. Instead of doing the hard work of self-scrutiny and healing emotional wounds, those stuck in selfishness and selflessness lean on another to complete them. If they are selfless, they look for a needy person to be the repository of their caretaking. If they are selfish, they look for one who will put up with their self-centeredness and is too weak to force them to grow. But the price of incomplete individuation and joining in complementary weakness is high. Codependency is found in marriages that more resemble legalized business contracts than passionate and intimate relationships. Codependency is found in families where one person's weaknesses and dysfunctions are glossed over by others trying to fix or take care of him or her. Codependency is found in work settings where autocratic management reduces workers to powerless children.

The root cause of codependency is incomplete individuation when people are only half-baked in terms of full human empowerment. Instead of whole, mature people who have fully explored their fears, interpersonal barriers and psychological defenses, codependent people are still at the starting gate. Empty and alone, they hide behind their masks. They need others to fill them up, make them feel whole, and make them feel happy. Most of us are raised by parents who haven't completed the emotional and psychological tasks of individuation. Their models of selflessness or selfishness imprint us with self-defeating behaviors that decrease our chances of forming deep and loving relationships. We tilt one way or the other -- too selfless to look out for our own needs and rights or too selfish to connect with the needs and feelings of others. When we balance the portions of self-love and other-love within ourselves, we can straddle the fence between self-protection and openness. Codependents aren't balanced enough to discriminate between being too selfish and being too selfless. They swing between the two extremes -- too other-focused or too self-centered.

Codependents are conditioned to control others or to be controlled by others. They know little about controlling themselves and trusting their own inner resources. They haven't learned to be independent, free, and self-sufficient. Therefore, they believe they must be in relationships, even though their relationships are most often unhappy and unfulfilling. Relating as an empowered equal with another is foreign to codependents, so they attract others who play one-up or one-down. These unequal and imbalanced relationships are plagued with control battles, anger, guilt, collusion, sickness, helplessness, loneliness, hurt and fear. Codependent people expect something or somebody external and independent of themselves to have the answers and to bring them peace and security. But peace never comes. Instead, the unattended problems of codependent couples, families, and organizations get swept under the rug and grow huge with fear and neglect.

Codependency has been described as an emotional illness characterized by denial, delusion, and repression. Instead of looking at ourselves honestly and confronting our own immature and undeveloped parts, we deny our shadow sides. Instead of looking objectively at another and the unsatisfying relationship that exists between us, we put on a satisfied mask and stay silent. We're particularly drawn to needy people who give us security and identity by depending on us. We spend inordinate amounts of energy and time trying to fix the needy dependents who cling to us and drain our life energy. By giving them our time and our life energy, we're actually feeding their dependency and keeping them weak and incomplete. We ultimately resent being used by parasitic dependents. Yet when our feelings of frustration, anger, and hurt emerge, we quickly repress them. Sometimes our repression doesn't work and the negative emotions come out in frightful explosions. Then we feel guilty, blame ourselves, and again push down the negative feelings that tell us something is wrong in our relationships.

Codependent relationships are the norm. Our guess is that ninety percent or higher of all couples are primarily codependent. Family, social, and work groups also tend to be codependent. Because it's so prevalent, people don't recognize codependency as dysfunctional and unhealthy. Before the 1970s Womens' Liberation movement, codependency was obvious on a broad scale with women being more dependent on men for economic survival, and men being dependent on women for emotional and social connection. But times have changed and women are out of their homes and more visible in the workplace. Economic dependence isn't a primary factor in codependent relationships (although it's somewhat a factor with women still earning substantially less than their male counterparts). In the last three decades, distinct gender roles have blurred and modern-day codependency is more subtle and harder to see.

People with codependent illness enter counseling complaining of depression, unhappiness, and boredom, but they are unable to point to the source of their problem. Debra and Daniel are a typical example of a modern day codependent couple. They are both employed full time in professional positions and have an eight year old son, Ricky. A bright child with attention deficit disorder, Ricky was beginning to have behavior problems at home and school. His grades declined as he became more and more despondent and belligerent. Debra called for a counseling appointment for Ricky. Donna noted in the first counseling session that Ricky had obvious academic and social problems. Those problems paled in comparison with Ricky's animosity toward his father Daniel. In a subsequent session with Debra alone, Donna pointed out that some of Ricky's difficulties were emotionally based and linked to his rage over Daniel's rigid and uncaring attitude toward him.

112

Unburdening herself of a heavy backpack of self-blame and hurt, Debra's words rushed out in an urgent and hurried surge: "I know I have two children rather than one. Daniel is so immature in the way he treats Ricky, and he's immature in the way he treats me too! He doesn't take time to talk to Ricky and find out how he's feeling or what problems he's having. He's always criticizing Ricky and if Ricky doesn't do things just the way Daniel wants him to, he gives him a beating. When I tell him to lay off Ricky, he gets angry, storms to the bedroom and slams the door. I know I'd better just leave him alone for several days while he cools down. Daniel won't take responsibility for growing up emotionally and relating to me or Ricky in a caring, loving, and rational way. Heck, he won't even take responsibility for physical duties either. Ricky wanted to play softball, but Daniel said Ricky wasn't good enough or old enough."

"Ricky begged to try out for the team anyway, and Daniel said he wasn't in favor, but it was my decision. You know what that means don't you? I have to drive Ricky to all the games and stay to see him play each week. Daniel slithers out of this responsibility by simply saying he's not in favor of Ricky playing. Daniel pulls this scene all the time and leaves me holding the bag. He can't help Ricky with homework because he gets so frustrated when Ricky doesn't understand his explanations. I do everything and I'm tired of it! I'm just sick and tired of not having an equal partner, a real grown-up to share my life and the family responsibilities."

Debra is describing modern day codependency. Daniel opts to be the selfish partner who draws energy and attention with his short fuse, pouting, and withdrawal from responsibility. Debra, the selfless partner, is afraid to confront him lest she incites his intimidating anger. So she continues to shoulder the burden of meeting the emotional and physical needs of the family. She gives up her wants, her time, and her energy keeping things going while Daniel selfishly does what he wants. Ricky is left confused -- he doesn't want to be like his gruff, intimidating dad, but equally distasteful is his doormat mom. Ricky seems to be modeling his dad more and more as he bullies kids on the bus and throws a fit when he doesn't get his way. The tension of Debra and Daniel's codependent relationship is emotionally contaminating Ricky who's responding to their dysfunction with anger and anxiety.

If a person's goal is to connect fully and deeply with others and intimately with a special partner, codependency isn't the path leading to the finish line. Codependency bolsters a person's weaknesses. The selfish partner refuses to look at himself because he'd have to put forth energy and change. Why should he change when he has others taking care of him and allowing him to remain a child? The selfless person gets sympathy from others for his plight and rewarded for his goodness and martyrdom. In taking care of other people's stuff, the selfless person doesn't have to look at his own stuff. Codependency is deeply ingrained and hard to change, but it must change if a person is to become fully empowered.

Some characteristics of codependents and their relationships include (1) imbalanced selflessness and selfishness within and between the codependent partners; (2) expecting others to meet their basic needs; (3) buying and earning love through *doing* ; (4) relying on simple thinking and rigid judgment; (5) fighting for power and control; (6) being unconsciously motivated by fear; (7) numbed emotions and emotional responses; (8) avoidance or intensification of risk-taking; (9) being externally oriented; (10) playing a role and acting normal; (11) reacting to others rather than acting on their own volition; (12) having inappropriate personal boundaries; (13) expecting someone or something to fill them up; and (14) avoidance of self-scrutiny and discernment of others.

(1) Imbalanced Selflessness and Selfishness within and between Codependent Partners

Those falling into codependent relationships haven't completed the individuation work of balancing the selfless/selfish proportions of their identity The two most frequent pairings are a selfish/selfless couple and a selfless/selfless couple. Selfish/ selfish pairings occur, but they tend to be short-lived, with each partner expecting the other to cater to his needs and wishes. When their mirrored expectations conflict, the selfish/selfish pair either separates or continues their cycle of volatile fighting. When one selfish partner leaves the other, he most often searches for a more willing victim from whom to draw energy and attention.

The selfish/selfless match is complementary. The self-absorbed member of a selfish/selfless couple demands that his partner center time, attention and energy around him. The selfless person is expected to pursue and serve, never requiring commensurate return for his energies.

Ginny and Bill were locked into the selfish/selfless cast. Coming from an emotionally deprived and physically abusive home environment, Bill was determined not to be one-down in adulthood. He built a very successful company and became rich. On his throne of wealth, Bill could impress others with his generosity. There were strings attached to Bill's giving, however. He only gave material things and was completely closed when it came to giving of himself. Bill didn't have anything to give because his self-esteem had been so damaged in childhood that he saw himself as worthless.

Ginny saw his neediness and responded with love, empathy, and understanding. But after fifteen sexless years of marriage, even Ginny's selfless understanding of Bill's inadequacies wore thin. She left him and hoped to find someone who would meet her emotional needs. Along came Dale -- handsome, smooth talking, complex, selfish -- and married. Dale had no problem giving in the sexual area -- after all, sex was for him. Dale expected Ginny to be there when he wanted her. It didn't matter to him that he was never available when she wanted him. Too selfish to look at the harm he was doing to his wife, kids, and Ginny, Dale kept up his double life for ten years -- and Ginny allowed it because she didn't love herself enough to expect any better. Then Ginny got into therapy and began to see the invisible scripts handed down in her Italian family -- men were gods to be served and idolized, women were merely the chattel of their male masters. Ginny got angry at the family script that had brainwashed her and rendered her selfless. She hated the inequality between the sexes that left each lonely and fearful of the other. She determined to rid herself of the selfless game and claim her power to stand alone. Only when she faced the lies (I'm worthy only when I'm helping needy men) and her own neediness was she able to break free of the codependent game. Today she's in an energizing professional position and involved with a man who respects her and treats her as an equal.

The selfless/selfless game is a bit different, but equally dysfunctional. Kay and Brendan are both selfless. Brendan tries to meet Kay's needs by waiting on her when she feels ill, assuming most of the child care, and bringing home the biggest paycheck. For a while this was acceptable to Brendan, but then he noticed he was continually short-changed. When he asked for a hug when he got home, Kay failed to respond. Then Kay started drinking and it became the focus of dissension between the couple. Brendan had finally had enough and was ready to leave, assuming that Kay was unable and unwilling to meet his emotional needs.

On the surface Kay looked like the selfish partner. In reality, Kay was the epitome of selflessness. Raped when she was fourteen, Kay had been robbed of her dignity, power, and security. Her self-worth plummeted and she became promiscuous with selfish, using men. Then she met Brendan and it looked as if life would end "happily ever after." Unfortunately, Kay couldn't give up her selflessness. She didn't love herself and she didn't know how to truly love another. When Brendan asked her to be more affectionate, she tried to acquiesce, but unconsciously she couldn't meet Brendan's needs because she couldn't admit or meet her own needs. She didn't know how to talk about her unresolved trauma. She stuffed her emotions and became numb to her own and others' needs. Kay only understood self-destruction and self-loathing. She needed to focus on healing her unresolved wounds. Only by balancing her selflessness with a heavy dose of self focus could Kay learn to give to herself and then to others. Both Kay and Brendan had to care enough about themselves to give up selflessness. They had to claim their rights to be listened to, focused on, loved and respected. First, they had to focus on themselves, listen to their own inner voice, and learn to love and respect themselves.

(2) Codependents Expect Others to Meet Their Basic Needs

Codependency is the disempowering connection between two people where one plays the role of *parent caretaker* while the other plays the role of *dependent child*. In codependent relationships, you could say that one partner is one-up while the other is one-down. Couples switch the one-up, one-down roles frequently, with one playing the parent in some situations and the child role in other situations. For example, the husband might play the one-up parent when it comes to mechanical repairs and the wife may be the parent in cooking meals. By maintaining separate areas of expertise, the couple stays dependent each on the other to meet some basic life skills. A crazy-quilt of enmeshed neediness and caretaking ensues with virtually no individual growth taking place. Each adult must assume responsibility for meeting all his or her basic needs. In codependency, people hide in childish dependency, expecting another person to meet their basic needs. Codependency rewards mutual weakness and stagnation.

Codependency is also an elixir for insecurity. As long as our partners are needy and we meet their needs, they can't leave us.

Not only are we rewarded for laziness and stagnation, we don't have to fear rejection or abandonment. The other person *has* to stay with us because he or she is too needy to break away and be autonomous.

From birth, we are taught we're incomplete, that we must have others around to take care of us and to do for us those things we can't or don't want to do for ourselves. The patterns of dependency we learn in early life become so strong that stage theorists, who study human growth and development stages, forcefully argue that the single most important task in our lives is to grow out of dependency and into fully empowered, independent adult status.

Significant adults in a child's life (parents, teachers, and other family members) should give children *roots* and *wings*. Human emotional and psychological roots are established when basic needs -- physiological needs, safety and security needs, and love and belongingness needs -- are met. With healthy emotional roots, we learn to value and care about ourselves and to trust others. The roots (psychological and emotional stability) atrophy when children are exposed to dysfunctional, self-centered or addicted parents who inadequately attend to the physical, safety, or love needs of their children. In such cases, children are developmentally delayed in a perpetual cycle of neediness, fear and distrust. When the roots of emotional and psychological stability are impoverished, the child grows into a codependent adult who is arrested in fear and neediness.

While some parents are able to meet basic needs and provide adequate roots, fewer are skilled at giving wings to their children. Wings are our sense of independence and empowerment. Few parents are themselves fully empowered adults. Most have emotional imprints of fear, hurt and neediness. They pass these emotional legacies down to children. The one-up caretaker is assuaging his powerlessness by controlling the child or his worthiness by having the child need him. There are ample examples of grown children relying on parents emotionally or financially to the point they're not able to make independent decisions or live without support. Robbed of independence, power, and unconditional love, children learn to be dependent on others and see themselves as insufficient. The dependency repeats throughout their lives, as they join with other codependent partners in adulthood.

Alexander tells the story of his former codependent marriage. The marriage relationship and relationships between Alexander, his wife and their children were codependent.

My former wife and I were together for twenty-four years before we divorced. Everyone around us thought we were a happy, model couple. Beneath the surface, our connectedness consisted of doing the right things for the children and playing out parts in our codependent rituals. We started out in a state of neediness. She felt rejected by her overly critical mother and wanted someone to love her. My alcoholic father had just died when I met her. I was feeling raw grief and needed a nurturing caretaker to salve my unhealed wounds. Within a few months after our marriage, she informed me she was pregnant. She said she had an allergic reaction to birth control pills and, unbeknownst to me, stopped taking them. I now see she tricked me by purposely getting pregnant. Her insecurity led her to take action that would permanently trap me. If the kids hadn't come, I would have left her early on because we were very different and had little in common.

Over the years, we drifted into a life where my wife did those things I was afraid to do or didn't want to do. I did the same for her. I didn't like answering the phone, she liked to talk. I never learned to cook or sew, she liked to do those things. I took care of the cars and mechanical repairs. Like most males, I hadn't done much work on developing my emotions. I didn't understand my own emotions -- much less the emotional needs of others. I'm sad to say I didn't connect with my children. My wife handled the emotional needs of the family, but she exacted a price for her caretaking. Because her whole identity centered around being the one-up parent, she made sure we were dependent on her. I finally broke out of her smothering

119

intrusions into my every private thought or action, but she continued to hover over our children and intruded on every part of their lives. They learned to believe they couldn't survive without her and became excessively dependent on her. She needed to be needed and their dependency made her feel useful.

We had a codependent business arrangement, not a real marriage. I wanted a wife -- an equal who was interested in growing and connecting intimately with me. It's pretty hard to connect with a woman whose whole identity is wrapped up in being everyone's mother, including her spouse. Well, you might guess, she puts all the blame on me for divorcing her. She's turned my children against me and now plays the "poor me victim" I'm condemned for standing up for my rights and needs. I finally told the truth about our relationship and got out of it. I've learned to accept her condemnation of me to our children and friends. I feel completely justified in leaving the smothering, codependent web that was killing me. If I had stayed much longer, I would have died -- emotionally and probably physically. Leaving her was the first good thing I've done for myself for over thirty years.

- Alexander, age 50

Although codependent relationships can be personal, emotional, and warm, *they are not love.* The undeveloped person needs to cling to another to be safe and whole. Equating neediness and reciprocal caretaking with love denigrates the sanctity of love. The paradox holding the world frozen is that we must give up our neediness in order for our real needs to be met. Before we can expect another to connect in truth and love with us, we must first be able to extinguish all neediness and become sufficient to meet our own needs. We must become fully empowered adults ready to join in wholeness and maturity rather than join in codependent neediness, insufficiency, and fear.

(3) Codependents Buy and Earn Love by Doing

For couples, a great deal of codependency results simply from accepting the socially dictated rules that govern being male and female, husband and wife, in this society. Men *do* some things, women *do* other things. Even with the fifty-fifty equality supposed to exist within some modern marriages, gender-based divisions remain. The unspoken assumption: if you do the right things, the relationship will last. But what are the rights things to do? If we cook nutritious and appetizing meals for our spouses and families, is that the right thing? If we remain faithful to our spouses, is that enough to ensure the longevity of the relationship? If we avoid conflicts and try to please our mates, is that enough to ensure love? While *doing* for others is fine, it's not enough to ensure true connections.

At the beginning of this chapter, Warren tells about his wife who *did* everything right but didn't connect with him honestly and forthrightly. Warren's wife wore the socially acceptable mask of the happy homemaker, but she hadn't developed who she was and couldn't connect with him on a deeper level. We need to get beyond merely *doing* in our intimate relationships. Going on trips together or buying gifts for each other will not ensure ultimate love and connection. Rather, we need to learn who we are at the core of our beings, and we need to offer our real selves to our significant others. We must learn to share openly and without fear-based boundaries. Only in connecting with our *being* do we truly touch each other. Our being includes all of us -- our good, our bad, our emotions, our thoughts and our dreams. Only when we're strong enough and developed enough to offer ourselves fully to another will we be able to connect.

(4) Codependents Rely on Simple Thinking and Rigid Judgment

Life is complex and people are complicated. The factors affecting human behaviors, emotions, and perceptions are unbelievably convoluted and intricate. Curiosity about the complex reasons for one's own or another's behaviors, beliefs, and feelings is a hallmark of intelligence and maturity. Yet most people have only rudimentary and simple understandings of themselves and others. More often than not, human behavior, beliefs, and feelings are judged in dichotomous terms of right/wrong or good/bad. Simple thinking is a sign of intellectual and emotional immaturity. Yet simple thinking predominates in a world intolerant of differences and without compassion for the needs and rights of others.

Codependents are generally judgmental and have the need to control those around them. This judgmental tendency makes them particularly prone to simple thinking. For example, codependent parents use simple judgments to control their children's behaviors. When a child leaves crayon marks on the wall or soils his pants, he's *bad*. The more emotionally and intellectually developed parent would refrain from simple judgment, and instead ask *why*. *Why* did the child have an urge to mark on the wall; why did the child soil his pants? Perhaps the child watched a television show about artists painting murals and was inspired. The parent could take this information and encourage creative talent while placing appropriate boundaries about suitable materials to use. Likewise, a child who soils his pants may be physically sick or emotionally distraught. The inquisitive parent opens up lines of communication and learns through their gentle questioning. A parent who's judgmental and has a simple answer (you're bad), closes communication and shuts off the opportunity to connect.

Simple thinking is lazy thinking - and it's unbefitting the mature and intellectually advanced adult. But simple thinking is prevalent as we watch parents blaming and shaming their children for "being bad." This tendency extends to societal organizations such as churches who label those who are dissimilar to them in race, religious beliefs, or sexual preference as wrong or sinners. Just as the child learns to accept and internalize shame, adults unfairly judged by simple thinkers are also damaged. Simple thinking and rigid judgment become a vicious and self-perpetuating cycle. The child grows up and uses the same simple thinking and manipulative shame or blame techniques to control others and get what he wants.

Simple thinking dulls our inquisitive pursuit of truth about the complexities that make us who we are. While simple thinkers exhaust their energies on judging or avoiding judgment, empowered individuals curiously examine the intricate and complex motivations that rule human perceptions and behaviors. The mature adult is unjudging, but interested in learning more about himself and about the lives of others. Likewise, he expects others to be unjudging and interested in knowing him on a deeper level. When he comes across those who are unwilling to be empathic and loving, and who choose to judge and label him, he nullifies their negativity by distancing from them. Simple thinkers are seen for what they are -- at a rudimentary level of human development and incapable of true heart connections. Empowered people don't allow their energy to be dissipated by simple thinkers. They merely reject shame, blame and simple thinking and decide for themselves what is right. Empowered individuals allow no one to steal their power or control their lives.

(5) Codependents Struggle for Power and Control

Codependents have an underlying quest for power and control in their interpersonal transactions. They believe there is limited power in relationships and they have to grab control and power to secure their own safety and dominance. Power grabs can be subtle or obvious. James Redfield, in the psychospiritual tale *The Celestine Prophecy*, and Virginia Satir in *Peoplemaking*, define common roles people play in their power games. Consciously or unconsciously, codependent partners manipulate others for attention and energy. The manipulation can be aggressive and overt or more passive and covert. The overt control dramas are easier to detect and resist. When people are more subtle and passive, they play on others' sympathies and draw energy to them in ways that are more invisible.

James Redfield outlines four primary roles people assume in codependent control dramas: *Poor Me, Aloof, Intimidator,* and *Interrogator.* Virginia Satir uses the labels *Intimidator, Blamer, Placater, Computer,* and *Distracter.* The *Intimidator, Interrogator,* and *Blamer* are more aggressive and visible codependent archetypes. The more passive and largely invisible codependent roles include the *Aloof, Poor Me, Placater, Martyr, Computer* and *Withdrawn* types.

Intimidator types demand all attention and energy swirl around them. They use verbal, emotional, or even physical threats or threatening innuendoes to control others with fear. Without fail, Intimidators are fearful of anyone who has any power or exercises independent judgment. Intimidators seek to destroy the energy and vitality of those around them. Like psychic vampires, they seek to steal courage and life energy from others and render others subordinate to them.

Interrogators put themselves in one-up positions and pull power from others by asking critical and probing questions. Interrogators don't value privacy needs or boundaries of others. They use information about others to trap them in blame or shame. The Interrogator invades another person's free-will and tries to influence him with judgmental innuendoes. The recipient of the Interrogator's control drama finds himself giving up his energy for fear of being judged wrong or insufficient by this one-up parent figure.

Blamers are more direct in their attempts to control, although they use some of the same tactics as Interrogators. They view the world in black/white, right/wrong, and good/bad dichotomies and use subtle manipulation to draw others into their judgmental frame of reference. When others buy the simple thinking of Blamers, they also buy into fear -- fear of negative judgment, fear of rejection, or fear of abandonment. Blamers divide the world into two camps -- them and us. "Them" becomes the enemy and all sorts of lies, manipulations, and slander are condoned in the war against "them." Many religions and religious leaders practice the control drama of blaming.

The *Aloof* personalities (also called *Withdrawn* or *Computer* personalities) are emotionally distant from others. They are mysterious, secretive, cautious, and vague in interpersonal transactions. Instead of feeling, they rationalize and intellectualize their life experiences. They pull others into their dramas by standing at a distance and forcing those who desire connection with them to approach. The pursuers are then forced to dig out their feelings while Aloof people resist. Hiding their thoughts and feelings becomes a game. They draw energy toward them by playing hard to get.

Aloof people often attract unacceptable and codependent partners because of their fear of intimacy or rejection. Their immature and undeveloped partners allow Aloof persons to stay in control by allowing their distancing and denial of relationship needs. Instead of recognizing and correcting their emotional deficits, they hide in the defensive control drama that protects their weaknesses, fear, and insecurity.

Another variation of the aloof type is the *Distracter*. Distracters are more cunning in their intimacy-evasive attempts. They evade true connection by avoiding direct expression of their emotions or beliefs. When cornered into expressing their inner truth, they make a joke, change the subject, or answer with an evasive variation of "I don't know." The effect of being in relationship with an Aloof or Distracter person is the same. The Aloof or Distracter types pull the energy of others toward them, without giving much of themselves. Those who persist in relationships with Aloofs or Distracters will eventually have to decide to get out of the relationship or give up hope for genuine connection.

125

The *Poor Me* personalities tell you about their troubles and the horrible things that have happened to them. You can be sure that the Poor Me is always the victim of other cruel and unfeeling people -- or so they would have you believe. Actually you are their victim if pulled into their "take care of me" game. They refuse to accept responsibility for controlling their lives. They continually need help from others. They have subtle ways of implying that you are responsible for helping them. If you refuse to rescue them, you are heartless and cold and become another in their long line of villains. The Poor Me type makes others feel guilty for not doing enough for them.

Martyr types elicit the sympathies and homage of others by selflessly caring for the needs of others while neglecting their own needs. In essence, Martyrs are similar to the Poor Me types, but their manipulations to gain attention are not as direct and are generally unconscious manipulations. They simply expect others to notice and applaud their selflessness. Always reacting to the needs and requests of others, Martyrs never take control of their own lives. They end up disillusioned, burned out and resentful that their lives were spent serving others. If serving others were a conscious decision, they wouldn't be Martyrs. A conscious decision to serve others is the mark of empowered persons. They give to others because they want to and choose to. There are no strings attached to the gifts of time and energy given by empowered persons. Giving by Martyrs is different. They feel trapped into giving and view taking care of others as mandatory. Martyrs don't take the responsibility of standing up for their own needs and rights. They expect the attention and adulation of others to fall on them because of their selfless giving. In actuality, Martyrs are disempowered and pull the attention and energy of others toward their negative void.

Virginia Satir uses the term *Placater* to describe another variation of the Poor Me/Martyr types. The Placater sacrifices herself or himself in the valiant attempt to smooth ruffled feelings

126

and be a mediator between conflicting people. The Placater always walks the middle ground -- reflecting both sides of an issue or argument, but never diving deep enough inside himself to find out his feelings about any subject. The Placater is a vital player in *triangulation* -- the game of pulling a third party into a disagreement or manipulative maneuver between two primary parties. The Placater's life purpose is to attend to the needs of others and get involved in the lives of others. But the Placater doesn't get involved in his own life. He doesn't do the hard work of developing who he is and standing on his truth. Because he's just the mirrored reflection of others' neediness, the Placater has little substance and is difficult to connect with.

All control dramas are unconscious or conscious manipulative efforts to avoid looking honestly at oneself and owning one's power. Codependent control dramas are prisons locking people into frozen levels of stunted development. Where there is fear, people fail to own their power. The codependent game of power and control robs each player of vitality, life, and love.

(6) Codependents are Ruled by Fear

At the root of codependency is fear. Codependents have learned to fear emotional pain such as rejection, abandonment, or negative judgment. They've also learned to fear for their physical or emotional safety and security. One adult child of an alcoholic father remembers her father loudly ordering her and her sisters to be silent and motionless while they watched him beat their mother. They were threatened with the same abusive treatment if they dared intervene in his sadistic ritual of intimidation. Children of alcoholics frequently grow up in stressful and traumatic environments that heighten their fear responses and increase their hypersensitivity. Other codependents live with more subtle fears that ultimately prove to be just as disempowering. Their fears are emotionally rooted. If they fail to conform and meet expectations of parents or significant others,

127

they fear negative judgment or rejection. One client in his fifties has been miserable in his marriage for the past thirty years. When questioned why he perseveres, he says he's afraid of being judged by others and afraid his grown children will reject him. His fear of rejection is rooted in parental expectations of conformity and perfection. He hasn't overcome his fears even though he's now a grandfather. Childhood lessons about codependent expectations die hard.

Fear blinds codependents to their inner truth. They live in accordance with the external expectations of the world. They deny their fears, their loneliness, and their depression. They're not empowered to live fully and joyfully. They only exist day to day in a gray and endless maze. If they break through denial and see the trap they've fallen into, their fear and neediness usually pull them back into their frozen state of codependency. Those heeding their inner voice enter a battle between mind and emotion when they finally admit the truth of their misery. The mind rationalizes that it's not so bad after all. But emotions don't lie. Emotions tell them that they've chosen a false and dreary path. Their choice is to follow the truth of their feelings or freeze in fear.

One codependent client said she refrained from speaking her truth and showing her real emotions because "I'm afraid I'll get killed or I'll kill the other person." When she ultimately risked voicing and living her truth, neither dire outcome happened. Taking the risk to confront imprisoning fears, even though frightful and stress-producing, is the path to growth and wisdom. Freezing in fear will most certainly kill the heart and soul. Self-imposed death is a terrible price to pay for worshipping fear.

(7) Codependents Numb Their Emotions and Emotional Responses

There are three primary rules in codependent families: don't trust; don't talk; don't feel. All three rules are based in fear -- fear of being vulnerable and fear of getting hurt. Early on, codependents learned their feelings didn't count. Expressing emotions and speaking one's inner truth were not valued or encouraged. In fact, independent thinking and emotional expression are actively discouraged in codependent homes.

Danielle's family show the lethal potential of numbed emotions. Her brother, cousin, and aunt had committed suicide. Danielle spoke in a soft, childlike voice and was chronically depressed. She was extremely afraid of confronting her tyrannical and egotistical husband. During a therapy session, she recounted the time in her teens when she argued against her father's opinion during a family dinner. The dinner table suddenly became deathly quiet. No one dared speak. The tension was incredible. Danielle didn't need corporal punishment or verbal admonitions to learn an indelible lesson -- she must not make her parents, particularly her father, uncomfortable by expressing a divergent belief or feeling. He needed to be in control and that meant every word and every emotion had to be regulated.

The price of acceptance in her family was complete subjugation of her individuality. She repressed her emotions and wore the mask of conformity. The codependent lesson -- don't feel, don't talk, don't trust -- was firmly ingrained into all family members. They dared not express their perspectives lest they be judged and sanctioned. The family was together, but beneath the surface, everyone was isolated and lonely. Danielle now sees that this repression of emotions probably contributed to the number of suicides in her family. When life became unbearably hard, family members closed up and allowed their depression to grow. They didn't know how to reach out and share their burdens with others. Problems swelled with neglect and fear until they became lethal.

When she was fifteen, her brother, Mike committed suicide after a jilted love affair. Eight years his junior, she looked up to her brother and believed he always had the right answers and did the right things. He was caring, sensitive, and always supportive of her. Her family environment was an emotional desert, but

Mike provided the oasis of hope and rejuvenation. In secrecy, she could talk to him about her fears and pain. Unfortunately, their communication was one-way -- probably because of the age difference. He never shared his hurts and concerns with her. Just before his suicide, his fiancee's mother told her to leave Mike because he wasn't good enough for her.

Mike accepted both the cruel judgment of his fiancee's mother and the broken engagement. He didn't express his hurt or resentment to anyone. After all, he had learned the family lesson well -- don't dispute the opinions of adults; don't express your feelings or beliefs; and don't raise your voice in defense or anger. He chose death rather than self-empowerment. Now, twenty years later, his sister is struggling to find her voice, tune in to her emotions and speak her inner truth. She's trying to unlearn the devastating lessons of emotional repression and recover her dormant emotions.

(8) Codependents Avoid or Intensify Risk-Taking

The "don't talk, don't trust, don't feel" rule thwarts emotional sensitivity and expression. Codependents incorporate the sanction against expressing emotion, particularly negative emotions. They end up largely unaware of their own emotions and insensitive to the emotions of others. They operate within a very narrow band of emotional awareness. Repression of negative emotions also results in repression of positive emotions. Feelings have been stuffed so routinely and completely that codependents don't know how to identify their emotions. If asked, they can generally name very few. When pressed, they are likely to misinterpret their true feelings. For example, most will say they are mad when they are feeling other emotions such as worry, irritation, hurt, or embarrassment. Emotional repression makes codependents more susceptible to avoidance or intensification of risk taking. Those who avoid risk taking are ruled by fear. It's as if they're sitting on a narrow chair and if they shift in one direction or another, they'll

130

fall off. The risk avoiders are afraid of change, afraid of the future, and afraid to hope for anything better in their lives. They don't want anything to change. Safety and security are foremost in their lives.

At the other end of the risk-taking continuum are codependents who are excitement-addicted. These people ride an emotional roller coaster -- they're either very high or very low. Because of their emotional restriction, they need to vacillate between the extremes of emotion to feel alive. They're attracted to people and situations that feed their addiction for excitement. Everyday occurrences are boring to the excitement addicted codependent. If given the choice of riding a treacherous roller coaster or walking through a beautiful park, the excitement-addicted codependent will choose the treacherous roller coaster each time. Any less than that high level of excitement and danger feels boring and dead to him.

(9) Codependents are Externally Oriented

In order to connect fully with another, we first need to own and express our inner truth. We need to know who we are and have the confidence to share our feelings and beliefs with other developed people. Yet, from early youth, we're raised to deny who we are, what we feel, and what we want. We're told what to do and what not to do as we're forced to conform to the dictates and desires of significant adults. Empowerment gets lost in conditioned responses that earn praise, acceptance, or in the most severely dysfunctional families, mere survival. Being ourselves is replaced with being what mom wants, teacher wants, or peers want. We are fed very subtle and manipulative messages of fear, neediness, and dependency. Our lives are structured "outside-in" by *external* dictates and rules handed down from generations of unempowered, dependent adults. We conform to subtle and overt messages that come from our parents, schools, churches, workplaces-- even from TV.

131

We blindly buy the externally-imposed fears, shoulds, and oughts without going within ourselves to find our inner truth. Rather than go inside and deal with the damage done to our self-esteem and power, we turn outward. We try to win favor and acceptance by pleasing others. We give up our independence and our freedom. We're imprisoned in the trap of giving ourselves away by conforming to external expectations. We conform to the rituals of marriage, education, and workplace without seriously considering if convention is right, fair, or consistent with our needs. We evaluate our worth by family connection, salary, job title, or educational level. There is little attention to the quality of our hearts or our commitment to truth. With our external focus, we squelch the small voices inside that tell us who we are and what path to follow. We surround ourselves with partners, children, friends, and work associates who condone our weaknesses and assuage our fear of loneliness.

Ginny exemplifies an externally focused codependent. Ginny's family looked exemplary. The five children did well in school. Her father worked hard while her mother stayed home and cared for the children. Presenting the right image to the outside world was important to Ginny's family. Early on, Ginny learned she would pay a big price if she embarrassed her mother. Sunday church services were particularly tense for Ginny. If she didn't act the well mannered and polite child, she always paid a price later. Ginny is now thirty-three and refuses to go to church because of the negative memories of her Sunday ritual. As the youngest, she found it difficult to sit still during the minister's service. Wiggling, stifling her laughter, dropping pencils and retrieving them under the pew was the repeated scenario on Sunday morning. Ginny still cringes when she remembers what happened after church.

As she hit Ginny with a belt, her mother chastised her for embarrassing the family with her unruly behavior. It didn't matter that Ginny was a hyperactive child who found it almost impossible to sit still. It didn't matter that she was only five years old. It just mattered that she brought her mother embarrassment from the perceived negative judgment of others. Following each Sunday experience, the bright, active, and curious child became quieter and more withdrawn.

Ginny lost her individuality and became the tamed and subdued shadow of family expectations. Enmeshed within the family tapestry of image and control, she lost her vitality and power. Her parents so feared external judgment, they traded their children's selfhood for positive image. Her parents weren't independent and empowered enough to encourage Ginny's independence and self-love. She learned she was bad and flawed. She learned to conform to gain acceptance and escape punishment. She feared her parents, yet she needed them to survive. She learned to play their game and she became externally oriented.

In adulthood, Ginny still gives herself away by caretaking others and pleasing them. She entered therapy after the collapse of the latest in a string of codependent relationships. When Donna instructed her to tell the truth about her feelings and to stand up for her own rights and needs, she replied, "No one will like me then." Ginny had long before learned the lesson of codependency -- if you're going to be safe and accepted by others, you have to play by the rules of others. She gave up personal power and became dependent on external validation. By committing to therapy and self-growth, Ginny grew past codependency and recovered the wonderful, energized, and highly intelligent person behind the mask of external conformity. Tragically, most codependents remain entombed in external expectations, never venturing into their internal world of lost dreams and lost power.

(10) Codependents Play Roles and Act Normal

Codependents are trained to give others what they want, so they look for cues about how others want them to be and they act the part expected. They value being good (as measured by others) rather than being real. Codependents aren't in touch with their emotions, beliefs, and inner truth so they have to fake being natural and normal. They have played an externally oriented role for so long they don't really know who they are outside their act.

Codependents don't know how to make deep and meaningful connections with others. Their relationships are defined by the personal and professional roles they play. If you ask them to define themselves, codependents will invariably cite their roles -- a wife, a boss, a doctor, etc.-- as their identities. Who they are outside their roles hasn't been examined. They become the social robe they wear -- the actor becomes the part he plays. Like the characters in Donna's *Oedipus Rex* dream, codependents act real, but they are merely robots repeating the words and actions programmed into them by the external world. Like robots, they're not aware of their separate and independent thoughts, nor are they in touch with their emotions.

Warren despairs about the quality of lovemaking between him and his wife: "I want her to tell me what she wants and how she feels. She just responds in a routine and mechanical way to what she thinks I want. She doesn't look inside herself to what she's feeling. I don't want her to just give to me because it's her duty and is expected. I want her to love herself enough to be able to receive and give love. But she won't make herself that vulnerable. She won't allow herself to get out of the control position of giving. She won't be open and real with me. She acts the way she thinks she's supposed to act. Where is the woman under the actress disguise? Where is her passion?" Warren's wife knows how to act, but she doesn't know how to reach down into the inner parts of her being and get in touch with her real feelings and wants.

134

Codependents pay a big price for acting -- they give up their real selves. Only by claiming our individuality can we distinguish the real self hiding behind societal encrustation. Only in claiming the "I" can we learn to relate to others with authenticity. Only in becoming real can we give up acting and start being who we truly are.

(11) Codependents React Rather than Act on their Own Accord

Consistent with acting normal and being externally oriented, codependents react to others, but lack the power and courage to act on their on accord. Instead of deciding a course of action right for them, they wait for others to make the first move. The one who acts takes all the responsibility and blame. The reactor slithers out of responsibility and blames the leader for wrong decisions or disappointments.

James tells of his experience at a dinner party that describes the codependent tendency to react rather than act. James arrived at the party while the host was engaged in another part of the house. As he stood near the front door, he became aware of his sense of embarrassment when none of the other guests welcomed him or introduced themselves. Then he became angry and indignant that no one had the common courtesy to acknowledge his presence. Finally one person acted by extending his hand and introducing himself to James. Others in the room then reacted, like dominos waiting for the first in line to fall.

Reactors wait for someone else to set the course before they act. They don't want to be blamed, shamed, or ridiculed, so someone else has to first take the risk of being vulnerable. Reactors are passive and allow the beliefs and behaviors of others to mold them. In group therapy language, we call this form of malleability being "easily led and misled." Reactors hide behind others and refrain from owning their own power and free will. Acting on your own volition requires connection with your inner truth, your principles, and your beliefs. Action requires you chart your course and commit to the journey of attaining your goals and wishes. Empowered people don't merely react to the beliefs and behaviors of others -- they decide what's right for them and they actively go after it!

(12) Codependents Have Inappropriate Personal Boundaries

People have physical and emotional boundaries that protect them from unwanted and unhealthy intrusion by others. An example of a physical boundary is the amount of distance between yourself and others that comprises your comfort zone. The comfort zone between people varies according to the intimacy of the relationship. For example, you may feel comfortable having little physical distance between yourself and your spouse. Holding hands, cuddling, hugging, and sitting close is comfortable within intimate relationships. Yet, if an acquaintance tried to invade your invisible comfort zone by moving too close, hugging inappropriately, or taking your hand, you would feel uneasy and back away from the intruder.

Our emotional boundaries are much the same as physical boundaries -- we expect to be able to share emotions openly in intimate relationships. We expect to share less with professional associates, strangers, or acquaintances. But codependents are warped in their idea of appropriate boundaries. Often they allow others to take unfair advantage of their time, energy, money, and attention. Others will ask too much from codependents, draining them of energy and resources. Codependents don't see that others are invading their boundaries because they aren't aware of their own rights and needs. Michael says that selfless codependents, in particular, have an unwritten sign on their forehead that says CHUMP. The chump message is written in their downcast eyes, slumping posture, and fearful demeanor. All the users in the world can see this sign and they flock to selfless codependents to get what they can. Lack of appropriate boundaries, failure to stand up for one's rights and needs, and giving when others don't

136

give back, is a reflection of the codependent's imbalanced selfishness and selflessness. While the selfless generally give too much of themselves, the selfish take too much. Only the balanced person is able to set appropriate boundaries, giving what they truly want to give, and judging how much is appropriate to ask of another.

(13) Codependents Expect Someone or Something to Fill Them Up

Because codependents are externally oriented, they believe that happiness and fulfillment are somewhere "out there." Their task is to find the right job, perfect partner, magnificent house, or comfortable situation AND THEN they will be satisfied and at peace. Their search for something or someone to fill them up and bring them peace is illusive. Peace comes only with following our inner truth. Satisfaction comes only in living in harmony with ourselves. The codependent spends fruitless energy looking for that person or thing to fill him up. In seeking empowerment, the codependent must accept the task of filling himself with inner wisdom and truth.

Instead of following the path toward full empowerment, most adults think that being adult means having an adult body. While they may talk about growth and wisdom, few make it their life priority to gain internal depth -- that balanced sense of intellectual, emotional, and spiritual maturity that makes them fully empowered adults. Carl Rogers aptly summarized the empowered adult as one who confronts each life challenge with the confidence that he is sufficient. Codependents may exude a self-confident facade, but deep within is a sense of incompleteness and insecurity. The codependent needs someone or something else to feel sufficient, normal, or secure. Looking for the right fit -- whether it be another person, job, religion or philosophy of life -- is important. Codependents put the cart before the horse, however. They first need to know themselves thoroughly. They need to compare who they are to other people, organizations, jobs,

137

etc. Instead of "filling up from the outside" and becoming what the outside world demands, sufficient people judge by the measuring stick of who they are and what they believe.

Matthew is an example of a person filling up from the outside. Matthew and Michael, coworkers at the university, considered themselves close friends for over twenty years. Matthew wasn't satisfied with his shallow, codependent marital relationship. His children were grown so he no longer defined his identity as the father caretaker. He needed something to define who he was and what his purpose was. Instead of doing the hard work of scrutinizing himself and looking at the truth about his marital relationship, Matthew ran. He ran to a fundamentalist religion and a dictator minister who told willing adult children what to think and what to do. Matthew refused to go within himself and fill up with his own inner strength and wisdom. He subjugated his inner truth and followed the dictates of someone outside himself. His image glistened. He dedicated many hours to mission work and attended church several times a week. He proselytized to others, expecting that they too would choose to be filled up from the outside and be brainwashed by the beliefs of others.

Then a situation occurred that revealed the fraudulent nature of his religion. A tyrannical administration pervaded the university, methodically replacing good and caring people with people who lied and twisted any thing and everything to get their way. Matthew and Michael both had the opportunity to speak out against the vicious persecution of their friends. Michael did speak out, but Matthew capitulated to fear and retreated further and further into his religion as a refuge. If his newfound religion was as great as he pretended, Matthew would have exhibited true empowerment. He would have known how to love and how to stand in courage. Instead, he hid in his cowardice and never connected intimately. He existed in the unscrupulous environment that surrounded him at the university and dared not be a force for change. Matthew never developed the courage to share his real self with others. He hid under a mask of codependency. He fooled himself into believing that "filling up from the outside" was enough. Inside Matthew was hollow, alone and unable to connect in truth with equals.

(14) Codependents Avoid Self-Scrutiny and Discernment

Denial is the arch-enemy of growth and empowerment. People lie to themselves and blind themselves to the truth of their problems. When codependents break out of denial and recognize their unhealed problems, they are more than half-way through their recovery struggle. Codependents must look at themselves honestly and impartially. They must scrupulously examine their relationships. When they're able to cast a critical and objective eye at their deficits, they can begin the work of clearing emotional traumas. With emotional clearing, the dysfunctional thought and behavioral patterns begin to change. Sadly, most people hide in denial and refuse to scrutinize themselves. They'd rather protect their defenses and stay in their blindness than move on to clearer understanding and truthful connection with others.

Donna objectively assessed a wife as selfish when she constantly complained about her husband's lack of ability to provide for her wants and needs. With grown children and a successful work history, there was no reason for the woman to avoid working and adding to the couple's financial well-being. Yet she refused to assume adult responsibility saying that she had the right to be taken care of like other wives in traditional marriages. Donna pointed out that she was repeating the selfish pattern of her mother, who expected others to meet her needs, but gave little in return. Her mother ended her life a lonely, bitter complainer who saw herself as the victim. Even though Donna's client could see her mother's problems, she refused to look at her own codependent behavior that caused others to flee from her.

People grow when they're ripe to grow. This truth is a salve for impatience when we're frustrated with those stuck in codependency. You can't change another person -- each person has the power to change only himself or herself. It's important to see that some people are stuck in second grade and are just not ready to progress forward to higher levels. The willingness to critically and objectively scrutinize oneself is a hallmark of a person's readiness to grow.

Complementary Control Dramas of Codependent Couples

Codependents attract others who complement their interpersonal styles and play into their power games. For example, the complementary game of pursuing and distancing is found in many Aloof-Interrogator dyads. Ginny is an Interrogator codependent who spent fifteen years with an Aloof partner, David. Ginny continually tried to pull David out of his intellectual armor. Recognizing his cognitive ability, she mistakenly believed he was capable of growing emotionally and connecting with her. So she spent the better part of her adult years asking him why he acted the way he did. She was there to salve his emotions when things were rocky. She shared her inner truth and feelings lavishly. What David gave back to her were mind games that rationalized his emotions and justified his distance from her. After years of therapy, she finally gave up the chase.

"It's sad to admit I've spent fifteen years chasing smoke," Ginny said. "He won't commit to me because he's never even committed to himself. He'll never become what I believed he was capable of becoming. He'll always hide in his mind games, with his defensive wall keeping me at a distance." Ginny broke the codependent game when she finally admitted that she couldn't change David. She decided her time and life were worth more than chasing David in his circular route that led nowhere and never ended.

Poor Me's attract both *Martyrs* and *Intimidators*. Poor Me victims believe they have an inalienable right to be taken care of

140

by someone else. They are conscious of using their victim status to capture the attention and energy of others. They are like black widow spiders, ensnaring others in their web of dependency and then killing them with emotional venom. Martyrs and Poor Me people are often found together. While these two may seem to be different in outward appearance (one sucking energy from others and one giving up energy to those more needy), they are two sides of the same coin. They are both codependent and base their relationships on mutual neediness and weakness. One acts as the parent figure and the other as the child. Their sense of self worth is defined by the codependent game of giving and taking. In other words, the parent caretaker ceases to have identity and ego meaning without having the needy child to take care of. They engage in a never ending and enmeshed do loop that consumes the energies of both.

Usually early in life, the Poor Me has given up his power and assumed the ineffectual victim stance. Dick's turbulent childhood was dominated by an abusive alcoholic father. Dick remembers many beatings. When he was seven, he was eating an ice cream cone when his father arrived home. His father asked for a bite of the ice cream. Dick, knowing his father would consume the entire treat, resisted and pretended not to hear him. His father came over to Dick and jabbed the burning end of his cigarette into the tender flesh of Dick's hand. Dick howled in pain and ran to his room to hide. His mother and three siblings watched the scene but never uttered a word of protest against the abusive intimidator. All were poor me victims lacking the courage, self love, or love for each other that are necessary to break away from a selfish intimidator. Dick's father succeeded in ruling the family with fear and intimidation. He was in control and no one was important except him. If anyone dared cross him in any way, he or she would be punished. He would punish them in such a way that a clear message was sent to others -- "bow to me or you'll pay a heavy price." Years later, the adult children celebrated when

141

their father died. Dick sipped champagne and clicked the rim of his glass to the glasses raised by his siblings. "We're finally free," they rejoiced.

But Dick wasn't free when his father died. The Intimidator/Poor Me game was indelibly etched in his emotional psyche. Unless people see control patterns and develop the courage to break away from them, those same control dramas repeat again and again in a person's life. Now in his forties, Dick is married to an intimidator wife. She doesn't work outside the home, but she continually chastises him for not being successful enough. Even though he waits on his wife hand and foot, she criticizes him for not doing enough, fast enough or well enough for her. All the energy and attention revolves around this leisure princess, while Dick bows and scrapes, trying to win some small sign of acceptance. When she complains, Dick defends her saying she's justified in complaining because he doesn't do things just as she instructs. Sometimes he forgets what her instructions are. The truth is Dick is full of rage and his passive-aggressive forgetting and half-way doing are his only ways to pay her back for her selfish inconsiderateness.

The Codependent Family

Codependency and family are like the chicken and the egg -- which came first is an enigma. When a couple has children, most often personal growth and growing together cease as they pour all their energy and attention into raising kids. Kids become their focal point and reason to exist. Parents find identity and meaning through their children, rather than taking on the task of individuating themselves. They come to the ends of their lives, having followed the rules of conformity and having taken care of others, but they never learned who they really were and what their particular purposes were. They are parents, they are teachers, they are spouses. Take away their association with others and the jobs that define them and they don't know who they are. Is

142

ignorance to our meaning and purpose what we really want to leave as our legacy? If not, why don't parents see themselves as people first, and parents second? Why are we so dependent on our children to complete us and fill our lives with meaning?

Much of our expertise in being codependent has its roots in our childhood and in our families. We must discard the codependent games that form family relationships. If our family relationships are real, if they have value, then all parties involved deserve more than mere ritualized, shallow connections. They deserve relationships with depth, relationships that honor truth above all things, relationships where emotional honesty and directness are the norm. They deserve true heart connections and no strings attached unconditional love.

Tragically, attempting to establish meaningful adult/adult relationships with our family members, particularly with parents, can be very frustrating. These are the people upon whom we were dependent as children and who were generally dependent upon us. The one-up/one-down parent-child relationships that were appropriate in our childhood years should evaporate into equal adult-adult relationships as we mature. More often, the one-up/one-down paradigm continues in codependent families with parents still exerting undue control and power over their adult children's lives. Claiming adult respect and the right to autonomy are often difficult for those raised in codependent homes.

A familiar pattern in codependent families is extension of sibling rivalry into adulthood. Favoritism and comparison between children are often used as control mechanisms in codependent homes. This sets an indelible imprint of jealousy and competition that lasts long into adulthood. Instead of learning to be supportive friends, codependent siblings have been scripted to be rivals. Often, adult children who play the codependent game are rewarded and those opting out of the game are punished or ignored by the rest of the family. For example, the Poor Mes, who remain ever dependent on their parents for support and nurturance (monetary as well as emotional), are looked upon with favor, while independent and self-sufficient adult children are ignored.

Codependent families are often isolated from others. Family members cling to each other rather than exert themselves to form meaningful relationships with outsiders. Codependents expect family members to meet their needs for security, love, and belongingness. "Blood is thicker than water" and "you can always count on family" are common mottoes of codependent families. Familial isolation is an extension of the "don't trust" rule. Codependents lean on family members rather than push themselves to reach out and make friends. Family isolation is counterproductive to adult empowerment. Adults take risks, and in doing so, they learn to trust themselves and they learn who they can trust. But codependent isolation nullifies the need for reaching out and taking risks with others. The isolated family or couple becomes the haven that makes risk taking and stretching as an adult unnecessary.

Codependent isolation heightens our dependency on family members who have stock in keeping us needy. As long as we're needy, family members control us. They aren't challenged to find their life purposes or to become autonomous because their life meanings are tied to controlling and caretaking us. As long as they caretake us, there's no need for us to become self-sufficient. Codependent family isolation is a vicious cycle that cripples progress to adult empowerment.

Codependent family isolation is invisible to those inside the system. Jason's story shows how difficult it is to see crippling family codependency. Jason, a seventeen year old, was popular with peers for his assurance, leadership and sensitivity. He was admired by his friends' parents for his respectful, but casually jovial nature. What friends and their families saw was different from what Jason's family saw. Jason was angry and defiant with them - particularly with his father.

Jason complained that his family was screwed up and said he didn't like any of them. His college-aged sister returned for holidays and summer breaks and it took only a few days for them to become combative. His sister was seen as the "good one" and he was seen as the "troubled one," according to Jason. More and more, Jason turned away from his family and toward his friends for support and validation.

Jason's parents divorced when he was twelve, and he decided to live with his father, who retained the family home. For years, Jason blamed his mother for the divorce and couldn't understand why she left his father. As Jason progressed through his teen years, he started having more and more problems with his father. His father was suspicious of Jason and looked for evidence of his misbehavior. Whenever his father talked to him, it was to complain or reprimand. Jason griped to his mother about the pressure and judgment he felt from his father. He was angry that his Dad didn't share more about himself - his feelings, his thoughts, his plans for the future. Jason's mother empathized. She too had felt the aloofness and anger within her ex-husband, but his outward demeanor was controlled and caring. Her ex-husband's inability to connect had confused her also. Jason angrily complained to his mother that something was wrong with his father, but he couldn't put words to his suspicions. All he could say was that "something is wrong with a man who doesn't have any friends."

"I think he's jealous of me because I'm able to take care of myself and I'm able to reach out to others and have friends," Jason exclaimed. His father, by contrast, isolated himself and associated only with his two children and a girlfriend who was thirteen years his junior. As long as he could control his subordinates, he felt secure. Jason threatened that security by being self-sufficient. Jason didn't need his father, so the ground rules of neediness and isolation that his father counted on to unite the family were violated by Jason. Jason continued to assert his individuality and sufficiency as an adult, and the father-son relationship withered. When codependents break free of the confining isolation of family codependency, they're often alienated. The awful choice in codependent families is to be smothered by the fear-driven codependency games or to break free and risk leaving undeveloped family members behind.

Summary: The Bridge From Codependency to Empowerment

Most of us arrive at early adulthood without completing the tasks of individuation that would balance us. Instead of balancing our needs for autonomy and unity with others, we become dependent on others and dependent on things external to us to make us feel normal and fulfilled. Unless we've completed the personal growth that leads us to wholeness and empowerment, we invariably seek another to complete us. In our state of neediness, we attract another undeveloped and disempowered person. Like two children playing grown up, we're not mature enough to understand the real key to connecting. We play games, we fix each other, we compete for power and control, but we're just playing at love and playing at life. Instead of confronting fears, we hide behind others and they hide behind us. We play a game we call love, but which is actually neediness. We cling to others because we're afraid to stand alone. We stay in empty, ritualized relationships believing there's nothing better.

Instead of looking deep within ourselves and uncovering the festering wounds within, we numb ourselves to our inner truths. We avoid looking at ourselves honestly. We put on our masks and act out socially acceptable games, hoping others won't detect our unhealed emotional and psychological basements. As we hide from who we are and from the experiences that have shaped us, our fear and need to control increases. Exposing the unhealed parts of ourselves to the light of truth will diminish the shadows that hold us captive. But a codependent relationship is not about

146

becoming empowered and independent. Codependents look for others with deficits and strengths that complement their own. Connecting with other codependent and incomplete people allows us to avoid the task of becoming fully responsible adults. Codependency is a trap that allows people to wallow in their weaknesses until they're completely consumed by them.

There are many strings attached to codependent connections. "I will love you if you do things my way"; "I will love you in trade for your taking care of me." Love becomes a social contract that is devoid of real connection. Codependency is the world's definition for love. A few people awaken to the terrible sense of isolation and separation in their relationships and tune in to an inner knowing -- what the world accepts as love isn't love. They know that connection isn't measured by a legal document or blood ties. They intuitively know that love is more. True love is a seamless connection that has no barriers. Love is the emotional, intellectual, and spiritual unity of two mature and complete people.

Given enough time, usually by mid-life, we can no longer drown out that quiet inner voice, that innate knowing that tells us we're living a lie. For some, there comes a point where the lie becomes too obvious, the unhappiness too great. That point, where the pain of continuing in codependency becomes stronger than the fear and sorrow of letting go, is one of the most bitter-sweet moments of life. It is here that we finally get it -- that *most of what we call love is really codependency.* It's at this point some of us choose to reject the script we've played so long and reach for who we can be -- complete persons empowered with truth and ready for love. If we awaken to our full potential, we will work to balance and center ourselves in mind, emotion, and spirit. We will claim the stability of our roots and the limitless freedom of our wings.

Chapter Six

Individuation Completion:
The Decision to Leave Codependency

Individuation Completion:
The Decision to Leave Codependency

If full empowerment and intimate relationships are our birthrights, then why do so many choose to spend their lives only partially fulfilled? How can we explain our willingness to enmesh ourselves in the vast array of addictions, habituations, and codependencies that arrest our journey to self-actualization? Perhaps it's because there remains one final wall we must pass through before we can own our power and truly love ourselves or another. It is a self-protective wall of unwillingness, fear, and laziness.

Years ago Michael became engrossed in studying how and why people and organizations change. He reversed the question believing the answer would be found in examining why people do not change. He'd spent fifteen years as an organizational training and development consultant and had become frustrated by the constant stream of clients who could so glibly verbalize the need for positive change, but who would not commit to the follow-through that was necessary to make change stick. They talked a good story about how things would be better -- if. But, talk and half-hearted efforts to move forward were frequently their only outcomes. Some did little more than relish in their belly-aching. The pattern was clear: most of us are content to tolerate and stay in situations we know can be better rather than exert ourselves and risk making a change. It is this final barrier, the wall of stagnancy, unwillingness, and fear that we must surmount before we can move to a fully actualized state.

John was one of those people who was discontent, lonely, filthy rich, and unwilling to change. Because of his money, his wife turned her head to his infidelities. As long as she got what she wanted, she didn't care what he did. She really didn't care about John at all. The other women who clung to him were dependent and selfless. They wanted his attention and his money, but didn't have the integrity or power to demand equality and respect. So John drifted for thirty years, until tragedy struck and he developed cancer. Suddenly truth mattered and having a real connection with someone who knew and loved him mattered.

Not long after his divorce, Patsy entered his life. Twenty years his junior and struggling to support her family alone, she seemed an unlikely equal to John. Patsy turned out to be more than his equal -- she was the one person who was strong enough to confront him about his problems and secure enough to leave him if he chose to stay frozen in his dysfunction. After dating for four years, Patsy and John had a committed relationship -- at least Patsy thought they did. Then she discovered John's relationship with another woman who had stayed at the periphery of John's life for the past twenty years. She caught John lying about this woman and about other petty issues. He closed up and refused to share his emotions with her. Even though John loved Patsy, his commitment to maintain his freewheeling and unconnected status prevailed. Patsy left John after he refused to go to counseling with her. She did what no other woman dared do with John -- she refused to put up with his immaturity and lack of commitment to their relationship. Patsy loved the real John hiding behind his mask of wealth and importance. She saw his money as a curse -- it anesthetized him to the need to scrutinize himself and to grow emotionally.

Everyone needs a Patsy in their lives. Instead of hiding in codependent weakness and game-playing, the "Patsy types" demand honesty and real connecting. They are strong enough to stand for their beliefs, even when standing up means hardship and pain for them. Patsy understands that truth and integrity don't mix with emotional repression and lying. She knows that love and fear are opposites. People like Patsy are tuned in to their inner truths. They discard their weaknesses and fear and follow paths to empowerment. Unfortunately, Patsy and those like her are exceptions instead of the norm.

Incentives for Staying Asleep: Why is codependency the norm? Why do people choose to stay in this arrested state of development? Why do they stay in miserable situations rather than follow the truth that will free them? Among the many possible answers to why people stay stuck in codependency are the following: (1) people are addicted to their power games; (2) it's easier to stay an undeveloped child; (3) selfishness or selflessness pays off; (4) people fear risk-taking; (5) people are too numbed out or lazy to make changes; and (6) there are few models showing others how to achieve true empowerment and human connecting.

(1) Addiction to Power Games: Some people are captivated by codependent power games and simply see no other way to be. For example, people choosing the Poor Me victim role continue to set themselves up to be victimized because their whole identity and way of connecting with others are based on victimization. Recall Warren's wife cited in the beginning of Chapter Five. She had a history of involvement with abusive men. Warren was in a social service occupation (law enforcement) and was attracted to victims because he could rescue them. A Poor Me victim fit his requisite of feeling needed and important. In the beginning of their relationship, Warren's wife readily talked about her past. He saw her vulnerability and neediness and was drawn to help her. After their marriage she closed up. There was really nothing else to talk about. She was a vulnerable victim, but once rescued, she became the undeveloped child unable to relate as an equal to another adult. Her only way of connecting was to act good and be pleasing. But she didn't give Warren what he needed -- a fully developed, adult female partner.

Warren asked Donna why his wife closed up after they married. Donna replied that she was probably addicted to being a victim. Warren was dumbfounded by Donna's reply.

"How could she be closing herself off from me because she's a victim? I don't victimize her!" Warren replied.

153

"She'll again be the victim if you leave her, won't she? And you are thinking about leaving. Everyone will blame you and gather around your wife to salve her emotional wounds. No one will see that she set herself up to be the victim by not growing enough to be a sharing, equal, adult partner with you," Donna explained.

Warren then understood. People are so accustomed to getting attention through their power games and control dramas that they don't know any other way of getting energy. Instead of being fulfilled from an inner source of self-knowledge and self-love, they expect others to fill their emptiness. Whether they are a Poor Me, Martyr, Blamer, Intimidator, Interrogator, Aloof, or Placating personality, they haven't learned the vital lesson: to get your real needs met, you must undo your neediness. You must become an empowered adult *and then* people will be attracted to you for your energy and vitality. A disempowered child only drains others of their life energies. It's a no-win battle when you're involved with others you want to change or save. Only they can change themselves. Only they can save themselves.

(2) It's Easier to Stay an Undeveloped Child: A client complained that she had worked for months making window treatments for her home with no offers of outside assistance. She'd just learned that her mother spent a few weeks at her sister's house making curtains. "Damn, I wasn't smart at all! If I had played the inept child who can't cook or sew like my sister, my mother would come to rescue me too!" she said.

This is an oft-repeated story. One person takes adult responsibility and finds himself or herself paired with a person who abdicates responsibility. In the preceding chapter, we read about Debra and Daniel, the example of modern-day codependency. Daniel did little around the house and lost his patience helping their son, Ricky, with homework. So Debra, after working all day, handled all the mundane household chores and all child-rearing responsibilities. Debra complained in therapy

154

about Daniel's childish irresponsibility. Donna asked Debra why Daniel should change -- after all, he got everything he wanted and she played the complementary martyr game. Why should a selfish and undeveloped person change if he can get by with taking the easy road? The answer is he doesn't change. The path of least resistance is very attractive. Most people choose the Easy Road!

(3) Selfishness and Selflessness Pay Off: The selfish resist change because there are enough selfless people around who will give them their way. They can stay on their throne and be "King Baby" while the attention and energy of others swirl around them. Only when the selfless get fed up with one-way giving will their selfish parasites see the need to grow up and treat others with consideration. As long as the selfish get what they want, they have no incentive to change.

Selfless people are likewise rewarded for their denigration of self-worth. With societal praise for long-suffering and humility, the selfless get ample reward. "She's had a hard life, but she's been so strong" and "He's so helpful to everybody" are esteemed comments. Suppose we instead focused on the destructive side of selflessness. Then we'd say, "She chose to be a victim and never became a positive and empowered role model for her children. It's a shame they'll follow her model and fall into the same caretaker trap!" Or we might say, "Why doesn't Fred allow anyone to help him? Maybe he's buying and earning love, and deep-down he doesn't believe he's lovable. Poor Fred, one day he'll learn that he must first love himself before he's ready to receive the love of others."

Suppose we stopped venerating selflessness and recognized it for what it is -- manipulative power games of the weak. When giving comes from an empowered person, it's his choice to give. When giving comes from a codependent, he's more likely hiding from his fear of loneliness and being unloved. Giving from a selfless person comes with strings attached -- you must give back or you'll be punished. Only when we recognize the neediness hiding behind selflessness will we stop rewarding and enabling this destructive behavior.

(4) People Fear Risk-taking: The biggest risk in committing to grow past codependency is the real possibility that you'll leave loved ones behind who aren't willing to grow and change with you. You may have to leave a marriage that enables weakness and dependency, you may no longer feel close to friends, and you may feel the need to distance from family members. When we stop playing our old codependent games and no longer enable the weaknesses of others, they get angry.

While you are changing and committing to truth, equality and growth, they want the old codependent you back. The fear of others may bring up your own repressed fears and questions -- who will I be when I change and rid myself of old games and defense mechanisms? Will I be all alone? Will I be loved? One client believed that no one would like her if she stepped beyond her selflessness and began to stand up for herself. The known, as miserable as it may be, is often preferable to the unknown. Growing into our power is risky. Stagnating in codependency seems safer. But it's not. Ultimately, codependent relationships become too painful, for all but the martyrs, and they wither and die.

(5) People Are Too Numbed Out or Lazy to Make Changes: People seem to have herd mentality -- if no one else is changing, why should I? Because codependency is so common, it's also invisible. It doesn't look too damaging or unhealthy. Most people choose to ignore their voices of discontent and numb their emotions. They lie and tell themselves they have it as good as it gets. The only way their lies succeed is if they numb their emotions and close their eyes to their inner truths. They may numb out on drugs, alcohol, work, or numerous other diversions from the work of self-empowerment. Above all, they keep so occupied and distracted that their nagging inner voice of truth can't be heard.

156

(6) *There Are Few Models Showing Others How to Achieve Self Empowerment and Empowered Love.*

Even when people commit to grow in truth and power, there aren't many human models to lead them in their journey to full actualization. Religious beliefs point to unconditional love and service to mankind as the way of God and the way to God. Unconditional love and service to others are indeed typical of the lives of empowered people such as Mahatma Ghandi, Sister Teresa, Martin Luther King, Jesus Christ, and others. When not exposed directly to powerful models of human love, courage, and truth, we must take the initiative to learn indirectly. We must be open to all opportunities to grow to our own highest level of development. It's our task to keep reading, connecting, and searching until we find models that point the way to true empowerment.

What is Individuation Completion? *Individuation Completion* is the process of opening to our inner truth and accepting our full power as a human being. It is recognizing all parts of ourselves -- the positives we readily show and want others to recognize, and the negative, dark sides we try to hide. It is learning to love all parts of ourselves unconditionally. We've been seeking unconditional love from others, only to be disappointed over and over again. At the point of mature individuation, we finally realize that before anyone can love us unconditionally, we must first love ourselves unconditionally. No one can give to us what we haven't first given to ourselves.

Before we're able to love ourselves unconditionally, we must stand in the light of complete truth. We must admit the truth of who we are to ourselves and others. We must look squarely at our fears of being inadequate, unlovable, abandoned, destitute, alone, ridiculed, unsuccessful, and successful, and at any other fears hiding in our emotional basements. Our task is to eradicate our unhealed parts during this stage of development. With our commitment to individuation completion, we affirm our intent to become whole and empowered.

An Overview of Tunnel Work: Of primary importance to individuation completion is committing to the *tunnel work* of psychological, emotional and spiritual catharsis. It's our task to uncover hidden fears and unhealed wounds. As we face our deepest secrets and most frightening fears, we remove the defenses that have become barriers to our growth. We begin to see ourselves more honestly and objectively, and we're also able to see others more clearly. Self-scrutiny and discernment of others are important to meaningful connection. During tunnel work, we acknowledge our hurts, pains and grievances that have accumulated over our lifetimes. We allow ourselves to feel the pain that we've stuffed into the recesses of forgetfulness. We immerse ourselves in the grieving process -- denial, anger, depression, bargaining, and acceptance -- and finally and completely let go of our defenses. What is left after catharsis is the true person. We can love and embrace ourselves fully. We own our free will and become what we're meant to be.

Therapy and Tunnel Work: The most formidable task confronting those of us choosing the path to wholeness is to rid ourselves of the fears and defenses that define our worldly persona. This is one of the most difficult things we will ever do, and generally, we need help in seeing and confronting the emotional defenses and protective masks that have become comfortable parts of the self. Seeing a counselor, joining a support group, or, if we are very fortunate, relying on the brutally candid feedback of an equally committed significant other or close friend, accelerates our insight and personal growth. The dilemma is that few others exist, including professional counselors, who have done enough of their own tunnel work to be of much real assistance during this stage.

Therapy helps us focus on the unresolved wounds that still

need healing. Sadly, most people learn too late that all therapists aren't created equally, and many get little from the therapeutic experience. Unless therapists have already walked the path of their own psychological, emotional and spiritual catharsis, they will not be adequate guides for their clients. One hallmark of the therapist who has completed individuation is humility. They shun the throne of expert and are real and honest with their clients. They present themselves as human and not as perfect and god-like. They join with and empower clients. The *expert-advice-giver* therapists do just the opposite. They heighten dependency in their clients by projecting that they have the answers and the client does not. Not only is this a lie, it takes away power from clients and makes them feel like helpless children.

Unfortunately, professional education and regulations in psychology, psychiatry, social work and counseling do the opposite of teaching client empowerment. The qualifications for diplomas, certification, and licensure in these areas falsely teach that the current body of knowledge will heal others. The professionals will admit among themselves that they really don't have the key to making a meaningful difference in most clients' lives. A popular admonition among beginning therapists is *fake it until you make it.* They are actually encouraged to pretend that they know what they're doing when they don't. They don't know because they've never taken the personal journey through tunnel work toward their own self-actualization. Instead of taking the difficult path to their own full empowerment, they hide behind titles and degrees. Following Freud, Jung, Skinner, or any of the other fathers of psychology is not the same as *walking your walk.* Those who haven't traveled the path to their own inner truth aren't able to lead others to full empowerment.

Dependency-promoting counselors are common. They're the ones who make you believe you need them to survive. One client told Donna that her ex-counselor had a technique he labeled *tantric counseling.* He told her that women needed attention and understanding and he believed it was his duty to give them this. His caseload was almost entirely female and they stayed with him for years and years. The client then offered her reason for leaving him. The counselor told her he was romantically attracted to her, but couldn't act on it because she was his client. He then added, "But wait until you're finished being my client." This is overt seduction and it's not only unethical, it's sick and manipulative.

Most counselors who promote dependency aren't as overt as the tantric counselor. Most counselors are blind to their dependency promotion. Whenever the counselor plays the role of parent or expert, the client is relegated to the role of the dependent child. Client empowerment requires counselors to acknowledge their clients' responsibilities to direct their own lives. Empowerment means honoring the client as the expert of himself or herself. Counselors are only guides who walk beside their clients and support them in their quest for truth.

Another ultimately disempowering game therapists play is the supportive advocate game. Like a friend or family member, the therapist supports the client's perspective and condemns victimizers that may be causing the client misery. Counseling becomes comfortable -- a non-confrontive, warm, fuzzy experience of being understood and affirmed. This approach may be helpful at times, but if therapy isn't also confrontive and uncomfortable, the client isn't being guided to examine his dysfunctional ideas, beliefs, and frozen emotions. Clients are invariably locked in repetitive codependent games that rob them of growth and vitality. Unless therapy helps them see their own unhealthy games, it's useless.

Another difficulty of traditional therapy is focus on sickness and the past without balanced focus on health, empowerment and the future. It's simply not good enough to point out emotional cancers and why they've developed. Emotional catharsis must be followed by *filling up* with healthy sharing and honest connecting.

160

Sadly, many therapists use disempowering therapies such as chemotherapy (use of drugs to mask pain) or psychoanalysis, where the therapist plays expert and tells the "sick child" what's wrong with him. The more effective therapists work with their clients to identify the traumas, fears, and inhibitors freezing him in uncomfortable stagnancy.

After the head work of identifying problem issues and tracing their origins, the therapist leads the client to emotionally clear himself of trauma or fear. For example, with a sex abuse survivor, hypnosis may be used to identify and recall the trauma. The client then owns her rage at being denigrated and sexually traumatized. Inner child work involves expressing the empowered adult's anger at the selfishness of an abuser. The client may express rage by hitting a blocking dummy with a soft bat, by crying, or by yelling.

Because people have been conditioned to repress anger and view it as dangerous, several attempts are generally needed before successful and complete catharsis of inner rage. A helpful exercise is writing a letter to the victimizer. The letter is then read in the therapy session and serves as the initiator of rage work. Anger is effectively exorcized in role playing when the counselor verbally acts the part of the victimizer. Particularly in sexual abuse cases, the survivor needs to own the power and fury that were repressed by her fear during the assault. After owning power to confront victimizers and emptying their repressed rage, clients need to learn skills that will fortify their healing. Joining a therapy group allows them to fill up on positive experiences of trusting and sharing their unvarnished self with others. In therapy groups they learn the skills of mutual support, honest and loving confrontation, and discernment.

All persons have an inner truth that serves as their guide throughout life. Therapists must encourage that inner truth to emerge by coaxing their clients to free themselves of emotional inhibitors. Therapists can offer their own truths only with the warning that "this is true for me, it may not be true for you." The therapist accompanies, but doesn't lead the client as he makes the journey into self-truth and empowerment. Those therapists arrogant enough to believe they can lead another maintain a one-up position that actually represses the client into a one-down position of dependency. All these therapists accomplish is self-aggrandizement at the expense of their clients' development.

The moral is *Beware the Expert!* Those who have to project the image of expert are undeveloped and insecure. They need continuous ego booster shots accomplished by fooling others into believing that they are important and knowledgeable. Those who have walked the self-enlightened path know that each person is his own expert and his unique way must be respected. The true experts wait for the path to be revealed and walk with -- not in front of-- their clients.

The Spiritual Wake-Up Call:

A spiritual wake-up call is a singular event (such as a near-death experience) or a growing awareness that has a transforming influence on a person. Generally, those experiencing wake-up calls turn from worldly pursuits and focus on personal and interpersonal development. They focus on their unique life work and have a heightened sense of urgency *to get on with it.* This persistent inner voice can be a real joy to the individual who hears it, but it can also be frightening. It is most assuredly challenging. For many, the wake up call comes at the mid-point in life when the goals set in early adulthood have been either achieved or discarded. For these individuals, it's the time to plot the course for the second half of their lives. Usually this means focusing on quality rather quantity -- and the quality of their relationships takes center stage.

Wake-up experiences come in varied forms. Some people experience a gentle awareness of dissatisfaction and discomfort leading them to search for something different and more meaningful in their lives. Some are jolted into an awakened state by a tragedy or trauma in their lives. Michael had a dream in which he was told, "It's time to wake up; you have work to do." Donna had a more subtle and symbolic wake-up call. She tells of her dream and the powerful effect it had on changing her life:

I saw myself walking down a long corridor lined with doors. The corridor looked like one you would see in a prison or mental hospital. Windows at the tops of the doors were reinforced with metal bars. As I walked down the hall, the slender arms of many women reached out the barred windows. The women began calling to me: "Help us, help us. We are being raped and murdered." I was enveloped by a cold chill and became very frightened. A sense of oppression overwhelmed me. I gazed at the wave of women's arms and winced as their desperate calls continued.

Finally I reached a door at the end of the hall. It opened to a descending stairway. At the bottom of the stairs, I entered a huge room that glowed with sunlit iridescence. A glare reflected off white marble floors and walls. No furniture was in the room, but it appeared full with streams of light pouring from windows that extended from floor to ceiling. In the middle of the room was a raised platform. Standing on the platform was a large, robe-clad figure. Like the room, the figure radiated light. His shining white robe extended to the floor, and a hood obscured the details of his face. I now say "he" but the figure actually had no discernible gender identity. I believed him to be masculine simply because of his large size. He extended his hand and beckoned to me. As I approached, I became aware of my own form. I was much like the figure on the platform. I was neither male nor female, but a large glowing spirit form. I felt that I was more powerful than a mere woman. I was intimately acquainted with the person in front of me and we loved each other unconditionally. He was larger than I and transmitted a greater power. In military terms, he would be the five-star general, while I was a four-star general. He was the one who gave the orders. Yet, the intimacy between us reminded me of a father-son or brother relationship.

His voice was calm and forceful as he spoke to me. "It's your job."

Like a petulant and stubborn child, I replied, "I don't want that job. Give me another."

This time he pointed a finger at me and repeated, "It's your job."

I protested. "It is too much for me alone."

He persisted. "You are able. The job is yours."

Again I protested, "I need help. I can't do it all alone."

He then nodded and, without any words exchanged, I felt assured that his nod meant that help would be sent and I wouldn't have to carry the burden alone.

The day after Donna had this dream, she opened the newspaper and read about Serbian militiamen who were systematically rounding up groups of Bosnian women and raping them. A later United Nations study revealed that over 20,000 women were raped in the Serbian ethnic cleansing campaign of 1992 and 1993. Donna was sensitized to injustice because of sex discrimination at the university which meant that she and other very capable women were denied tenure. She believed the dream was inciting her to awaken others to the world's atrocities and injustices. No longer was she content to exist day to day without focus on a larger purpose. She wrote a book, *Injustice for All*, that aimed at awakening people from their lethargy and urged them to accept their responsibility in creating a just world.

In recent years, we've witnessed a growing number of people who wake up and critically examine themselves and their purpose in the world. The reasons young and old are subjecting themselves to deep self-reflection are frequently the same, spiritual and life renewal. They are all looking for a life that is more truthful and for relationships and connections that are genuine and grounded in candor and honesty. For those able to overcome their fear, the wake-up call beckons a time of emotional, intellectual, and spiritual catharsis -- it's a time of transformation.

The paths that seekers of truth take are as varied as the

number of people responding to the call. Yet all paths merge on the common ground of finding life's deeper purpose and rejecting the veneer we wear as we play out worldly roles. It takes faith to persevere on the path to inner truth. First, they have to have faith that there is a meaning and purpose in their life. Second, they have to believe that their lives will be guided to an outcome better than any they could achieve purely on their own. Regardless of the words they use to describe their Higher Power, they are maintained on their journey by faith. Along the journey, they hold each of their fears to the light of inner truth and find themselves increasingly less fearful and less controlled by external forces. As their fear diminishes, their faith and ability to feel secure in who they are and who they are becoming increases.

Wake-up calls frequently come in dream messages. In the first chapter, Donna and Michael's stories of dream and vision awakenings are examples. Many therapists encourage their clients to keep a dream journal and record their dreams soon upon awakening. One archetypal dream has been reported by several women clients. While there were minor variations among their dreams, the common theme was a wake-up signal.

Dream of 45 year-old woman: *I was visiting the home of a childhood friend. I walked toward the back of the house and into the kitchen, but no one was at home. I then went back toward the front of the house where I saw the outside door open. Suddenly a large, dark figure blocked my exit. As he came toward me, I knew that he meant me harm. At first I panicked and froze. Then, garnering all my courage, I ran toward him at full speed. He was shocked and didn't respond when I sped by him and out the door. He had counted on my freezing in fear and giving him no resistance.*

Dream of a 20 year-old woman: *I was in the college library. I was concentrating on my studies and didn't realize that everyone else had left the library. Suddenly I heard the bell ring signaling that the library was closing. I tried to get my books and papers together, but must have taken too long. As I descended the steps from the fourth floor, the lights went out.*

I carefully descended the remaining steps by feeling the sides of the wall. When I reached the bottom floor, I could see light coming through the glass entrance doors. As I walked nearer the entrance, a large figure stepped between me and the door. His darkened figure was silhouetted against the outside light. I couldn't see any features, just an outline of a big person. Somehow I knew he was sinister. I dropped my books and started back toward the stairs. I heard him say, "You can run, but you'll never get away from me." I ran as fast as I could up the stairs, but when I reached the fourth floor, there he stood at the top of the stairs. I couldn't figure out how he got there because he hadn't passed me on the stairs. He laughed and said, "You'll never get away from me." I was terrified and saw no way out. Then I woke up.

The two dreams revolve around the issue of individuation completion. The issue of pushing past fear into a more empowered state was the task of each woman. The signal from their subconscious (or the spiritual realm) was that it was time to grow beyond their fears and become empowered. The forty-five year old was strong enough to push past the dark figure, which symbolized her own repressed emotions, fears, and denial. The twenty year old was too terrified to confront her dark internal self. The silhouetted person kept telling her she couldn't get away from him. None of us can escape our own dark, unenlightened parts.

The forty-five year old decided to leave a twenty-three year, codependent marriage that suffocated her emotional and spiritual development. The dream signaled her willingness and readiness to courageously push past her fears and bolt to freedom and empowerment. The twenty year old froze in fear. She stayed in a codependent relationship with her alcoholic boyfriend. The dark side of fear prevailed. She did not yet have the courage to risk following her truth and her power.

The lives of those who hear and respond to their wake-up calls are never the same. Those who see the world's sham, yet refuse to grow toward full empowerment, are destined to live a life of torment. Their armor of denial, rationalization, and passivity becomes increasingly ineffectual. Some try to numb out with busy-work, alcohol, or other diversions. Eventually they come back to the same realization they had during their initial wake-up: they are not happy, they are not honest, and their relationships are not connected. They learn they cannot run from the dark figure of internal fears. A client going through the pains of tunnel work once told us, "You get to a point that turning back is more painful than going forward into the unknown." When you hear the wake-up call and see the truth of the world's false messages, it becomes too painful to play the game anymore.

The Struggle between Eros and Thanatos:

This process of cleaning out ones' emotional, psychological, and spiritual basement is dominated by two powerful and opposing forces. On the one side is the urge to risk and grow. On the other side is the fear of the unknown and the comfort of familiarity. These two contrasting forces are known by the symbolic Greek figures, Eros and Thanatos. Eros, the life force, is in constant conflict with Thanatos, the death force. Eros urges us to take risks and move onward into uncharted regions of Truth. Thanatos, the death force, urges us to retreat into the known regions of dependency and escapism. In the pull and push of these two competing forces, we inch through the thick mire of tunnel work. For most, the path is dark and the journey hampered with mirages that appear real and inviting, but actually trap and delay us in our fear.

Triumph of Eros - the Personal Struggle to Live Truth: Jane's tunnel work is a good example of the push and pull of Eros and Thanatos that occur during this stage of self-growth. Jane is very intelligent and competent. She can master any problem and meet any challenge. Her super-competence was recognized and used by those who desired her care giving. Jane acquiesced to the codependent caretaking role because it felt comfortable and familiar. Her family of origin was codependent and Jane was molded by their demand of conformity. Everyone depended on Jane and she always came through. But then Jane hit her forties and realized her one-up caretaking didn't allow equal connections between her and others. She felt alone and depressed. Anger simmered just below the surface as her "good but weak" husband continued to unfairly lean on her to keep the family going. Slowly, she realized that an unwritten marriage contract called for her to be the parent and her husband the child. He wanted to change, but he was too locked into the *good boy* syndrome of pleasing parent authority figures. Although rankled with fear, Jane became more and more determined to break out of the codependent trap that drained her of life and vitality. It took much courage for her to break away from the marriage, but after nine agonizing months in therapy, she did break away. Since her husband wanted no part of the dissolution of the marriage, he refused to leave their home. Jane knew she had to be the one to leave. Her two daughters elected to stay in the home and assume Jane's place of taking care of their father.

Jane initially thought the decision to move from the house would be her most difficult transition. She later learned that prolonged resistance to her decision from family and friends was her hardest test. As the forces of Eros and Thanatos competed, Jane waffled between her determination to live her truth and fear of losing everyone she loved. Some friends applauded Jane's courage to expose the falsity of the happy ever after image. Far more people condemned her actions. Once very active in her church, Jane got letters from former church friends telling her to repent and follow the Lord's will for her life (which meant return to her husband). Her husband echoed the familiar refrain that Jane was going against the Lord's will and doing something very wrong. Her two daughters expressed their anger at her by becoming more distant and non-communicative. Jane struggled against the force of Thanatos. She knew it would be much easier to return home. Her supportive friends would understand and still support her. Her judgmental friends would applaud her for finally coming to her senses. But Jane stood firm. She was committed to her search for truth. She looked at her friends and asked which of them were really loving -- the coercive ones who arrogantly tried to force their version of truth or the supportive ones who were understanding and non-judging. She looked at her husband and questioned his capability of supporting her search for truth when he never searched for his own truth. She looked at her daughters and wondered what she would be teaching them if she stayed in a loveless marriage that caused her depression and irritation.

Jane knows that her choice is causing others discomfort -- there is no question that family and friends are hurt by her decision. Trained to please others, she often feels she's doing something wrong by standing up for herself. She asks herself whether the short-range discomfort outweighs the long-range discomfort of living a lie. Jane is now struggling to stay on her path of truth as she confronts the resistant forces urging her to return to her empty marriage. The world's rejection is equipoised with the hope of future happiness and a connected relationship. The struggle between Eros and Thanatos is real and painful for Jane. It's also confusing because she's battling the selfless conditioning within herself as well as external forces that expect her to forego her needs and capitulate to external expectations.

Shortcuts through Tunnel Work that Don't Work

Tunnel work is the hardest work a person will ever do. The world is not constructed to support truth and love. The world is based on controlling power plays between people. Those who reach inside themselves for inner truth can reject the lies and cruelty they see in the outside world. But they have to have an extraordinary strength to resist the force of Thanatos. That strength comes only through completing the tasks of purging oneself of fears, defenses and hurts. Most people want to avoid the strenuous work of emotional, psychological and spiritual catharsis necessary to reach inner truth. They want a short cut around the strenuous tasks of tunnel work. Common shortcuts (that don't work) are denial, numbing out, faking it, martyrdom and passing go and collecting $200.

Denial: Many seekers begin their journey weary of the emptiness of codependent relationships that have trapped them for years. Deep within they desire truth and genuineness in their relationships. Unfortunately, many do not do the hard internal work necessary to attract and support the deep-level human connections they so passionately desire. They remain permanently trapped in the stagnant relationship, or they desperately move from one relationship to the next, perhaps finally giving up on relationships altogether. They finally deny that there is any ideal such as unity and true connection. They give up on themselves and buy the lie that what they have is all there is.

One example is Joe, a medical doctor in his sixties, whom Michael counseled. Joe felt disconnected and unfulfilled in a forty year marriage. He and his wife communicated only on a very superficial level, mostly about their grown children and their problems. During counseling sessions, Joe would talk about anything -- except his true feelings and desires. Like most men, Joe had done little work to develop his emotions or to look honestly at his life situation. While something within Joe prompted him to call, make an appointment, and come to several counseling sessions, Joe believed in the mask he projected to the world: successful doctor, responsible spouse and parent. His inner truth didn't buy the mask and tormented Joe with symptoms of despair and internal conflict. He was depressed, lethargic, angry and unhappy. He wanted to break out of denial but was too fearful to speak his truth. His few counseling sessions were more like social calls than opportunities to engage in serious discussion about real life issues. The fact that he came at all attests that, on some level, Joe knew what he wanted. Tragically, his fear kept him from honestly confronting the source of his unhappiness and accepting responsibility to do the hard work that lay in front of him. He stopped coming, choosing to remain stuck in the status-quo rather than rock the boat and jeopardize the familiar codependent life he knew so well. He repressed his pain and denied his inner urge to follow the path to an empowered self and empowered love.

__Numbing Out:__ In an attempt to avoid facing pain, many seek refuge in such diversions as alcohol, drugs, television, work and other dependencies. They all choose to remain dependent children, trapped in a self-defined world of personal inadequacy and neediness. Charles presents a typical example of one who chose to numb out rather than do the hard work of individuation completion. Charles never quite grew up, even though he was now in his late twenties. He was fired from several jobs for being late and undependable. He incurred large debts with legal difficulties stemming from two drinking while driving charges. In each case of financial or emotional need, his mother came to the rescue of her only child. After going through a divorce and two unsuccessful jobs, Charles had hope of getting his life together when he met Sarah. Sarah had been in therapy for some time following her divorce from an abusive husband. She was determined, caring and strong. Charles was sure he could make things work this time. He and Sarah became engaged, but soon thereafter, Sarah left him. She said he was still too much a child and too dependent on her. She loved him but she wasn't going to make the same mistake that she did in her first marriage -- being a mother to a little boy husband.

Charles became depressed and saw no hope for his future. He spent more and more time with his drinking buddies. Before long, he found himself sitting in jail again, charged with driving under the influence and speeding at 100 miles per hour down a country road. He didn't remember anything about his arrest or the

171

circumstances of the incident. He just remembered being at his friend's home and drinking some shots of bourbon.

Charles' mother had sought help from Donna who advised her to have an alcoholic intervention and place Charles in inpatient alcoholism treatment. She was unable to consummate the intervention because family and friends refused to participate in the intervention session. All of his friends were alcoholic. They said they'd be hypocrites if they told Charles that he needed treatment when they drank just as much as he. Family members said they were too uncomfortable to confront him in an intervention session. So Donna and Charles's mother confronted him alone. Typical of an alcoholic, he replied that he didn't have a problem. He only got drunk and in trouble when he drank hard liquor, but he was now going to drink only beer. Donna told Charles that his depression was obvious and that he needed more than drinking only beer to solve his problems.

With a dejected attitude Charles replied, "I don't think there is anything better. All of my friends are like me. In fact, you are the only person that I know who seems happy."

Charles was numbing out and avoiding his pain. He wouldn't accept the challenge of seeking something better. He had convinced himself that there was nothing better to seek. He saw his life as an endless series of losses and disappointments. It was safer to stay numb than to feel the pain of hoping and failing again.

People numb out with phobias, diversions, and addictions. The escape "isms" -- workaholism, alcoholism, shopaholism, perfectionism, and others -- give refuge for those who want to avoid their feelings and the hard tunnel work of healing themselves and becoming whole.

Martyrdom: Many people see themselves as victims of a cruel and heartless reality and deny their power to create an exciting and happy life. Melissa presents a classic example. Melissa

172

married Alvin shortly after college and quickly committed to living the American Dream. They were an attraction of opposites. Melissa was quiet, somber and conservative. Alvin was fun-loving and outgoing. He leaned on Melissa to support them financially while he tried one job after another. None of the jobs seemed to fit Alvin, who always dreamed of the next perfect job that would fulfill his every wish. After several years with Alvin searching and Melissa holding the anchor, their marriage started to go sour. Alvin could not hold a job and quickly ran through the family's savings in failed business attempts.

Melissa had been willing to be the caretaker in the early years, but now there were also two children to care for and she was simply burned out. It was always the same story with Alvin. The only luck he had was bad luck. No one would give him a chance. In reality, Alvin was not the victim of destiny, but rather, a classic poor-me. His failures were always someone else's fault and he took responsibility for as little as possible, including the welfare of their two small children.

After a bitter divorce Alvin disappeared, moving to a distant state to avoid paying child support. Melissa struggled to make it on her own and provide for her children. She received no help from Alvin. When he reappeared in their lives after several years, he once again started his poor-me theatrics and manipulations, pulling the children's sympathies to him. He blamed Melissa for being angry at him. It wasn't his fault for being unable to send her any money to support the children. She had to understand the pressure he had been under. She had to be a Christian and forgive.

Melissa saw through his victim manipulations and got fed up with his irresponsibility and childishness. But instead of going through her own tunnel work and dealing with her anger, she became increasingly bitter and jaded about all men. She believes that they all try to use women. She has a thick wall of martyrdom that separates her from the possibility of genuine bonding with a man. She has no hope of ever finding the true, honest heart connection she sought when she first married Alvin years ago. Melissa believes that she has no choice but to stay stuck in an untenable and powerless position. She has chosen to avoid taking any risks. She has accepted the status-quo, and it is both disappointing and unfulfilling. She complains about Alvin and his irresponsibility. She's determined that another Alvin won't burn her, so she stays alone and lonely.

Pass Go and Collect $200: Some believe God will do their work for them, that all they need do is pray, focus on the light, and disregard the dark sides of themselves and the world. They want to believe that attainment of wholeness is done by a force outside them. Many religious and spiritual people seem to fall in this category. Instead of empowering themselves, they look to others to give them advice and make them whole and happy. They turn to a preacher or guru to give them the hard answers about truth and love and peace. They turn to God and expect him to protect, defend and heal them of inadequacies and fears. The problem is that God didn't put us here on earth to be whimpering children. He expects us to grow and to become empowered agents of His will on earth. That means accepting the task of becoming whole.

Danny is a good example of a spiritual person who attempted a detour around the hard tunnel work of emotional healing. Danny came from a home with a passive mother and very domineering and critical father. All the energy of the family swirled around the father. A bank president, he was revered in the community, and he expected no less adulation at home. Danny and his three older sisters cowered under their father's stern admonitions. Danny grew up believing he was inadequate and feeling he was never quite good enough to measure up to his father's expectations. He unconsciously chose to model his father's selfish and domineering pattern rather than become like his selfless and adoring mother. In his early twenties, he started

174

several successful businesses and became ruthless in his pursuit of power and recognition. Everything looked fine -- money, women and power were his. Then he made a tactical mistake. He overextended in one of his businesses and the whole house of cards tumbled. Danny had to file bankruptcy. His mounting fear and feelings of inadequacy surfaced. Danny sank into a consuming depression and was hospitalized when he lost contact with reality. Bolstered by antidepressants and long hours in therapy, Danny was still unable to regain his confidence and return to the business arena. He decided to try something different -- he turned to God for help and direction. He spent hours a day in prayer and listened to the quiet voice within to guide him into health and wholeness. His faith in God's healing power restored him to health.

Several years after his healing, Danny came for couple counseling with Sandy. Even though he was in his mid-forties, this was the first significant relationship of his life. All the other women throughout his life were merely conquests. But Sandy was different. She was deeply religious and spiritual and supported Danny's devotion to God. Donna had counseled with Sandy and pointed out to her that she was always in the one-up caretaker position with others, particularly with men. She was ever ready to listen, understand and help others, but she never expected reciprocal giving. During the course of her therapy, it became obvious that Sandy believed the only way to receive love was to be perfect and giving. She felt rejected by both her mother and father, who were selfishly consumed with their own problems and gave little attention to their children. Sandy was anxious, confused and lonely in the family setting that was unperceptive and callous to the emotions of others. When her feelings were hurt or when she cried, she was shamed by her parents. "What's wrong with you. Toughen up. You're so different. What rock did you crawl out from under?" With each shaming statement, Sandy built a thicker protective wall. With each shaming statement, she also attempted to win love by conforming and becoming more perfect.

While Donna worked with Sandy to help her rid herself of perfectionism and one-up caretaking, Michael worked with Danny to help him get in touch with his repressed emotions. Danny tightly controlled everything around him -- his daily schedule, his interactions with others, his adherence to prescription drugs and his almost incessant praying. There was little room for spontaneity and flexibility. When Michael asked him why he needed to be so regimented, Danny replied that he was afraid of going crazy again and this would keep him functioning like others. He also added that his rigid prayer schedule was going to help him be like Jesus.

Most therapists would have given up on Danny and labeled him psychotic, but Michael could only see the mountain of fear that kept Danny's mind, heart and soul captive. Michael gently led Danny to a point of believing in himself and reclaiming his adulthood. Michael suggested that Danny give up some of his rigid compulsiveness. Gradually Danny learned to let go of his need for unbending rules to guide his life. Michael suggested that Danny might be less spaced out and more in control of his life if he progressively reduced his drug prescription. Danny was immensely proud of his accomplishment in slowly letting go of the drugs. The psychiatrist that monitored Danny's drug needs saw him every three months and was amazed at his tremendous progress. Danny came to his first joint counseling session with Sandy, Michael, and Donna with many triumphs under his belt.

Sandy began the session. "I asked for this joint meeting because I'm feeling so inadequate. Danny has made a lot of progress in the last six months. He's gradually freed himself of his dependency on antidepressants. He's grown so much spiritually that I feel left behind. I still have unresolved emotional pain that blocks my spiritual path, but Danny just takes his problems to God in prayer and they are magically resolved. I'm left behind and unable to catch up with Danny."

Danny smiled in acknowledgment and in sympathy for Sandy's plight. He felt proud of his accomplishments and was secure in his connection with God.

Donna spoke up first in answer to Sandy's opening statement: "I think you need to get away from hierarchical thinking -- Danny is *higher* than you or you are *lower* than another. Think in terms of what you have already accomplished and what you want to accomplish for yourself and the relationship," Donna offered Sandy.

Sandy looked amazed. "But Danny's connection with God is so direct. I can't do that. I am slowly working my way through the thick sludge of my stunted emotional development and there are times I don't feel God's presence in my life at all."

A feeling was brewing within Sandy that was not yet fully developed or recognized by her. Donna tapped into her yet unformed feeling with the question: "How does that make you feel when he takes all his problems to God and they are instantly solved."

Sandy's emotional truth bubbled up. "I feel cheated. I want him to connect with me and not with the 'heavenly host' all the time. I want the old Danny back -- the one who struggled with his feelings and shared them with me. I want a genuine emotional connection and I think he's short-circuiting the emotional connection by going up to heaven instead of outward to me and to others."

Sandy is highly intuitive and full-blown ideas come to her without much conscious thought processing. Her problem with Danny was known on the intuitive level. While she supported his spiritual devotion and development, she knew it could not substitute for his emotional development. He was trying to avoid his emotional tunnel work by "going up" instead of "going inside." In tunnel work, there is no way to "Pass Go and Collect $200" without first making the long, hard journey toward inner healing and wholeness.

Being Good Instead of Being Real: Anne's four-year old grandson, David, became angry when she scolded him for jumping on the bed.   Embarrassment, hurt, and shame welled up and erupted in a spontaneous "I hate you, Grandmommy!"   Anne was shocked at the unbridled emotion coming from her grandson and determined then to tell her daughter, Lynn, about the incident.

Lynn's nonchalant attitude about David's hate message disturbed Anne.   She judged Lynn as too permissive with her son.   "Lynn, you must set boundaries for David.   You can't let him go around telling others that he hates them."

"Mom, I remember hating you at times, but I dared not express it.   You would have punished me for getting angry and venting my emotions.   I learned to be good, but I wasn't allowed to be real.   I have a choice with David.   I can force him to stuff his emotions, or I can allow him to express his emotions and learn how to deal with them honestly.   He's a small child and his emotions come out as "I hate you."   He says that to me when I discipline him, but I'm an adult and his immature words don't hurt me.   I just listen and tell him I understand his anger and frustration.   I'm a good person and he won't hate me forever.   I trust the love between us.   I don't punish him for having feelings or for speaking them out loud.   If we stop talking about our feelings, both of us will suffer.   It's more important for David to be real than to be good."

Lynn is an unusual mother.   Instead of molding David into a square peg of conforming goodness, she encourages him to connect with his feelings and express them to her.   Then they can resolve difficulties and disputes out in the open.   This is not how most families operate.   Children are expected to be good -- which translates into children conforming to parental expectations.   One of the prerequisites of "being good" is not expressing negative emotions.   So children stuff their feelings, learn to withdraw and

178

hide, and learn to judge themselves as bad when natural emotions arise.

One of the most difficult impasses for clients to surmount is expressing negative emotions - particularly anger. Donna has a karate tackling dummy and a soft bat that facilitate anger expression. She asks clients to vent their anger by hitting the dummy. Its very effective, but many clients are petrified of doing anger work. In obvious discomfort, they often laugh to cover up their uneasiness.. When pressed, they simply say they can't get angry. All the while, they are seething inside about years of cumulated hurts and injustices against them.

Psychotherapy is right in advocating emotional catharsis. Negative emotions need to be expunged before healing begins. The psychotherapeutic environment provides a safe and neutral outlet for anger. Anger doesn't dissipate when it's pushed down. Repression is damaging to the person and it's dangerous to the objects of their anger. The angry person awaits the chance of revenge, ever ready to balance the power imbalance with their attacker. People stuff their anger because they've been taught they have to be good to be accepted. So they go around seething until they develop high blood pressure, ulcers, or other physical or emotional problems.

Anger expression separates psychology and spirituality. Whereas psychology emphasizes the benefits of anger expungement, spirituality and religion urge people to forgive trespasses. Forgiveness and anger seem contradictory. When the stages of grief -- denial, anger, depression, bargaining, and acceptance -- are viewed as a continuum, we see that psychotherapy is short-sighted when it stops at anger expungement. The person needs to move past anger and depression (anger turned inward), understand the true origins of their grief, and move on to acceptance and forgiveness. When psychotherapy stops at anger without moving beyond to the place of understanding, acceptance and forgiveness, total healing is thwarted.

On the other side, religious and spiritual leaders often urge forgiveness without explaining the process of getting to that final place of peace and acceptance. The result is "cheap forgiveness" -- feigning forgiveness by playing good instead of being real. The mask of forgiveness will crumble if people bypass the grueling grief process. Being real means feeling pain, anger, hurt, disappointment, and sadness. Owning the strength to feel deeply is the conduit that helps people rise above anger, judgment and vengeance to a state of true forgiveness and peace. Psychotherapy often truncates the process, spirituality often takes a detour around the process. Being real instead of playing good mandates our completion of the entire grief process.

Conclusion:

We believe these shortcuts circumvent the *tunnel work* of emotional catharsis and eventually prove to be false paths. Individuals don't become empowered by expecting a parent substitute or God to do the hard work for them. They don't become empowered by avoiding truth and freezing in denial and numbness. They can't hide in martyrdom or be above the human condition by donning a mask of perfectionism and spirituality. They become empowered when they dive into the dark recesses of their inner being and clear away the fear, hurt, and neediness that live there. Commitment to tunnel work means being real instead of acting good. Negative emotions need to surface and be expunged. The dark sides of our selves cannot be dismissed in tunnel work.

To surmount our walls of unwillingness, we must first recognize the codependency within us. We must reject the control dramas and power games that have frozen us in disconnected and meaningless relationships. Our commitment to overcome our laziness and numbness honors the sacred within us. We're committing to our Divine power and to our faith in following the higher purpose of our lives. Out faith supplies us with knowledge of our sufficiency to grow to individuation completion. We become a small peg that moves the world one notch closer to truth and love. With our commitment to leave codependency, we move from the darkness of separation toward the light of unity.

Chapter Seven

Tunnel Work: The Path through Darkness into Light

Tunnel Work: The Path
through Darkness into Light

I'm almost embarrassed to tell you about my dream, but you were in it and I think you'll be able to tell me what it means. I was at my high school graduation. Some girls told me everyone would be naked and I had to come naked too. When I walked into the high school auditorium, I realized I'd been duped. Everybody else had clothes on. I scanned the audience and saw you sitting beside my father. Somehow that gave me courage to walk across the stage unclothed. 'What the heck, I'm not going to let it bother me or keep me from graduating,' I remember saying. As I walked onto the stage, you and my father clapped loudly for me, but others were booing. I just held my head high and kept walking. After the graduation I went to a celebration party. By this time it didn't bother me to be naked. I saw the girls who had fooled me across the room. I marched over and confronted them about their cruelty. What do you think such a bizarre dream means?"

- Sarah, age 28

This dream struck Donna as an exciting affirmation of Sarah's unconscious commitment to self-empowerment. "Sarah, your dream seems to be a message from your inner self, your soul level. I believe it's telling you of a deep spiritual vow you've made to graduate from the disempowering worldly traditions of codependency and fearfulness. You're ready to abandon the "shoulds," take off your false social mask, and show your real self.

You're willing to be totally vulnerable and fully scrutinize yourself, hence the image of being naked. Your dream told you that you can be naked or real without being ashamed. You're ready to move past the world's traps and give up your fears about other peoples' judgment. In the dream you even confronted the lies and cruelty of others who tried to hurt you. Congratulations, Sarah! Your dream self is saying you'll escape the gravity of the world's negative energy. You'll graduate to a higher level of

185

knowing and being."

Sarah first came into counseling two years prior when her relationship with Roger was unraveling. Sarah is an adult child of an alcoholic father and she learned early to be selfless. The ingrained one-up/one-down pattern of control was a family legacy handed down for generations. A needy "poor me" claimed all the energy, robbing other family members of attention, identity and affirmation. Sarah grew up believing codependency was normal and right. She attracted Roger who also came from an alcoholic home. Roger's alcoholic father played the role of arrogant and selfish intimidator role. Roger imitated his father and became the intimidator, while Sarah modeled her powerless, poor me father. Roger was domineering, jealous and miserly with showing affection. Sarah was accustomed to neglect and understood the unspoken message -- she was unimportant, unlovable, and powerless.

In subtle ways, Roger robbed her of self-confidence. He found one thing after another about Sarah to criticize. He alleged she wasted time on idle pursuits and that she needed to develop her mind. His advice - she should read more. Each time he said it she felt dumber and dumber. Even though she was quite slim, he persisted in calling her chubby until she started to believe it and became bulimic. Roger's standards were always just a little higher than Sarah could reach. Bit by bit she lost power, self-esteem, and confidence. She felt drained when she was around him but found it increasingly more difficult to break away.

Sarah had one thing going for her that saved her from the abysmal pit of codependency. Her father was in recovery and was growing more empowered and confident. He urged Sarah to go to therapy and to untangle the confusing threads binding her to Roger. Donna talked with Sarah about codependency and the devastating effects it has on personal empowerment. She also told Sarah that Roger wasn't ready for a truly loving connection with an equal partner. His own low self-esteem led him to seek control in relationships, which translated into putting women down and claiming the superior one-up position. Unless they both committed to moving past codependency, they were destined for a life of misery.

After Sarah decided to leave Roger, Donna advised her to stay in counseling and learn the reasons for her attraction to an unsuitable partner, but neither she nor Roger continued counseling. Two years later, she called after her new fiancé abruptly broke their engagement. After a few minutes of conversation, it was apparent Sarah had chosen another man who looked good on the surface, but who was emotionally undeveloped and codependent. This time Sarah committed to stay in counseling long enough to understand and break the repetitive trap she found herself in.

When she first came for counseling, Sarah would stiffen when Donna hugged her good-bye. She looked to the floor when painful subjects were broached and never risked expressing feelings. Yet this time was different from her first counseling endeavor -- her hurt was too great and her anger was too uncontrollable. This time, she knew she had to get in touch with the inner truth of her emotions. Slowly she became more and more comfortable expressing her feelings. She was muted and embarrassed at first, but then her catharsis rapidly climbed to a crescendo of passion and volatility.

A lifetime of repressed feelings came boiling out. Previously meek and conforming in demeanor, Sarah now risked confronting and disagreeing with others. She learned to protect her time and energy from unwelcome intrusions. Instead of stuffing her feelings and being the poor me martyr, she began standing up for her own needs and wants. One by one, she moved past her fears of abandonment and rejection. Sarah's dream prophesied her commitment to clear old beliefs and habits enslaving her into codependent powerlessness. The road to inner truth and self-empowerment is like traveling through a dark, twisting tunnel.

Along the walls of the tunnel are dark cracks, recesses, and holes out of which come hidden fears, unhealed hurts, and embarrassing secrets -- the dirty stuff we all like to deny and keep hidden from ourselves and certainly from others.   We call the process of moving through and clearing out our emotional basement *tunnel work*.

Successful passage through tunnel work involves eight steadfast commitments: *(1) to ongoing inner vigilance and self-scrutiny; (2) to a critical assessment of one's balance between selfishness and selflessness; (3) to expunge repressed emotions; (4) to move past the control and neediness of codependency; (5) to conquer the fears holding one captive in unhealthy patterns; (6) to change behaviors detrimental to empowerment; (7) to learn and to speak one's inner truth; and (8) to learn to love oneself.*

This chapter explains these eight basic tasks of tunnel work. In them, we examine what's involved in each step and why each is so important to the process of empowerment.   In addition to describing what to do and why, we also examine the "how to." We use personal stories and the stories of clients and friends to illustrate how one converts these principles into positive self-growth and action.

(1) Committing to Ongoing Inner Vigilance and Self-Scrutiny

Self-scrutiny is the first step out of the ego's denial. The commitment to look at oneself critically and objectively is essential to the therapeutic process. Without this commitment, there will be no change and no progress toward expanded understanding and meaningful connection.   We all develop ego defenses early in life when we have little real power. They emerge as twisted forms of self protection.   In later years, these ego defenses anesthetize us from feeling, and they shield us from examining the real truth. Since they feel as if they're protecting us against attacks to our well being, we find it hard to release them. Denial, rationalization, and intellectualization are three of the most common defense mechanisms that often block the urge to examine ourselves objectively and grow. The commitment to look honestly and critically at our own behavior is the first step out of other-focused codependency.

The personal struggle that inevitably occurs when one begins the process of self-scrutiny is much like one's ego waging war against one's soul. The ego has a vested interest in keeping things the way they are -- static, predictable, and in control. The soul intends that we grow and become our fullest potential. We can't arrive at our fullest potential without letting go of fear, control, and apparent safety. Like a swimmer standing safely on the shore, if we desire to reach an island we must let go of the known and immerse ourselves in the water of the unknown. We must take risks and break the worldly rules that imprison us in conformity.

Joyce and David faced a common struggle between the ego and soul, between the commitment to self-scrutiny and the opposing pull of codependent defenses. Both had come from alcoholic homes. Joyce's alcoholic mother wanted to party and leave the raising of younger children to Joyce. After the family split apart, the father disappeared. Resentment grew within Joyce when her mother went out at night and came home late and intoxicated. Her siblings were burdens and rivals for limited attention. This view of other people stayed with her into adulthood. David was the product of a nearly identical situation, except that his alcoholic father was physically abusive and intimidating. He withered in fear and adopted a detached "I don't care" attitude about himself and others. Joyce and David came together, married, and stayed together for twenty years in a disempowering codependent relationship -- David playing the poor me and Joyce playing the intimidator. When they came into counseling they were in a financially precarious predicament. Reductions at David's workplace resulted in a substantial salary cut. Joyce came in each week and berated David for being a

189

helpless, childish, poor me. "If David would only confront his boss -- if David would only look for a new job -- if David would only grow up -- if, then the problem would evaporate!" Joyce was always focused on David's weaknesses and the pain he caused her. Nothing Joyce said was untrue -- even David admitted that. Of course, Joyce's public (in counseling) beratement only reinforced David's status as a poor me. In their codependency, he had become accustomed to Joyce's emotional abuse that mirrored his father's abuse -- this game was very familiar and he secretly relished his helpless victim role. After all, Joyce came off looking like the bad guy and he got pity for having such a bitch wife. Joyce's reward was being able to play the pampered princess and sit at home while directing him to do the hard adult work and provide for her. She was in her mother's role -- "I don't want adult responsibility; you take it for me."

Joyce beamed when Donna got on David's case for his passive aggressive tactics, such as feigning incompetence and frequently forgetting what he'd promised to do. Her expression changed when Donna told her to look at her own selfishness in expecting another adult to take care of her and then berating him when he didn't do the job well enough. Joyce didn't want to look at herself. She said her priority was to her spiritual journey and she had the right to have a leisurely life to pursue her goal. When Donna asked her if she was willing to starve for that goal, or be willing for David to have the same luxury of not working, she got angry and accused Donna of abusing her as her mother had. When Donna held her ground and asked her to assess whether her actions were loving toward David or whether she was acting like an empowered adult, Joyce called Donna a bitch. Joyce was fighting like a crazed dog when the mirror of self-scrutiny turned toward her. While she merrily pointed the finger of blame at David and at others, she revolted wildly when the spot light focused on her.

Expect this resistance to self-scrutiny, for it's inevitable.

Expect it within yourself and be ready to stand firm against it. People naturally resist change, particularly when it means giving up the known patterns that have provided them a sense of safety and security. Some people will vigorously resist committing to self-scrutiny while others, like David, passively agree with everything, then promptly forget it and do what they have always done. Resistance is resistance in whatever form -- passive and invisible or active and aggressive. Unless we willingly and energetically dedicate ourselves to looking at our own flaws, and unless we use critical assessment to move beyond our own self-inhibiting behaviors, we won't grow.

It's hard to look at yourself critically. We all like to see ourselves as innocent and flawless. The fact is none of us are -- we all have flaws and deficits. Our blindness to them allows the negative aspects of our person to grow until they encompass our entire personality. If we own our blemishes, we can cleanse them in the light of truth and self-love. When we're able to say, "I'm imperfect and human like everyone else," we let go of the fear of being found out. We can finally relax in the truth of who we are, unvarnished, imperfect -- and growing better each day. Self-scrutiny and admitting our imperfections are the first steps out of denial and into truth. These are the hardest and most vital elements of tunnel work. Without committing to looking at ourselves openly and objectively, we won't grow and change.

When someone is considering leaving a relationship, we ask him or her to assess one basic trait about his or her partner: is he or she honestly and actively committed to self-growth and change? If the answer is yes, we advise the client to look closely at the decision. All of us have flaws and all of us make mistakes. That's no reason to leave a relationship. But if the other person continues to play games, refuses to look honestly at him or herself, and fails to change patterns of behavior leading to interpersonal tension and self-protective distancing, then it's time to go.

Self-scrutiny leads us to a point where we examine the

formative individuation of childhood and admit our leaning toward selfishness or selflessness. We then go on and recognize codependency characterizing us and our relationships.

(2) Critical Assessment of Selfish/Selfless Imbalance

The emotionally immature tend to be at the extremes of selfishness or selflessness. Those who are selfless are hollow repositories for others' needs and wants. They continuously give themselves away because they believe they have no worth or meaning except through others. The selfless seem to be long-suffering, benevolent, and caring. If you observe them long enough, you'll see their caring facade dissolve. Once they're provoked, their caretaker mask shatters and their true nature appears. They tire of being used by people who don't appreciate what they do for them. Those who play the selfless game eventually revert to passive-aggressive vengeance when their caretaking is rejected or taken for granted. On a subconscious level, selfless caretakers hold tremendous pent-up rage against those who use them, even though they may have personally created, willingly entered, and fostered continuance of their offensive situation. The selfless caretaker controls others by making them needy. They enable weakness and glean the reward of finding identity and meaning through others' needing them.

Selfish people wear a different mask and outwardly look the opposite of selfless. In actuality, selfish and selfless are two sides of the same coin. Both are concerned with ego-gratification -- how others see them, what others give them, and being in one-up or one-down control. Selfish people are self-absorbed and little concerned with the feelings and needs of others. The self-protective ego boundaries surrounding them form an invisible, but opaque, shield preventing them from seeing beyond themselves or establishing any real connections with others.

In the last chapter, we told about Sandy and Danny's dilemma when he tried to circumvent his emotional work by developing spiritually and ignoring the rest of his development. Growing up with an egocentric and achievement-driven father, Danny followed his father's model and became a self-centered person. His two sisters mimicked their mother's selfless model and incorporated the unspoken message that women aren't worth much. Danny got little positive attention and affection from his father, but his mother made up for it sevenfold. He came to see himself as the center of her universe and when he reached adulthood, he expected every other woman to idolize him as his mother did. He was in his forties when he met Sandy. By this time, Danny had accumulated a long list of romantic conquests but he'd never married. He told Sandy his mother was the most important woman in his life and would always be. Then two things happened -- his mother died and Danny suffered business losses that plunged him into depression. He turned to Sandy and expected her to make him the center of her universe, but she didn't. In therapy, Sandy had explored her selfless pattern and her attraction to selfish egomaniacs. She resolved to break her selfless pattern and pushed Danny away. She told him she no longer needed to be a caretaker for Peter Pans -- spoiled boys who refused to grow up.

Danny was astounded! This novel reaction shocked him and propelled him to look at himself and his emotional issues. In the past Danny would abandon women who refused to play his codependent game, but this time he was more desperate. This time he needed truth and love to get him past the point of hopelessness and despair. He came to realize that Sandy was right. His selfish, ego-centered personality was not only disastrous to relationships, it was the primary reason for his business failure. Danny made the commitment to get past selfishness and learn to connect in empathy and understanding. In this case, the union of selfish Danny and selfless Sandy worked to bring both to a healthier balance. Sandy was balancing her own selflessness by demanding that he grow to become sensitive to her needs, wants, and feelings. He was balancing his selfishness by being open to her request for emotional attachment.

There is generally an imbalance in the selfish/selfless dimension in one or both members of a couple. While the selfish person is generally judged more harshly by others, the truth may be that the selfless person is setting his or her partner up to look bad. A person who has a healthy balance may look selfish in contrast to the selfless doormat who gives without boundaries. This sort of imbalance causes deep resentment within each partner and brings out the worst in both. Each partner in the punishing pair blames the other for their woes. For growth to occur, each partner must look honestly at his or her own shortcomings and the contributions they make to the deteriorating relationship. Selfish partners send messages of unworthiness, unlovability, and disrespect to their partners. Selfless partners give their partners nothing to connect with. They're so other-focused they haven't stopped to consider who they are, what they want, and what their needs are. They survive by becoming masters of giving and doing in the codependency game -- but they spend precious little time developing their *being*. Like the robots in the *Oedipus Rex* dream, they're hollow and without substance. Balancing the imbalance of selfishness and selflessness caused in beginning individuation takes commitment to look at ourselves honestly and critically. It takes courage to get past our egos and defenses, and it takes courage to break the old habits that separate us from others. It's the first step at getting past *I* and reaching for *we*.

(3) Expunging repressed emotions

The head work of analyzing and understanding unhealthy and self-defeating behavior is easy compared with the work of clearing oneself of emotional repression. Most of us have learned to contain emotions, be rational, be in control. We believe we'll gain acceptance from others if we conform to polite social mores and we'll be rejected if we unleash the shadow self brimming with rage, hurt, fear, and sadness. We go through life adhering to the rules of emotional repression and hiding from our emotional truth. The world tells us it's good to repress and deny feelings -- they're dangerous, a risk to our control, and uncomfortable for us and others to experience. Probably the most difficult passage in tunnel work is to defy the world's rule about emotional repression and to learn to express our feelings appropriately and without shame, guilt, or discomfort.

In therapy, people travel down a path of increased understanding of how unconscious programming stunts their full empowerment. Like Sarah who dreamed of going to her graduation naked, they may learn they've been programmed to be selfless, and this quality attracts one selfish person after another to them. Understanding what patterns are programmed into us is relatively easy. What comes next is much more difficult. We must work to change those programmed messages. The only way we know to change emotional imprinting is to pull the cork on emotional repression. Each of us needs to undo our emotional constipation by owning and expressing our emotions. It's at the point of emotional catharsis that most clients want to run and hide.

Donna usually asks clients to write letters to people who have caused them hurt and pain. They're relieved when she tells them not to mail the letter -- at least for the time being. The letter becomes the focal point in emotional catharsis. Donna then asks the client to read and share the letter aloud. Through role playing, the client tells the letter recipient how she or he feels about their relationship. Clients are armed with a plastic bat while Donna stands behind a tackling dummy. Donna urges then to hit the tackling dummy and release anger, sadness, and pain. The words they say aren't as important as the emotions they express. Almost always they say they can't get angry. But with prodding, the anger begins to emerge. One young man, abandoned early in life by his father, finally unplugged his repressed emotions and beat the tackling dummy for a full five

195

minutes before he collapsed into his chair and cried. A recovering addict, he later acknowledged that inner rage was destroying him. He was just too fearful to let it out -- it might kill him or kill someone else. After his initial catharsis, he was less fearful of his anger and more confident he could appropriately control it. He learned he could do so by expressing his grief in safe environments with strong people. He didn't need to kill his father to rid himself of the toxic rage caused by his father's neglect and abandonment.

Tuning in to original hurts and expunging repressed emotions help us move to a more honest and empowered emotional response.

We believe emotional repression restrains us from realizing our full power. It's not emotions that are dangerous -- it's harmful intent and inappropriate action that are dangerous. We hide in fear from our emotions because we fail to separate the emotion from the possible harmful consequences of emotions gone amuck. Our fear and repression become a self-defeating circular process: we're afraid of our emotions so we deny and repress them, emotions then become bigger with fear pumping up their importance, and we try with more difficulty and more energy to push them down and deny them. If we do the opposite, express the emotion in an appropriate way and in a safe setting, we lose our fear of the emotion and it decreases in intensity and magnitude. We then have control over the emotion -- it doesn't control us.

Repressed emotions become a powder keg that can ultimately destroy us. Expungement of repressed emotions is important because: (1) repression of negative emotions also mutes expression of positive emotions; (2) our negative emotions build in intensity and volume when not expunged; (3) we remain fearful of a natural part of our inner truth when we repress emotions; (4) we must embrace our shadow side and expose it to the light to heal; (5) repressing emotions causes mental, physical, emotional and spiritual harm to self and others; (6)

196

repressing emotions enables us to play at being perfect, a self-defeating lie; (7) through expressing them, we learn to appropriately channel emotions into productive behavior; (8) we encourage full connections with others by allowing them access to our emotional selves; (9) when we repress emotions, we increase others' fear of expressing emotions; and (10) we get in touch with our inner truth when we feel, understand and express our emotions.   In summary, repressed emotions are toxins that diminish and destroy our human potential. The trick is to allow emotions to surface and learn to transmute them into tools of empowerment.

Jack's story illustrates the healing power of emotional expression and the dangerous potential of stuffing emotions. Jack is a therapist who works primarily with drug- and alcohol-addicted adolescents.   Over dinner he expressed his concern about the anger he was feeling toward some rebelling teen-age boys in the residential treatment program he supervised.   His anger was spilling over to his wife and he found himself frequently snapping at her over minor issues.

"I'm worried about controlling my anger with those kids. They've pushed me to the breaking point several times in the last two months. I'm afraid I'll grab one of them by the collar and slam him against the wall. I'd be fired, for sure, but that's not what I'm most concerned about. If I lose it, I'll be destroying myself. I won't be able to trust myself anymore. I lost my temper only once with my former wife. She was afraid I'd kill her. Our marriage deteriorated soon afterwards."

Among Jack's most endearing qualities were his openness and honesty in revealing his shadow side. Even though he was a therapist, he didn't play perfect and he didn't play god. He was mortal and he owned his imperfections. After a few questions, we learned that Jack had a physically abusive, intimidator father and a religious, selfless mother. Jack feared his father's rage and meekly conformed so his father's monster emotions wouldn't be provoked. Fear engulfed the family, as Jack and his mother centered attention and energy on the volatile father. He and his mother were selfless, invisible, and powerless. He subverted his power, his emotions, and his truth, but it took increasing energy to do so as the years passed. Now he was like his father -- bottling up his emotions, not feeling in control, ready to explode. Jack's fear of emotions needed recognition and deflation.

"Jack, I think anger is like a fever," commented Donna. "It's alerting you that something is wrong and needs attention. Anger is your early warning system. If you can see it that way, you can develop an investigative attitude whenever it comes up. Feel the anger and ask yourself what it's trying to teach you. Think back to your childhood and what you learned about emotions. Think back to the time you lost it with your former wife. What could your father do to hurt you? What could your ex-wife do to hurt you?"

Jack hesitated only a minute. "I learned that emotions are dangerous. I believed my father would kill me if he got mad enough. My ex-wife was small. She couldn't physically kill me, but she killed me with verbal abuse. She was always criticizing me. I couldn't do anything right. I felt inadequate, unloved, and powerless around her. In fact, I felt inadequate, unloved and powerless around my father also. Both of them hurt me by taking away my power, my self-esteem and my confidence."

Donna reflected on this and said, "So you think others can steal your self-esteem, confidence and power? Can the boys also rob you of these valuable assets?"

"I guess I'm giving them the power. They're such brats! If I had talked to my father the way they talk to me, I'd be creamed!" Jack was yelling by this time.

"So you're angry they get to talk back and you didn't? You don't know how to handle people who don't conform to the rules like you did. Your anxiety about loss of control is snapping you

198

back into your father's role. How did you feel when your father dumped his rage on you?"

Jack admitted he wanted to fight back, but was too afraid. "I just wanted him to care about me. He intimidated me and made me feel worthless and powerless. I hated the way he treated me. Damn it, he could have grown up and gotten control of his anger. He was so damned selfish, he didn't think of anyone but himself."

Jack allowed his emotions to surface, and once his hurt, anger and depression cleared a little, he relaxed. The bottled-up rage of fifty years emerged and it didn't destroy him. In fact, it freed him to see his own current situation more clearly. He came to see the boys as fighting for their independence and integrity -- a necessary transition step from boyhood to manhood. He despaired that no one had been strong enough to allow him to get angry and to stand up for his rights and needs when he was a teen. He acknowledged the inner pain caused by living with a selfish father and selfless mother. He modeled after his mother who hadn't grown sufficiently to get past her own fear of anger. She gave up her self-worth, confidence and self-love to an intimidating, selfish husband. Jack recognized his anger and fear were rooted in the emotional heritage handed down from his parents. Once expressed and acknowledged, his anger and his fear of anger subsided. He decided his fight for dignity and self-worth was with his parents -- not with the boys at the treatment center. As an enlightened and confident adult, he could understand and connect with the boys rather than fight for superiority and control. He resolved to applaud their struggle toward maturity and, at the same time, set appropriate boundaries on their possibly harmful and destructive behavior.

(4) Moving past the control and neediness of codependency

We were recently asked to tell about our own tunnel work that occurred at the beginning of our relationship. The couple making this request was having difficulties getting past codependent control and avoidance issues. Ann complained that

199

Evan ran away when she tried to talk about problems. Most of the time he fell asleep in front of the television, not bothering to come to bed. Obviously, their love life had something missing.

Michael began, "One of the greatest things Donna taught me was how to fight. I don't mean vicious, hurtful fighting. I mean staying with a disagreement until it's resolved. I always fled conflict before. Growing up in an alcoholic home, I learned that conflict was dangerous. So whenever I saw a disagreement brewing, I took off. But Donna wouldn't let me run away. She said if I was committed to the relationship, I'd stay with her until our disagreements were resolved. So I learned to stay. The more I stayed, the more I learned how cut off I was from my emotions. I needed to get in touch with how I felt and share those feelings with her in our disagreements. Thankfully, she recognized my emotional underdevelopment and prodded me to name my feelings by saying, 'You seem to be angry, depressed, confused -- or whatever.' In response, I answered yes or no and gradually learned to label my feelings and share them with her. Then I had the task of guessing how she felt, and I'll tell you, I didn't have a clue. I would try her technique of guessing feelings and sometimes it worked. Other times I just asked her to give me a hint. I'd say, 'If you were in my place, what would you say to you now?' She'd tell me what she wanted to hear and I'd say that. Gradually, I learned to give sensitive and accurate responses to her emotions."

Donna was eager to add her thoughts about tunnel work. "There were two qualities about Michael that made me endure the tunnel work. I knew without a shadow of a doubt that he loved me and I knew that he was absolutely committed to his growth and our ultimate connection. He would say over and over again, "You are the most important thing in my life. Without you, nothing matters!" How could I push away a man who's that vulnerable and that determined? He never backed up into false pride when I tried to push him away. He kept telling me he loved me and he wasn't about to leave. He also made me face the truth that my abandonment fear was sabotaging our unity. His strength and determination to make our relationship work helped me trust him. I began to look at my contributions to our disharmony. I knew that Michael's intent was not to blame or shame or criticize me. He honestly wanted to look at any impediments to our relationship -- from his side as well as mine."

Ann broke in, "But Evan doesn't have that commitment to anything -- not me, not to fixing up the house, not to anything I want."

"That's not true," Evan shot back. "I just get tired of you telling me what to do. You treat me like a child. And if I don't listen to you and do what you want, I'm criticized."

Donna chimed in at this point. Most relationships are unequal, one-up/one-down, parent/child relationships. These are codependent relationships and will ultimately be unhappy or end. People need to grow to full self-sufficiency and then seek people at equal developmental levels for adult/adult relationships. They need to give up trying to control each other. You have to accept the fact that you really can't control another adult -- and if you try, you're destroying the relationship. I learned that the hard way. I call my lesson the Valentine's Day Massacre.

Michael and I had a tentative relationship at the time. It could have gone either way. I asked him what he was doing the next Tuesday which was Valentine's Day. He said he was going out to eat with his male friend, John. I then asked him if he knew Tuesday was Valentine's Day. He didn't know, but he'd already made the commitment to his friend and wanted to keep it. As the days passed, I got angrier and angrier. Of course I didn't tell him I was angry and he didn't have a clue about my emotions, so he mainly ignored my grouchiness and critical snips. On Valentine's Day night, I had a major case of self-pity.

Then I got angry -- very angry! I wanted to scream and throw and tear things, but I went driving instead. I drove about forty miles, cussing at God the whole way. I remember blaming God for deserting me and leading me to a place where I was all alone. I cried at His abandonment, and asked Him what type of father He was anyway. I accused Him of being uncaring, aloof, and cruel. In the midst of my ranting and raving came a knowing that silenced my tirade and jolted me into silent reverence. The voice rang clear within me. 'You are not alone.' A moment of peace was followed by desperate fear. 'I know I'm not alone, but damn it, I need others to be with me. Not just wispy spirits, either. I want real people -- people I can touch and talk to.' The conversation between me and my Inner Self continued. 'Donna, you have people around you who love you. Just reach out, give up your self-protective fear , and they'll be there for you.' This was truth. I counted the number of friends and relatives who really loved me. I could tell them my darkest secret and they'd still love me. I could call and wake them at 3:00 a.m. and they would be there for me. I hadn't reached out for them because of my codependent beliefs -- if I'm not perfect, I won't be loved; if I show need, others will run away. I realized my codependent neediness was sabotaging my relationship with Michael. I needed him to *do* external things *and then* I'd be assured of his love. I needed affirmation on Valentine's Day to be assured I was really special to him. When he was oblivious to my need, I angrily pushed him away and protected myself from further hurt.

Somehow the voice inside my head got me in touch with the truth -- I was sufficient, I wasn't alone, and I was loved and lovable. I didn't need Michael to prove to myself that I was loved and lovable. Michael was still at a point where he was struggling to decipher his own and others' emotions, so I couldn't expect him to satisfy my emotional neediness. I could meet my own needs by reaching out to others in truth, mutual compassion and strength. I came face to face with my greatest emotional need (my fear of abandonment) and I found it a false idol imprisoning me and stagnating my growth to full empowerment.

202

On that Valentine's Day night, I turned my car around and transformed myself from a demanding "poor me" to a more confident and empowered being. Michael was waiting at the condo when I returned. He tentatively asked me what I had done, all the while emotionally shielding himself from an expected attack. Instead, I calmly told him of my experience and the lesson I learned. I told him I would no longer expect him to meet my expectations. I was letting go of my need to control him. I also made it clear I wanted him, but I only wanted an empowered Michael -- one who could feel, and one who was strong enough to push himself, as well as me, to grow. My tranquillity convinced him of the sincerity and conviction of my words. I consider this my Valentine's Day Massacre because I slaughtered my codependent neediness and it was replaced with faith and inner knowing about the strength of love and truth"

Codependency locks us into believing we're inadequate and powerless. We push down those inner fears by becoming the one-up, controlling parent or the one-down, controlled child. We expect others to meet our unmet needs and we blame them when they don't. Codependency ceases when we recognize the patterns holding us captive in a variety of messy control dramas. Codependency is rooted in unfounded fears. If we empower ourselves with truth and faith, we'll defeat fears that blind us to our power.

(5) Conquering fears that arrest health and growth

Emotional purification of our unresolved fears requires that we bring up memories of all those past terrors and dark emotions we'd rather not re-visit. Our efforts to avoid our fears, to deny they exist, and to keep them pushed down, drains us of tremendous amounts of energy. Instead of extinguishing them, this repression does just the opposite -- it empowers our fears and they grow to consume us.

Men perhaps have a more difficult time purifying fear than

203

women. Unfortunately, our society is structured in such a twisted way that men are denied access to and expression of emotions. If we view this situation honestly, we see an entire societal system of disincentives and penalties for men who feel. When young boys are hurt, the messages they receive are to stuff pain, suck it in, and not show any emotions. As boys mature, they're discouraged from acknowledging either pain or fear in sports. In fact, boys are often openly ridiculed for even the smallest display of emotional honesty. The result of this enculturation is that many men, especially the older ones, are almost completely walled off from their emotions. They feel and can name anger, impatience, and frustration -- but little else. Men's emotional unavailability is most certainly a major factor in many stuck and unfulfilling relationships.

We conduct an exercise in our Relationship Workshops that requests participants to identify and inventory their fears. Fears of abandonment, rejection, ridicule, failure, success, intimacy, vulnerability, autonomy, being unloved, and others are included on a sizable worksheet. It is the participant's task to name a fear, trace its origin, and share information about that fear with his or her partner or with another participant. Women readily identify several fears and have little trouble tracing their origin to a childhood trauma or a hurtful parental model or message. Most men find this a difficult exercise to complete. Upon closer scrutiny, however, we've found that male participants have many of the same fears as women -- they just label them differently. Since society does not allow boys (or men) to be afraid, they view their repressed fears in more acceptable forms, such as frustrations, hurts, or anger. Men use the more aggressive and externalized emotions (frustrated at, angry at, etc.) to get them in touch with their fear. Remember the story of Jack, the therapist who was angry at the rebelling boys. Jack wasn't aware of fears at the time he began talking about his concern. He was only aware of his anger. As he explored the origins of the anger, it became apparent that he was also afraid of losing his self-esteem, power, and confidence. Jack traced his anger to forgotten childhood fears that arose when his father yelled or hit him.

Michael writes about his formula for identifying fear: "Committing to understand my feelings was the first step. I was tired of feeling exhausted, frustrated and confused, and I wanted to know what was behind those feelings. It finally came to me that many men fail the emotional literacy test because they live in their heads. They define intimacy and believe they understand what it means. But they only understand on a cognitive level. They haven't felt intimacy. The word has no connection to experience. They "think" they feel. But, except for anger and frustration, they're not in touch with their feelings. So each time I experienced tension of any sort, I put all of my attention and energy into tracing it. The difference was that I did the tracing with my body, not my mind.

I looked first within my body and tried to discern where the feeling originated. Sometimes I could localize a feeling in my stomach region; sometimes from my upper chest. The where was really irrelevant. The point was that I was feeling, not thinking, where my emotions were coming from. For example, I noticed a tightness in my jaw and recognized my frustration, or a knot in my stomach signalled anxiety. This opened the door. The second step was to then trace the feeling deep within and follow the fleeting images that tied it to an emotional source somewhere in my past. With persistence, I began to see that my tensions linked with childhood feelings of inadequacy, fear of not being loved, or the desperate feeling that I was unlovable. With each success in tracing and naming a new emotion, I learned how to feel it and identify the feeling when it touched my life. What a great source of truth! What started slowly picked up speed as my emotional sensitivity increased. My repertoire of emotions grew rapidly. As the truth of my life and my despair came into focus, I began the equally difficult task of cutting the emotional strings that had

205

previously welded me to relationships and patterns of behavior that were damaging and intrinsically untruthful."

Emotional competence helps us recognize and name our emotions. When we commit to a process of cleansing and purifying our unhealed wounds, we rid ourselves of repressed negative energy. The following story follows Carl from a level of fear that rendered him phobic and unable to trust or connect with anyone.

"I was so frustrated in college. Everything seemed fake and superfluous. I dropped out my sophomore year and went back to live with my mother and father for awhile before I could find a job and support myself. I don't remember what the disagreement was about, but I remember yelling at my father that he'd better not expect me to take care of him in his old age because I wouldn't be there."

Carl was in his early thirties and adept at introspective self-scrutiny and analytical observation of others. His mind constantly surveyed others for clues about their intentions and motivations. He also examined his own inner motives and passed harsh judgment on himself when they were less than pious.

"Carl, tell me about your father," Donna said, guessing the roots of Carl's mistrust lay somewhere close to home.

"My father was a very strict man who was religiously upright in the eyes of the community. But I saw him differently. He frequently had outbursts of rage and he hit me and my brother. Mom just went in the other room and pretended she didn't hear. We never talked about our hurt. Even if we cried he told us to shut up or he'd give us something to really cry about. All he cared about was his own power and control over us. I don't remember anyone there for me when I was hurt or scared. I was all alone. My mother cared more about her fear than our security. I don't remember happy times, but there must have been some. I just remember criticism, judgment, fear, and abuse. To this day,

I'm not sure of my worth and I don't know who to trust. There are times I want others to go away and leave me alone. They're all hypocrites - acting kind and caring when they'd just as soon destroy you. I remember Dad saying 'I'm doing this because I love you' while he beat me. People just deceive and hurt you, so I stay on edge for the next betrayal."

Donna told Carl the rules in a codependent family: *don't talk, don't feel* and *don't trust*. He'd thoroughly learned and internalized all three of these enslaving rules, but by entering therapy he was signaling his readiness to break free. He was passing the first test by speaking his truth to Donna. His second test was to get in touch with his feelings. Because he was deprived of the elemental ingredients of healthy development, he would need to grieve the loss of not getting what he had deserved as a child -- mature, fully developed parents who could give him love and guidance.

Using Dr. Elisabeth Kubler-Ross's grief process paradigm, Carl's first task was to admit his loss and bring to the surface the anger and hurt of being neglected and abused. Carl used the letter technique and beating on the tackling dummy to expunge his anger. His emotional catharsis was followed by a period of depression. After experiencing his emotions fully and wallowing in self-pity for a while, he was ready for bargaining -- a period of analyzing and objectively understanding the roots of his parents' fear and dysfunction. Carl struggled, but persevered. He went through the process of tunnel work and allowed himself to express his repressed anger and pain in role plays. He finally got to a point he could forgive his parents. Only then did his paranoid fear and mistrust of others subside.

We have an iron-clad rule about fear: *go straight into and through what you fear most*. Most people would rather avoid the painful grief work that brings to light their unhealed wounds and hurts. What they fail to realize is that avoidance just leads to magnification of our fears and fortifies our defenses. With courage, we need to face each unresolved wound and go through the emotional catharsis of grief work. Only then will we be able to forgive and accept. Only then can we free ourselves from emotional bondage and grow to a higher level of empowerment.

(6) Changing behaviors detrimental to empowerment

As previously discussed, the three primary rules in a codependent home are: don't talk, don't trust, don't feel. These rules and their resultant behaviors are detrimental to self-empowerment and are formidable blocks to true intimacy, vulnerability, and bonding between people. We can see this very clearly if we observe the ways we interact with those who should be closest to us -- our spouse, children, parents, siblings, and close friends. If we observe ourselves in a detached and objective manner, we will probably discover that our discussions with these intimates are superficial and devoid of honest sharing.

Jay was oblivious to his contamination by the self-protective game of not talking, trusting, or feeling. However, he was aware of his growing irritation with family members for not reaching out and genuinely connecting with him. After listening to his end of the phone conversations with his mother, brother and sister, Jay's wife commented on how superficial and awkward his communications with them really were. Jay admitted he felt tense and bored when talking with his family. His physical demeanor while on the phone mirrored his discomfort as he groped for words and anxiously paced the floor. The phone receiver seemed like a hot potato in his hand -- he couldn't get rid of it soon enough.

When his wife, Diane, laughed at his unease, Jay took immediate offense and started verbally attacking her for her insensitivity. She urged him to trace the reasons for his discomfort, but Jay tried to avoid the spot light of self-examination by focusing on Diane. Diane didn't allow the focus to change because she was genuinely concerned about Jay's distress and she expected Jay to be as committed to self-scrutiny as she was. She pointed out that Jay's uneasiness with his family was in direct

208

contrast to his openness with her.   After a feeble attempt to evade, Jay finally joined the search for truth.

"It hurts me that my relationships are so shallow and strained with my brother, sister and mother.   I want more, but they all want to stay on safe, concrete subjects such as family or church events, work, or the children. No one dares talk about how they really feel. They've never let me close to them, and I'm damn mad about it!"

The plunge into emotional catharsis cleared Jay's denial and within minutes he was ready to tackle the analytical task of investigating the origin of his avoidant pattern. The answer came fast and clear to Jay.

"We don't know how to talk. We don't know how to express our real feelings. No one talked about Dad's drinking. We all suffered in silence. We dared not speak the truth -- and we're still afraid to speak the truth! We spend our time making silly jokes, or discussing things that have no substance. How can I change this pattern that's so deeply ingrained?"

Diane suggested he recall a feeling that rose during family conversations. Jay remembered getting angry when his sister told him that no one remembered her birthday with a gift or a cake.

"That really made me mad! She's the ultimate caretaker -- she gives and gives and no one gives anything back to her. No one bothers to help her feel important and loved. She told me she feels old and she's only thirty-two. She's probably drowning in depression and sees little hope for joy and vitality in her life. God, I felt that way all my life too. Life was just an endless journey of obligation and duty. Dad was the only one who got out of being responsible -- and we surely didn't want to be like him. So what did we all do? We married people who made us responsible for them, while they stayed undeveloped children. We were groomed to be selfless caretakers attached to emotionally immature and irresponsible people. We believe that relationships

209

are about taking care of someone else. We have to be strong, one-up, and in control. We can't be scared or vulnerable or hurting. No, we just put on our responsible mask and pretend everything is OK." Jay was starting to talk and feel. He uncorked the stuffed emotions that had held him captive in codependent games.

The next day Jay eagerly told Diane about calling his sister and telling her how he felt when she told him about her birthday fizzle. She got nervous when he said they were both chumps and needed to demand more attention and respect. On an unconscious level, his sister must have realized that Jay was breaking the family rules. He was talking and feeling -- and urging her to do the same. She wasn't ready for the challenge and got off the phone as quickly as possible. Nevertheless, Jay had done what he needed to become more empowered -- he'd shattered the fragile codependent tension and dared talking, feeling, and trusting. He was stepping into truth that would ultimately lead to connection with anyone else willing to do the same.

(7) Learning to stand in your truth

When we ask clients if they are honest with others, they invariably answer yes. Their definition of honesty and truth revolves around the definition of not telling a lie. But standing in your truth is more than not telling a lie -- it goes beyond cognitive truth and includes emotional truth as well. As we've already discussed, the world doesn't encourage us to know or express our emotional truth. An honest display of emotion is awkward, confrontive and challenging. So the world trains us to tell emotional lies, and we lie so frequently we forget what emotional truth is. Tunnel work leads to complete truth, not merely half truth. Before you can love and be loved you must own your truth and be willing to give that truth to another who is ready for a relationship without boundaries and self-censure.

In Chapter Six, we discussed Jane's tug of war between the

inner forces of Eros and Thanatos. She finally developed the courage to leave the codependent and hollow marriage. Jane paid a big price for standing in her truth. Her daughters blamed her for the dissolution of the marriage, her husband bombarded her with guilt for disobeying God's will, and former friends wrote letters and telephoned her urging her to return home. Throughout this, Jane stood tall in her conviction that she was living her truth. Jane learned how powerful the world's demand for emotional dishonesty was during a group therapy session.

Jane proudly told her fellow group members about standing her ground with her former minister's wife, Anne, who had called the night before. Anne began the conversation by telling Jane she was concerned about her and wanted her to know she cared. As the conversation unfolded, Anne told Jane she was praying for her and Thomas and for their eventual reunion. Jane then spent a half hour convincing Anne that her decision was her truth and that she further believed she was being led and protected by God. Anne listened and replied with her own arguments for why Jane should return home. After forty-five minutes, the conversation finally ended in a stalemate.

After Jane finished reciting her story to her fellow group members, Donna asked her how she felt during the conversation.

"I wasn't surprised. That's what I expected of her," Jane replied.

"But how did you *feel* at the time, Jane? I'm not asking what you think about the encounter after it's over." Donna pressed her to get in touch with her inner barometer of emotional truth. Jane was blocking her emotional truth and she needed to break through.

"Well, I really didn't feel anything. She had her message and I had mine. I didn't allow her to back me into a corner." Jane was drawing on intellectualization rather than her emotions.

Susan spoke up. "I find it offensive that Anne thought she

had the right to present herself as caring when what she really wanted was to steal your free will and impose her truth on you. I don't consider that caring. It's manipulative and disrespectful in my book."

Again Donna pressed Jane for the truth hidden in her emotions. "So how did you really feel when Anne was trying to persuade you to go back to your husband?"

Jane dug deeper this time and blurted out, "Well, I was irritated at the end of the call that she'd taken up forty-five minutes of my time!"

"So you were angry that she consumed your time and energy. Why didn't you put a stop to it sooner rather than engage in a debate that was fruitless for both you and her?" asked Sandy.

"Well, what could I say to her? I didn't want to be rude!" replied Jane.

"Taking up your time and your life, pretending to be caring when she really wanted to make you feel guilty, and trying to steal your free will to decide your truth -- that's not rude?" asked Sandy incredulously.

"Well, yes, when you put it that way, it was rude, but I didn't see it at the time. I do remember hearing her voice when I answered the phone and I immediately felt trapped and full of dread." Jane was now finally admitting the emotions that would lead her to her inner truth.

"Jane, that was the truth you needed to get in touch with at the beginning of the conversation. Your dread told you to brace yourself in readiness for defense. The suffocating feeling of being trapped told you she was going to attempt to impose her will on you. When Anne voiced her desire that you reunite with Thomas, your suspicions of her manipulative intent were confirmed. At that point, you could have chosen to take control of your life rather than play into her power game. If you were aware and in touch with your truth, you could have told Anne: 'You have your truth and I have mine. I give respect for differing perspectives and I expect the same in return.' Then, without argument or cajoling, you could simply bid her good-bye. At most, you would have wasted two minutes." Donna's words were disconcerting to Jane.

"But that seems so abrupt and rude to me," Jane responded.

Sandy eagerly piped in: "Jane, what would you lose by being truthful? You might lose Anne's acceptance, but her acceptance comes with strings attached. It comes with the big price tag of giving up your free will. She wants you to conform to her version of reality. You'll have to give up you and become like her before she'll accept you. Is Anne's acceptance what you really want -- or do you want to stand strong and confident in your own truth?"

"Gosh, this becoming truth is a hard thing. It means I have to reject all of the world's messages that I've held so dear -- do the right thing, be a good girl, win friends and influence neighbors!" By now Jane was laughing at herself. She had spent forty-five years trying to please others and win their approval. Now she was finally getting in touch with the price she paid for living the world's truth and ignoring her own. She was learning to listen and respect the inner voice that would lead her down the path to real empowerment. She was now seeing the subtlety of the world's indoctrination and manipulation. She could be pulled off the path of truth very easily. She could be trapped by the world's games that waste time and lives. The incident with Anne also taught her to trust her internal compass, her emotions, to point the way to truth.

The postscript to Jane's story is her return call to Anne the following week. Before the call, she wrote out what she wanted to say and rehearsed her script. When Anne answered the phone, Jane began by telling Anne she was convinced that her decision was right and that she was being guided by God along this path. She asked Anne to pray not for the outcome she desired, but for the outcome God intended. Anne was stunned, but readily agreed to pray that God's will be done in Jane's life. Anne thanked Jane for being candid and asked her to call again. The conversation took two minutes. Jane stood firm in her truth. Anne was confronted with her own indirect coercion and she backed down. Hopefully, Anne learned a lesson about respect. Certainly, Jane learned to stand confidently in her truth. Jane became clearer and stronger about what she wanted and what was right for her.

(8) Learning to Love Yourself

Learning to love ourselves is not about narcissistic self-adulation or wearing a mask of superiority. It's about embracing the fullness of who we really are -- both our light side that's beautiful, loving, giving, and capable, and our dark side that's vengeful, jealous, afraid, and imperfect. Learning to love yourself is about learning to love you the way God loves you. Pure, deep love is based on knowing who and what you are at your core. It appreciates the uniqueness of your total being. It is looking at ourselves the way loving parents look at their child -- full of wonder and tenderness with hearts brimming over with emotion. The power of this love is almost incomprehensible to we humans who insist on giving love with external conditions or strings attached.

Loving ourselves the way God loves us can best be illustrated by Betty's story of her spiritual encounter. At the time, Betty was severely distressed about her marriage to Bob. Bob was psychologically disturbed and was causing much fear, pain and confusion for Betty and their teen-age son. She had been with Bob for twenty years, but his paranoid symptoms and isolation had grown more pronounced in the last few years. Protected by a family business, he continued to hold a job, but home life was a disaster. He yelled at Betty and Bob Junior constantly, accusing them of taking his things or of trying to hurt him. He refused to get help and his condition wasn't obvious enough for an involuntary commitment. Betty was worried for her safety as well as Bob Junior's well being. Still, she was mortified to admit the failure of the marriage and embarrassed for friends to learn the true story of her situation.

As she prayed in church one Sunday morning, a blissful peace enveloped her. It was as if she were inside a luminous bubble. It felt as if she were both in this reality and outside it at the same time. Noise ceased and the light within the church took on a supernatural hue and intensity. Words formed inside her head and told her she was fully known by God. He knew the dark, unhealed parts she tried to hide from everyone. He saw the bright, loving light within her also. He knew and loved all facets of her total being -- not just her shiny perfect side but also her shabby side; not just her healthy self but also her defective, unhealthy self. With this assurance of His love, Betty was able to leave Bob. She had faith that empowered her to confront each fear with courage, commitment and determination. Gaining permission to recognize her weaknesses also gave her the power to move beyond them.

Betty hadn't known this kind of love before. She had been a poor student and her parents had low expectations of her academic success. Later in adulthood, she learned she had learning disabilities and attention deficit disorder that obscured her school performance. A psychological scar remained from childhood reminding her that she was dumb, inadequate, and different from others. Betty now had to disavow those messages and see herself as adequate, strong and able. She got a job and felt relieved to be able to support herself and Bob Junior. As administrative assistant to a company executive, she was capable and organized. However, the luck of the draw wasn't with her because she was stuck with an arrogant, critical, and insensitive boss. His dictatorial style was obnoxious to everyone, but he viewed Betty as an underling and was particularly condescending with her. One day he made a derogatory comment about her to one of her friends. When Betty heard his comment, she marched into his office and demanded an apology.

"You think you're better than anyone else because you have a fancy title and lots of money, but let me tell you, when you leave this world, you won't have any more in your suitcase than I will! You must treat me with dignity and respect, as I treat you." Betty stood up for her self-worth and dignity. Love for herself overshadowed the fear of her boss and losing her job. Even though her boss did apologize, she decided to quit the job. His dysfunction was too entrenched to change and she loved herself enough to leave his verbal abuse. Within two weeks she found the perfect job with people who appreciated her special qualities and organizational skills.

Love and fear are opposites. They will not coexist in the same space. It's for you to decide if you believe in love and its power to vanquish the fear in your life. If you give in to fear, you will never learn to love yourself. Betty's spiritual experience helped her get in touch with her essence. She became aware that God could see every particle of who she was and He still found her worthy of His love. This knowing fortified her to take the risks leading to happiness and empowerment. Her love for herself was tested several times and she passed each time. Betty learned what we all must ultimately learn -- only when we love ourselves and fearlessly stand up for our dignity and self worth, only then will we be ready to truly love and join with another person.

The Outcome and Rewards of Tunnel Work

The mandatory tasks of tunnel work are formidable and we can easily become discouraged unless we see the light at the end of our tunnel. It's the light of promise, of hope, of true happiness -- and it's ours if we persevere through the tunnel to claim it. The rewards for completing this journey are well worth the struggle. We emerge stronger and wiser. By confronting our deepest hurts and fears, we are able to (1) truly own and feel good about ourselves; (2) bond genuinely with others; (3) see where we and

216

others are in the growth process; (4) let go of fear and step into truth and love; (5) relinquish the need for control- and need-based codependency; (6) see ourselves clearly and use that understanding to direct our lives; (7) deal forthrightly with repressed emotions and unconscious motivations; and (8) change the behavioral patterns that separate us from those we love. In other words, we empower ourselves to transcend the darkness of our lives and transmute that darkness into power and light. Love, happiness and peace are finally an attainable goal.

Chapter Eight

Discernment: Seeing, Sifting and Separating

Discernment: Seeing, Sifting and Separating

Discernment is defined as perceiving distinctions or differences. The Latin translation means to separate by sifting. Discernment means we have "eyes to see" the truth about our own level of development as well as the developmental levels of others. Without discernment, we blindly stumble through the maze of life without direction, understanding or meaning. We keep repeating the same pattern handed down from generations past: using or being used by others, not connecting in truth and candor with friends, choosing the wrong people for relationships, feeling irritable and awkward around spouse and children.

Discernment requires we look honestly at the forces that have shaped our perceptions of ourselves and others and our interpersonal relationships. In the preceding chapters, we've talked about behavioral conditioning early in life that predisposes us to be more selfless or selfish. If we tilt in either direction, our ability to bond in truth and love is hampered. Without balancing selflessness and selfishness, we inevitably fall into codependent relationships. The trap of codependence lures us to follow a path of weakness and disempowerment. Tunnel work starts with our commitment to change disempowering messages, to understand the unconscious motivations holding us stagnant, and to remove blocks to self-control through emotional catharsis. After tunnel work, monster fears have been reduced to squeaking mice, annoying but not life threatening. Our cleared vision of ourselves enables us to more accurately judge the motives and intents of others. Our growing ability to see our deficits in emotional, intellectual and spiritual development helps us see others more accurately. Discernment is truly the stage of seeing, sifting and separating.

The Stages of Discernment

The first stage of discernment is to understand what our final empowered state looks like. The image of full empowerment serves as incentive to spur us on in times of doubt, confusion, and exhaustion. Our second task is to evaluate the level of development of significant others. Just as parents hand down genetic and material inheritances, they likewise bequeath intellectual, emotional, and spiritual legacies. What we know about being human and navigating the river of life comes largely from what parents and other significant people present in our early life. We need to look honestly and objectively at the lessons and challenges they have passed on to us. For example, if we grew up with one selfish and one selfless parent, a life challenge for us will be balancing the two: learning to stand up for our needs while being sensitive to the feelings and needs of others.

(1) We Must See What Empowerment Is

Like the popular book title, *If You Don't Know Where You're Going, You'll End Up Somewhere Else,* we can't accomplish our goals if we don't clearly define them. For us, empowerment means the positive end of the continuum between good and evil. It is about being a fully charged, focused, loving and impassioned human being. Empowerment -- the state of possessing power -- remains an abstract idea until we translate it into a set of qualitative criteria that give it purpose, substance, and meaning. To do this, we begin by examining what we already know about human power and energy.

At an early age, our energy level and the direction it will take (+ or -) begin to take form. Because we're raised in a world with few fully empowered adult models, most of us arrive at early adulthood with a crazy quilt pattern of positive and negative energies. We're sometimes too selfless, at other times too selfish. By the time we reach middle age, we know something is very wrong. Our energy, and the energy of those around us, seems false, diffuse, and unsatisfying. In contrast, Mother Teresa is an example of one with consistent and focused energy that flows from the positive. She knows what her mission is and steadfastly pursues it. Her sense of purpose is so strong that those who come

222

near her become empowered by her presence. Hitler stands at the opposite end of the spectrum. He also had high energy, but chose to direct it in a negative direction. His destructive power consumed others with fear and robbed them of dignity, hope, and life.

In the past decade science has documented the existence of the human aura. Our aura consists of colored bands of energy surrounding our physical body. To those who see can see these energy bands, they tell a great deal about our health, our emotional condition -- our general vitality and dynamism. Some people have bright, pulsating bands of energy surrounding their physical bodies. These are Sun People. Other peoples' auras exhibit a softer light of lesser intensity. These are Moon People. The colors and intensities of others, however, resemble dark, angry, swirling vortexes. These are Black Hole People.

Sun People shine with energy, enthusiasm and hope. Like the sun, their power emanates from a deep internal source of energy. The source of their unlimited power is love - love for themselves and love of others. They understand the transient nature of material things and the deeply rewarding and lasting value of love. More than others, Sun People are models for what we all can be at our highest. Like coastal lighthouses, their radiant glow draws others to them because of their strength, caring, and vitality.

Not content to merely exist, Sun People are fully impassioned and go through life with gusto and fervor. Never static, their commitment to growth is unwavering. They're not satisfied until they reach the summit of intellectual, emotional and spiritual maturity and balance. In a world satisfied with passivity and status quo, Sun People stand out as different. They restlessly create new ideas and deeper understanding of life's meaning. Like the sun, they exude the intensity and verve of fire. Their passion for truth has led them through life's hardest challenges and they have emerged purified and fearless.

223

Unlike the sun, the moon is dependent on an outside source of energy and light. Likewise, Moon People are dependent on sources outside themselves for support, sustenance, and affirmation of worth. Externally oriented, they react like ships without rudders or sails as they face life's turmoil and challenges. Because of their dependency, they spend their lives trying to pull energy and attention from others. There is little time or energy left for exploring and finding their own inner truth and radiant power. Even though they possess the same capacities as Sun People, Moon People are blind to their own vigor and potential. They shrink from the painful lessons of life that afford each of us repeated opportunities to grow and be of service to each other. They freeze, never daring risk what is for what could be. They are need- and fear-oriented. Self-protection becomes their driving force. They erect thick defensive walls, needing to control everything and everyone around them so their weaknesses won't be exposed. Their dark cave of self-protective anxiety, control, and worry becomes a prison.

Moons have traded authenticity and inner truth for social image. They go through life playing a game of normalcy -- trying to fool others and themselves into believing their "good enough" compromises are truth. Underneath they're scared, lonely and confused- buying the lie that others are just as empty as they are.

Black Hole People are represented in Michael's story of the ruthless university administrators. Like astral black holes, these people are almost invisible on the surface. They know how to project an acceptable image, and confuse people regarding their true intentions. Like a swirling vortex of black energy, these people suck others into their self-serving manipulations. The university administrators didn't care when they ruined the reputations of others or robbed them of their careers. They cared only for their own power and advancement. Like Ted Bundy, the mass murderer of young women, Black Hole People see others as pawns who exist only for their manipulation and use.

Unlike magnetic energy, similar human energy forms attract. Black Hole People attract other Black Hole People until, like a spreading cancer, a whole family, work organization, or community turns dark and ruthless. Likewise, Moon People seek codependent support from others who will accommodate and reinforce their own weaknesses. Sun People need the strength, determination and passion of other Sun people.

In this book we've described the process of tunnel work that is necessary to clear emotional blocks to inner empowerment. Once on that path, those growing toward empowerment begin to see others more clearly and more easily discern Moon and Black Hole energy. Those who have gone through the process of tunnel work become more radiant -- more visible. They're empowered with more and more Sun energy and their luminosity draws other compatible souls.

The most distinguishable thing about Sun People is their balance. Of all human beings, Sun People have progressed the furthest in balancing their intellectual, emotional, and spiritual development. Balanced development, in fact, is what distinguishes Sun People from Moon People and Black Hole People who are undeveloped and imbalanced. For example, those with high intellectual development combined with low emotional and spiritual development are highly ego-centered. Their unbalanced Black Hole energy cuts a wide swath of destruction in personal, corporate, and governmental spheres. Moon People are also unbalanced, but instead of being negatively empowered like Black Hole People, their power is diffused and largely without effect. Their energy is tied up in self-protection, status, and control. They don't actively hurt others, but they fail to help themselves or others grow in strength, wisdom, and positive effectiveness. Moon People can choose to grow and seek balance but the path isn't easy. The journey to full empowerment is taxing, difficult, and painful. It is definitely the road less traveled.

225

For those on the narrow road upward, it is important to see human dynamics clearly.   In sports, if you want to better your skills, you play with those at or above your level of expertise. Likewise, if you consistently play with those at lower levels of development, you're not challenged to stretch beyond your current capacity.   Those who want to move upward and progress in emotional, intellectual, and spiritual maturity will seek out Sun people as guides and mentors.

(2) Seeing Maturational Differences

When Michael first asked why people couldn't connect honestly and genuinely, Donna answered, "Because people are at different levels of maturity."   A kindergarten student can't be expected to connect at a deep intellectual level with a graduate student.   One is not better than the other -- they're just at different maturity levels.   Like intelligence, people also vary greatly in emotional and spiritual maturation.   The upward path to self-empowerment requires balanced, integrated growth in all three areas.   Like the athlete who "plays up" in order to advance, we must join with others at or above our level of maturity.   This doesn't mean we judge others who are less developed as inferior or bad. They are simply in the second grade and have a longer path before reaching graduate school. Since our highest goal is to love and be of service to mankind, it's appropriate to teach others who are open to growth.   But we must balance our giving with our receiving. The balance required for us to grow is again one of selfless/selfish equilibrium.   While we selflessly serve others, we must also selfishly consider our own needs for continued growth. We're challenged to grow when surrounded by other graduate students.   In the company of those more intellectually, emotionally, and spiritually advanced, we become aware of the gaps in our own development.   For this reason, our second task in discernment is to see the emotional, intellectual, and spiritual maturity of those around us and to choose to bond with those at or above our level of development.

226

Emotional Maturity : The *emotional sphere* encompasses our ability to feel and understand both our own and others' emotions. It is here we transcend our ego boundaries and learn to truly connect with others. Aided by coterminous intellectual and spiritual growth, we develop the ability to see and understand the unconscious emotional motivations of behavior.

If you look closely, you will see that most people are emotionally numbed out and unaware of their own and others' emotions. They conceal their inability and unwillingness to feel for others by wearing social masks. While they may appear caring and sympathetic, it's only a facade. Their interest and compassion toward others are feigned. Their behavior is merely a disingenuous mimic of the more developed individuals they have observed. Emotionally immature people are motivated by self-preservation. As a result, their interpersonal connections remain shallow and superficial. With self protection a priority, spouse, family, friends, and co-workers become foes to guard against, control, conquer, and use. Emotional immaturity negates any capacity for higher level motivations such as love, fairness, integrity and justice.

In contrast, emotionally mature people continually scrutinize themselves and monitor their feelings and intentions. Scientists label this heightened level of self-awareness *metamood*. *Metamood* is the ability to objectively and accurately assess our own internal emotional state. Obviously, such self-awareness is mandatory for the appropriate control of emotions. Yet many in today's society are far from achieving this basic ingredient of emotional maturity. When emotions aren't understood, when they're denied or repressed, they grow in strength and eventually rule the person. Emotionally mature individuals can name their emotions and are able to express them appropriately. They are sensitive to others' emotions and their friendships are deep, connected, and genuine.

227

The emotionally mature are guided by the higher principles of love, justice, fairness, and respect. Emotional maturity requires balance between the extremes of selfishness and selflessness, so emotionally mature individuals are neither consumed with self-interest nor self-preservation. Constant internal vigilance enables them to discern the underlying motives as feelings, wants, and needs arise. With these insights, they readily avoid manipulative, controlling and disempowering behavior in themselves or from others. While they may choose to help others, they fully understand and respect the principle of free will and never impose their ideas, beliefs or feelings.

Intellectual Maturity: The intellectual sphere embodies the cognitive abilities of reasoning, planning, and analyzing. Intellectual maturity, more than emotional or spiritual maturity, is loosely tied to age. Young children are intellectually concrete. If a ball is in front of a young child, the child is aware of its presence. If the ball rolls behind a sofa and out of view, the ball no longer exists for the child. With maturation, the child becomes more able to understand abstractions. He knows, for example, that you don't have to actually see the ball for it to exist.

The ability to think abstractly opens up a new world of seeing possibilities, associations, and patterns that infuse life with meaning and purpose. As one grows in intellectual maturity, it becomes possible to see beyond the "what is" to the "what can be." Unfortunately, many adults stop maturing intellectually, choosing to see the world and life's meaning in simplistic, concrete terms. The dilemma is those stuck in concrete thinking tend to remain more materialistic, naive, and unable to understand or internalize abstract moral principles. Intellectually mature people can understand and integrate abstract principles such as love, justice and truth. Rather than merely acting as if they're just or loving, their whole essence is infused with justice and love.

228

The intellectually mature are keen and accurate observers. They understand human dynamics and can read others' intentions. They intuitively project into the future and anticipate likely consequences of behavioral choices. They value wisdom over knowledge. In a concrete and undeveloped world, knowledge is easy to gain. The intellectually immature often possess advanced degrees and much accumulated knowledge. Often emotionally and spiritually immature, they use knowledge for self-aggrandizement and personal gain. For those who have sought balance, however, knowledge becomes a tool for the continuous betterment of self and humankind.

The authors of our constitution were wise. Modern day lawyers purporting to uphold the constitution are merely knowledgeable. Wisdom requires introspection and adherence to higher moral values. Knowledge only requires memorization and regurgitation of the thoughts of others. One uplifts. The other maintains. The intellectually mature person always strives for growth, empowerment, and higher understanding -- both for himself and for others.

The intellectually immature are child-like, naive, and blind to internal human dynamics. They simplify the complexities of life into a never ending series of judgments regarding what is right/wrong, good/bad, appropriate/inappropriate. Unable to appreciate the layers of complexity in human problems, they offer mundane and simplistic solutions. Having little visionary or creative ability, they merely mimic and follow the lead of others. They measure life's meaning by their accumulated possessions, worldly achievements, and the reflected praise of others. Their world view is compartmentalized and based on superficial opinions or fads. You'll see them climbing onto the popular bandwagon, but you won't see them ever stand up for convictions or for the rights of others when doing so might be unpopular or dangerous.

The intellectually undeveloped drift through life asleep. They don't see or grasp what is really happening around them. Unfortunately, the intellectually immature seem to be in the majority. Although individually they have little power, their collective mass pulls the whole downward toward intellectual lethargy and denseness. Like glue inside a watch, the intellectually immature gum up the works.

<u>Spiritual Maturity</u> : Spiritual maturity is more difficult to define than emotional and intellectual maturity. This difficulty may arise because religion and spirituality are often viewed as interchangeable terms. In reality they are very different, and may even be antithetical. *Religious* is an adjective referring to those who subscribe to a specific institutional and/or cultural dogma and doctrine. Religious people acknowledge an externally defined belief system and endorse it as their own. The term *spiritual* is more broad and diffuse. A truly spiritual person is one who seeks an intimate, personal relationship with a divine and universal power. Thus, a spiritual person is not necessarily limited by a particular church or doctrine, but rather seeks to find the truth transcending all religions.

A person can be spiritual or religious, or both. Mahatma Ghandi, while identifying himself as Hindu, was knowledgeable of the doctrines and traditions of other major world religions and acknowledged the common thread of truth among them. Ghandi was spiritual as well as religious.   His beliefs in passive non-compliance and non-violent intervention were anchored in universal truths that transcended religious doctrine. Spiritual truths are no less true to Muslims, Jews, and Hindus than to Christians. Ghandi is reported saying that he liked the man Jesus Christ, but he wasn't so sure about those Christians! His statement exposes the difference between religion and spirituality. The essence of the life of Christ was love: love of God, love for all humans, service to others, and belief in a spiritual world that transcends and supersedes the material world.   This is the

230

spiritual aspect of Christianity. Yet look at the history of Christianity as a religion, replete with the Crusades and the Inquisition. Were those Christians modeling the love of God and expressing that love to their fellow man? Were they spiritually committed to serving others and advancing the well-being of all? Were their sights on the spiritual world or the material world?

The basic nature of many contemporary religious movements represses personal and spiritual empowerment. Religiosity, as many know it today, places all power and control in the hands of an external God. God is the supreme judge. We're taught to fear our shortcomings lest we incur the wrath of a critical Father. We play the helpless child who needs an intermediary to interpret God's message and intercede on our behalf. This disempowering view of God repeats over and over in dogmatic, controlling, and exclusive contemporary churches. Ministers, pastors, priests and rabbis arrogantly proclaim they have the "real truth" and they judge and preach exclusion of others who are different. Congregations are brainwashed into believing that God -- the cosmic policeman -- will punish them if they fail to follow the letter of church law. This brand of religion rules by fear and denunciation. It steals power and free will by placing itself in the "one-up, parent role" and by subjugating their followers into the role of the "one-down, powerless child."

This is not what it means to be spiritually mature. Spiritual maturity can be measured by the extent moral integrity is integrated into a person's essence. A spiritually mature person stands for fairness, justice, compassion and truth in a dark world that cynically uses these words as a deceptive mask to secure self-advancement. Spiritually mature individuals act out of love and compassion for others as well as self. They emphasize common threads of love, service, and truth between and among religions. Their inclusive nature is tolerant and accepting of differences between people. Spiritually mature persons go within to find the truth of God rather than relying on an external

231

intermediary. God becomes an integrated part of self -- and a very personal force within their lives.

(3) Sifting through Differences in Essence

Essence is also known as soul, inner truth, or higher self. Our essence is the very core of who and what we are. Our ability to accurately see our own essence and the essence of others is dependent on the level of emotional, intellectual, and spiritual balance we've attained. Deep within each of us, within the recesses of our intuitive unconscious, lies a full understanding of who we really are. Yet we allow ourselves to remain trapped in a much lower, more fearful and needy state of being. Ironically, it's the very things we fear and seek to control against that provide greatest opportunity for growth. Turmoil and stress are often tools for our awakening. In the depths of despair and depression, concern for the material world recedes. To survive the pain and anguish, we seek meaning and find refuge in our inner truth. We know the path inward is the one we must take. We have a choice. We can either see life's hardships as opportunities to become powerful or we can forever remain the victim.

Have you noticed how you become aware of some people's essence when you meet them for the first time? Depending on our own essence, we have an instinctive attraction or repulsion to another. We size them up and quickly decide to put up our defenses or to be open and joining with them. Unfortunately, discerning the essence of others is most difficult with those we love most. Discerning the essence of those closest to us is challenging. But it's something we must do, for discernment is a critical component of growth.

In the last chapter, we talked about Jane who separated from her fundamentalist husband, but then found herself engulfed in unbridled guilt and doubt. She knew how she felt around him -- smothered, irritable, and defensive. Yet, there was nothing overt in his behavior that could easily explain her overpowering need to

232

leave.   Church members hounded her with subtle and not-so-subtle criticism and advice. They admonished her to return to her marriage.   Donna decided to gently lead her to an understanding about the elemental differences in essence and maturation between her and her husband.

"Can you discern the essence of others, Jane?" Donna asked.

Jane blinked and looked puzzled at the question. Donna pushed forward. "For example, what is the major theme -- or essence-- of your brother Ron's life?"

Ron had spent the better part of his fifty years on a spiritual journey.   He'd rejected worldly rules and imprisoning expectations. He now lived simply in the California mountains and worked at odd jobs when he needed money. He made a decision early in his life to reject externally imposed truth and to go inside himself for answers.

Jane quickly responded, "Ron's life is about truth."

"And how about your essence, Jane? What is the major theme of your life?"

Without hesitation she replied, "Truth also. I am seeking the truth of who I am and what is real in my life. I'm committed to finding truth at all costs."

Jane was right in her self-assessment. She has a razor-sharp mind that quickly and accurately dissects the intentions and motivations of others.   She's always scrutinizing her own intentions and motivations as well. Jane's search for what is real and true is the major propelling force in her life.

"And what is your husband's essence?" Donna asked.

Again she answered immediately as if the question had been stirring in her unconscious for years. "His essence is fear. He is afraid of everything. That's why he's so religiously narrow. That's why he's so conservative politically. And that's why he's always trying to please everyone else. He's afraid of disapproval. He's afraid of risks. He's afraid to go after the truth and stand up for his convictions. In fact, I'm not sure he really has any convictions. I don't think he knows himself well enough to stand up for his own beliefs. He just mirrors the beliefs of others and lives according to the expectations of others."

"That's really why you left him, isn't it? Your essence and his essence weren't the same. You couldn't connect with him in truth and love because you're two very different people. Your essence is truth -- his essence is fear. Truth and love go hand-in-hand. Fear is the enemy of love and truth."

Jane looked down and sighed. "You are right. I've known his essence and I've known we're different for a long, long time. I remember walking by the bus station about fifteen years ago. The bus was pulling out and a man was running beside the bus trying to get the driver's attention. The bus stopped abruptly and the man slipped and fell beneath it. My husband froze in fear. I immediately ran in front of the bus, and like a mad woman began pounding on the window to get the driver's attention. The driver stopped immediately and paramedics were summoned. When they got the injured man out from under the bus, his leg was broken, but he lived. Something in me snapped that day. I think the illusion that my husband was brave, kind and caring was shattered with that one incident. Since then, I've seen him as fearful, weak, and self-centered. Even when he looks like he's helping others, he's doing it with strings attached -- he's doing something nice to bolster his own image or with expectations of a future pay off. He's so immature and blind. Yes, his essence is fear." Jane's words dropped to a sad whisper. Donna and Jane looked at each other and both knew the truth had been spoken. Jane also knew her decision to leave this man was justified. A pretend connection with one so different would be a lie. Jane couldn't live a lie and she couldn't pretend to be married when she was only connected legally.

Discerning the essence of others is important if a person wants to own full empowerment and connect in truth and love with others. An understanding of different essences and the degree of intellectual, emotional and spiritual maturation of each essence type helps understanding and discernment. We've observed five primary essences labeled Disciples of Darkness, Power Mongers, Disempowered Dependents, Armored Awake, and Disciples of Light. These essence categories describe how people at differing maturational levels interact in the world.

Just as the kindergartner can progress in educational level, those at less developed maturational levels have the ability to progress to higher levels. Their willingness to scrutinize themselves and their commitment to grow in love and truth will determine their progress. While these five primary essences are presented as different types, it's important to recognize that people exhibit different essences within themselves. A person who is ordinarily the essence of truth (the Armored Awake) can regress under certain circumstances to more closely resemble a Disempowered Dependent (the essence of fear). People who are seriously committed to their own growth will spend as much time looking inward and examining their own essence as they spend looking outward and judging the maturational levels of others.

Essence of Evil: Disciples of Darkness: Disciples of Darkness are the essence of evil and embody black hole energy. While possessing some attributes of intellectual development, their emotional and spiritual maturity is virtually nonexistent. Their ego-focus is single minded, targeting only the accumulation of power and control over others. They are adept at manipulating and using others to serve their own purposes and destroying those who get in their way. In times of social disorder, they display their intentions openly and ruthlessly. Under other conditions, like chameleons, they blend into and take charge of the control systems in society. They steal power from others through manipulation and intimidation, or with promises appealing to the human frailties of dependency and greed. They are the epitome of self-centeredness.

On the surface, Disciples of Darkness are quite adept at looking acceptable. They say the right words and con others into believing they are morally upright and are merely looking out for what's best for others. They understand and rely on the ignorance and blindness of the masses who allow them access to more and more power. Once entrenched on their throne of power, however, they rule by fear and fill lower power positions with their loyal lieutenants.

If there are no constraints of civilized society to hold them in check, Disciples of Darkness can rise to considerable notoriety in the world. Ruthless tyrants like Sadaam Hussein and murderous demagogues like Adolf Hitler are all too familiar. Ted Bundy, who murdered many attractive young women, charmed his victims into willingly following him to their death. Jim Jones brainwashed his religious followers and persuaded them to move with him to the jungles of Guyana. Once isolated from outside help, he held hundreds captive by convincing them he held divine powers. When he gave the order to destroy themselves with cyanide, his followers blindly obeyed like unthinking cattle following each other into slaughter.

Disciples of Darkness are not limited to psychopathic murderers and demonic leaders. These people are found in virtually every organization, and are often found at or near the top. Their chameleon-like abilities to package and disguise their evil intentions as tough business practices or strong leadership readily explain the cut-throat environments found in many private and public-sector organizations today. Their subordinates, damaged and weak themselves, overlook their cruelty and arrogant disregard for ethics. Seeing themselves as dependent on the

Disciple of Darkness for social or economic survival, they concede to and support one despotic manipulation after another. Either fearful to stand up, or enamored and corrupted with negative power, these subordinates facilitate the spread of darkness within society. They must share blame for the abuses that result.

The *emotional sphere* in Disciples of Darkness is highly undeveloped. They are unaware of their own emotions and are even less sensitive to the feelings of others. They have an almost robotic demeanor and express only anesthetized or fabricated emotional responses. They don't show anger, joy, sadness, or love. Both the negative and positive ends of the emotional spectrum are deadened. Love and truth are not within them. Totally ego-centered, they have no compassion for the needs and rights of others.

As previously noted, Disciples of Darkness have amazing chameleon-like qualities enabling them to blend into any environment. When relating to a group of union workers, they can emulate and adopt a fitting demeanor and attitude. When meeting with executives, they can exude an air of autocratic authority. They are able to blend with others because they are keen observers of human behavior.

Yet, since they have no moral conscience, they have no compassion for others. If they thought they could get away with murder, they would shoot another person in the head without flinching. They view their absence of emotions as positive. They can efficiently execute their plans without the bother of messy emotions or the restraint of integrity. Disciples of Darkness differ from others in their absence of fear and lack of moral conscience. Fear and conscience are two major limitors of behavior. Without such limitors, Disciples of Darkness are capable of unimaginable atrocities. In fact, one of the reasons they're successful in achieving their goals is that others can't fathom anyone doing what Disciples of Darkness readily do.

237

They are so slick that others fail to see them until it is too late. This is their greatest protection. By wearing a suit, by holding high office, by filling an important post, the Disciples of Darkness are able to disguise their real intent. The civilized world simply does not wish to see that such base savagery exists right in its midst. The incomprehensible nature of a person without conscience and fear is why unsuspecting girls followed Ted Bundy to their deaths and why the world allowed Hitler to get away with unspeakable acts of human destruction. Most of us can't believe there are people so morally deplete they can look you in the face and stab you in the back simultaneously. These demonic monsters are without the emotional foundation that underlies moral structure and compassion. If you acknowledge the distinction between good and bad, the Disciple of Darkness is darkness and evil personified.

Confronting them is a test for those who would choose light over darkness. To do so requires we confront our own fear and reject the status quo and victim mentality of the world around us. To be empowered against Disciples of Darkness we must see them as they truly are -- and we must have the courage and inner integrity to speak what we see. Disciples of Darkness maintain control on the thin threads of ignorance and fear. If others see and become empowered, the Disciple of Darkness has nothing.

Picture the scene in the Wizard of Oz where Dorothy inadvertently throws water on the witch. Once smug in her capacity to destroy any threat, the witch now screams in pain and fear as she shrinks into nothingness. Disciples of Darkness know their image is a hollow facade that will evaporate if their power is challenged. With courage and conviction, a critical mass of empowered individuals can break the hold of evil and fear. Unfortunately, there are not yet enough people who see evil and understand the compounding destruction inflicted on us all by allowing Disciples of Darkness to stay in positions of power. Tragically, those who are dark themselves, or who are dominated by insecurity, fear and neediness, misguidedly view the Disciples of Darkness as strong leaders and good businessmen.

Disciples of Darkness do have some aspects of *intellectual development* that are advanced and others that are seriously retarded. They are retarded in understanding and controlling their own unconscious motivations. Tragically, it is his lack of understanding that almost totally obviates their chances of growing and changing. They simply can't or won't critically analyze themselves. This deficiency in seeing themselves is sharply and paradoxically contrasted with their keen ability to read the motivations of others. They have an almost uncanny ability to hone in on the weaknesses of others. They accurately read the emotional triggers, values, and fears of others. Instead of using this knowledge to empower others, they use it to manipulate and gain control. They are experts in deciphering power dynamics and using subtle manipulation to gain the upper hand. While crudely stomping on those beneath them, they smoothly cater to superiors, with always an eye toward self preservation and even taking the superior's place. They skillfully diminish the powers of others until likely foes are impotent to contest them. They carefully consider each move they make. Life is a chess game to them. A move that is too obvious could give them away and even lead to their downfall. So they move slowly, carefully, and deliberately. Subtlety is their motto.

When *spiritual development* is defined as moving toward qualities of unconditional love and service to others, Disciples of Darkness are the least spiritually mature of all beings. The value orientation of the Disciple of Darkness is very clear. They value only self.

In summary, Disciples or Darkness are the embodiment of evil and black hole energy. While they are moderately developed intellectually, they are at the lowest levels of emotional and spiritual development. Like children, they haven't moved past the initial stages of individuation. They are extremely selfish people. Their power is their ability to read and manipulate others' fear and ignorance. We need to see them, confront their destructive force, and disempower them until they've grown sufficiently to warrant our trust.

Essence of Power: Power Mongers: Power Mongers value worldly power above all else. They represent a cross between black hole energy and moon energy. Left to their own devices, they would probably not choose to be destructive forces. However, they find themselves enmeshed in the worldly illusion that happiness and self-preservation require power, status, and control over the world around them. Like Moons, they believe they need something external to themselves to live and prosper. Their answer is to attach to the negative black hole energy of worldly leaders. Instead of renouncing the world's false and shallow ways, they embrace materialistic values and means. If Disciples of Darkness are the generals, Power Mongers are their sergeants. They hitch their wagons to the star of Disciples of Darkness or to others who have what they want -- power, money, influence or prestige. Power Mongers are yes men who step on others to get recognition and rewards. The officers who served under Hitler come to mind as obvious examples. Virtually all government agencies and private businesses are riddled with Power Mongers who cull favor at the expense of others. They are morally vacuous and will do anything that promotes their cause or feeds their sick need for approval.

Emotionally underdeveloped. Power Mongers aren't aware of their emotions or their unconscious motivations. They feign sensitivity to others' feeling only when this effort gratifies or glorifies them. Because their lives are externally focused on power, status, or money, Power Mongers ignore development of their inner selves. Like Disciples of Darkness, they present a hollow image. Their civilized mask hides emotional emptiness. About the only true emotions Power Mongers feel and show are anger and frustration. They often vent their anger and frustration at others in their efforts to intimidate.

Power Mongers generally have authoritarian or emotionally distant parents who showed them little love and respect. They are profoundly insecure and emotionally immature. Unconscious feelings of being unloved motivate them to seek the approval of authority figures. By pleasing authority, they seek the parental love that was absent in their childhoods. This makes them easy prey for the Disciples of Darkness who must have a following to subjugate and control others. Power Mongers believe love is based on achievement and only those in power can measure whether their achievements are adequate. Since they are hollow, only someone in power can award them the love and recognition they so desperately seek.

Power Mongers are also *intellectually underdeveloped*. Their intellectual pursuits are shallow, going only deep enough to give the appearance of knowledge or expertise. They drop names and spout worthless facts. They are not intellectually curious people, and thus, they have little interest in deeper meanings and inner workings. Concrete thinkers, they stagnate in the known, never venturing into the unknown. If questioned in depth, it becomes apparent that Power Mongers are neither wise nor in possession of relevant or timely knowledge. They are stale. They steal the appearance of wisdom from the ingenuity of others. They have no inspirational genius of their own.

Unfortunately, Power Mongers are largely unconscious of their toxic behaviors and may even see themselves as pillars of their community or workplace. Because they are intellectually, emotionally, and spiritually blind, they generally live out their lives in denial about their undeveloped states and their deep interpersonal problems. Without self awareness, they have no motivation to change and grow.

Power Mongers are as *spiritually undeveloped* as Disciples of

Darkness. Their only real commitment is to serving themselves. Instead of following the guidance of a Higher Power, or a set of empowering moral principles, they are guided by their own self interest. If this means stealing power and dignity from others, they don't wince. On the conventional level of moral maturity, their values are externally oriented. This means the prevailing morals and sentiments of those around them largely determine what they do. They follow orders without thinking about the consequences their actions have on others. If the boss tells them to do something, or if rules demand some action, they blindly follow. They differ from Disciples of Darkness in one major way -- they are generally reactors rather than instigators. Not having the intellectual development of a Disciple of Darkness, Power Mongers are typically the disseminators of darkness -- not the initiators.

Power Mongers use blame, shame, intimidation, and manipulation to coerce others into subservient positions. Self-righteous, they often assume the self-appointed duty of judging others. Unconditional love is unknown to these people and well beyond their capacity to understand. They may, however, resort to caretaker patterns that give the appearance of loving others. Their caretaking has strings attached and Power Mongers always exact a price for whatever they give. The person who succumbs to the Power Monger's manipulative caretaking will ultimately feel guilty when he doesn't want to give in to the eventual demand for repayment. Life has no greater purpose for a Power Monger than collecting the most marbles, satisfying their emotional neediness, and being one-up.

In summary, Power Mongers are as undeveloped as are Disciples of Darkness on the emotional and spiritual levels. They also embody black hole energy. They are even less developed intellectually because they're unable to see the motives, intents and unconscious motivations of others. Alone they don't have the destructive potential of Disciples of Darkness, but they are often accomplices. Their power is an illusion built on the fear and ignorance of those around them. Their power will crumble only when the fearful become empowered.

Essence of Fear: Disempowered Dependents: Disempowered Dependents embody moon energy. They believe power and energy originate outside themselves. Fear and dependency eclipse their internal power and they feel safe and powerful only in the presence of someone they perceive as being more powerful. Unfortunately, the power they cling to for sustenance may be Black Hole energy since manipulative lies may be more appealing than the truth delivered by Sun energy. Codependency renders them impotent to confront and challenge negative patterns within themselves or in others. They are oblivious to their need to change and tend to cling to familiar, static, and self-defeating interpersonal patterns for an entire lifetime. Disempowered Dependents probably are the most populous group. They comprise what one politician labeled the silent majority.

Because they're not in touch with their inner truth, Disempowered Dependents are full of fear. Like rudderless ships, they change course with the changing direction of the wind. Outside forces determine their stand on issues, their feelings, and their perception of themselves. Outwardly, they present an agreeable and socially appealing facade. Tuned in to the external expectations of others, they are vigilant about pleasing others and winning approval. While their neediness and external orientation make them similar to Power Mongers, they differ in intent. Power Mongers seek power at all costs while Disempowered Dependents avoid power and the responsibilities that come with power. Since Disempowered Dependents comprise the majority, their passivity and willingness to be used by others (particularly by Disciples of Darkness and Power Mongers) explains much of our current personal and societal abuses. While they might inadvertently hurt others through their blindness, timidity, rationalization, or denial, they don't purposely intend harm. They defend their

243

unwillingness to stand on principle by disavowing any power to impact and change situations. They see themselves as pawns in a cosmic chess game in which they're moved around by outside forces. Fear and helplessness thwart their efforts to grow intellectually, emotionally, and spiritually.

The *emotional development* of Disempowered Dependents is truncated by their neediness and inability to claim power. Disempowered Dependents give the appearance of having weak ego boundaries. Others seem to continually take advantage of them. In reality, they are self-absorbed people who have thick ego-boundaries. Their codependent games keep others at a safe distance, never really knowing who they are. They generally fit into the Parent or Child role. The child role solicits the energy of others with their neediness, incompetence and naiveté. Some of these "poor me children" are obvious in their attempts to steal energy and attention from others. The more subtle "children" suck energy from others with illness, bad luck, and a projected image of fragility. Those choosing the Parent/Martyr role are different on the surface only. Their whole identity revolves around their need to be needed. While they may complain about being used, they won't own the power to just say no and break the dependent pattern that weakens those they take care of as well as themselves.

On the *intellectual level,* Disempowered Dependents choose immaturity. They don't understand human power dynamics and appear naive, likely victims to others. They can be controlling or controlled, depending on whether they are playing caretaker or victim. They don't anticipate long-term outcomes of their decisions or actions. Their inability to become empowered results in their floating through life without much meaning or direction. They give circumstance and luck credit for their successes and failures.

The Disempowered Dependents are stuck in concrete

thinking. Material possessions and worldly success are valued higher than are abstract principles of justice, honor, and love. Economic security, physical health, and material comfort are their dominant concerns.

On the surface, some Disempowered Dependents may appear *spiritually developed.* Many are dedicated church-goers, while others have given up on religion and spirituality altogether. Those who are religious display the same dependency pattern present in their interpersonal relationships. Disempowered Dependents are often religious zealots who are brainwashed by the beliefs of others. They believe they cannot interpret religious messages themselves nor can they connect directly with God (however they define God). They need someone as intermediary to tell them what the words and life of Christ, Mohammed or Buddha mean. Religious doctrine and dogma anesthetize them to the need to connect personally and deeply with a Divine Source.   God is viewed as external to them and their religious beliefs are often formed around fear of God.

Throughout the ages, Disempowered Dependents have fought religious wars in the name of their god or sacrificed themselves for their beliefs. What they fail to understand is that their model -- whether Christ, Mohammed, or Buddha -- was an empowered being who rose above ignorance and fear and who, through example, challenges them to do the same. Instead, they cling to child-like dependency, refusing to accept their responsibility and power to follow their teacher's path and become the model of love, truth and power.

In summary, Disempowered Dependents are developmentally frozen in fear. Fear arrests their emotional, intellectual and spiritual development. They view themselves as powerless and unable to change their negative situations. As Moon people, they believe power, light, and energy exist in other people, but not in themselves. They are arrested at beginning individuation and tend to be at the extremes of selflessness or selfishness. They need to confront and move past their fears, own their power, and commit to becoming sources of energy, hope and light.

Essence of Truth: Armored Awake: The Armored Awake people clearly see the motivations and intents of others. They are not taken in by the Disciples of Darkness, Power Mongers, or Disempowered Dependents. They see and avoid the control dramas of others, readily admitting the shallowness in human relationships. They see others as inherently undeveloped and immature, and consider themselves intellectually, if not emotionally, beyond most. Their energetic frequency approaches sun energy, but falls short because of their self-protective fear. They frequently present an aloof demeanor, as if uninterested in others when they are more likely to be protecting themselves from manipulations and power plays.

On the *emotional level,* Armored Awakes are moderately aware of their emotions and their unconscious motivations. They avoid needy relationships and balance their needs with the needs of others. They seek autonomy and self-reliance and are attracted to equals who have the same values. Armored Awake people have no need to control or have power over others. They protect their rights and their freedom from encroachment by lesser developed persons. They could have tremendous power to influence others in a positive direction, but they often fail to do this because their energies are too wrapped up in self-protection. Seeing the cruelty and stupidity of most of the world's inhabitants, Armored Awakes are aloof and detached, ever studying the intents of others. This fear-orientation consumes much of their energy and prevents them from attaining full empowerment.

The Armored Awakes have few peers on the *intellectual level.* They are keen observers of others and can accurately read their own and others' motivations and needs. They are acutely aware of the ways of the world and understand the interpersonal power games that make up life's drama. Because of their intellectual acuity, they are most often very capable in their careers. However, they fail to have the courage to speak out and commit to leadership service in changing the injustices around them. They see and understand, but fail to act. They do not own their power, and thus, they allow the injustices perpetrated by others to flourish. Without inner courage, they may rationalize injustice and take a political stance rather than stand up for what is right and just. Their silence allows Disciples of Darkness and Power Mongers to flourish. They are special in that they have the potential to counterbalance the evil in the world and provide leadership through example to others. One may argue that the Armored Awakes have more responsibility for changing injustice because they are capable of seeing it clearly. Yet, because they haven't committed emotionally to others, they feel no overt need to stand in defense of those less endowed than they. Failure to stand on principle and confront the injustices they see ultimately exacts a high price on the conscience and spirit of the Armored Awake.

Armored Awakes are abstract thinkers. That which the world prizes -- material goods, status, and power, mean little to them as long as they have enough. They value truth above all else, and because of this their conscience aches when they don't stand for truth and justice. Armored Awake persons can find themselves trapped between what they know to be true and finding the courage to speak that truth to others. If they fail to stand up for justice, it's an act of omission rather than an act of commission. While they don't speak out when they should, they rarely commit a deliberate wrong against another. The Armored Awakes look at life from an idiosyncratic standpoint based on their internal moral structure and acute intellectual perspective. They're not easily persuaded to follow the crowd or to adapt to the conventions of the group.

On a *spiritual level*, the Armored Awakes are more advanced than the other three types. The moral values of the Armored Awake are internally oriented and they fully ascribe to abstract values of fairness, justice, equality and personal freedom. However, the full expression of love and service is blunted by their need to self-protect.

Their spiritual underdevelopment often results in disillusionment and depression. In their state of intellectual and emotional advancement, they see but don't have the internal strength to act that comes with spiritual awakening to a higher mission in life. On a secular level, they believe the primary purpose of life is to understand the world and its inner workings. Yet, they need to move beyond their aloof intellectual understanding of life and commit to heartfelt connection with others. They need to commit to the united uplifting of mankind. Before they can become agents of change in the world, they must transcend the world's illusion that others have power over them. Only through full spiritual development can they give up this illusion and their fear attached to the illusion. A few Armored Awakes make the transition from fear-orientation to faith-orientation and rise to a new level of courage that enables them to stand and radiate truth and love. Most, however, buy into the illusion that others have power over them and thus they fail to actualize their real transformative power in the world.

In summary, Armored Awakes embrace the guiding principle of truth and are reaching toward Sun energy. They are highly developed intellectually, but need further work on emotional and spiritual development. They have completed the work of beginning individuation and are balanced in selflessness and selfishness. They demand respect and give respect to their own and others' rights, feelings, and needs. They have committed to tunnel work and are engaged in the process of growing past their fears. When they conquer their need for self-protective aloofness, they'll be ready to own Sun power.

248

Essence of Love: Disciples of Light: The world has seen only a few Disciples of Light, but their power and influence are immense. These are people who speak the truth and commit to love and service. They are total Sun Energy -- bright, warm, powerful, and self-sustaining. They're about as fully developed on all three levels -- emotional, intellectual, and spiritual -- as any human can be. They adhere to a higher calling and unite with a Higher Power. They have little interest in man's illusion of power and control. They shun materialism and live a mission-centered life. The Disciples of Light are the uppermost exemplar of evolved humanity.   Depending on a person's religious or cultural attachments, this ideal is found in Confucius, Buddha, Jesus Christ, Mohammed, Ghandi, or the many others who have taught and demonstrated selfless love and service.

Those embodying the essence of love are fully awakened individuals who see the world and the humans around them clearly. They understand the underlying motivations of behavior and, instead of judging or controlling, gently lead others to a more enlightened position.   They are fully empowered people who know and directly confront their fears.   They're not bound by the rules and conventions of worldly reality. Rather, they transcend myopic and narrow human understanding and become visionary leaders for a better world. While encouraging others to transcend fears and blindness, they don't allow the blindness of others to cloud their vision and distract them from their missions.   They are cause- and service-oriented. Their cause centers on widespread intellectual, emotional and spiritual evolution of mankind. Through example and teaching, they raise generations of people to higher levels of understanding and godliness.

Disciples of Light are at the highest level of *emotional development.* Their ego boundaries are permeable. They feel and understand their own emotions and needs, and they are equally adept at feeling and understanding the emotions and needs of others. They expect to both give and receive respect and caring.

Never imposing their beliefs and will on others, they expect the same consideration. When reciprocity of love and caring is absent, the Disciples of Light forgive rather than retaliate.

Disciples of Light have complete awareness of their own and others' motivations. They see and name control dramas, particularly those harmful to others. They lack fear and believe in their ability to help others grow in understanding, love, and service. They have absolute control over themselves and seek no control over others. They seek to empower others and they shun idolization by others. They serve as catalysts that activate empowering qualities within each person.

They are in the superior range of *intellectual development*. They're completely aware of their own and others' unconscious motivations. Continuously examining their own motives, they urge others to look truthfully at themselves and to consider whether their actions are based in love and service. Because they have tremendous power to attract kindred spirits, and by example raise those less developed to a higher plane, people seek them out. The collective Sun Energy of Disciples of Light and their followers has tremendous transformative power. Like spreading electric current, the power, hope, dynamism, and idealism embodied in a Disciple of Light radiates and extends outward to others.

Disciples of Light are the only fully mature spiritual beings. Their strength emanates from their belief in a Higher Power they define as the Source of Love and Life. Because of their identification with the Love Source, they don't seek power over or harm to anyone. At the same time, they don't shrink from their responsibility to confront others about moral and spiritual shortcomings. This reflection of others' deficits is done without self-righteousness or judgment. With fortitude and conviction, Disciples of Light stand up firmly and confidently for those in need.

When compared with others, Disciples of Light have the

greatest capacity to love. They know how to give and receive love without conditions or strings attached to their loving. They've learned the lesson of loving themselves, regardless of their human blemishes, which enables them to love others without conditions or judgment. They seek loving connections with no ulterior motives except truth, support, and desire for genuine bonding.

The moral values of the Disciples of Light are internally oriented. They possess an inner well-spring of morality that transcends human ego-centeredness and fear. They live their moral conscience, often sacrificing much for their moral and spiritual beliefs. The central life purpose of Disciples of Light is to spread understanding, growth, love and enlightenment to others. Their visionary leadership has inspired masses to leave behind the dark illusion of materialism, hate, fear, control, and prejudice. They inspire people to reach toward full intellectual, emotional and spiritual self-actualization.

An acquaintance recently told us about the new director of her international organization. "He has a joy and confidence that is uplifting to us all. Everyone is respected and valued -- from the biggest financial contributor to the most powerful politician to the janitor. In fact, I was with him when he stopped to talk to the janitor the other day. He told the janitor that he had noticed the exceptionally good job he was doing. He declared that the janitor's job was one of the most important in the organization because a clean and organized environment inspired visitors and employees. He credited the janitor with creating the lovely physical and emotional environment so many in the organization enjoyed. He thanked the janitor several times before he left."

This new CEO sounds like a Disciple of Light. Seeing no status distinctions, he empowered another with loving and appreciative comments. He made others feel noticed, important, and honored. As a truly empowered being, he didn't have the need to steal energy and disempower others. Instead, he empowered others and started a domino effect that spread empowerment throughout the entire organization.

The problem we have with Disciples of Light is not theirs, but ours. We insist on putting them on pedestals and believing they possess capacities far beyond our reach as mortal beings. When we do this we disempower ourselves. As highly evolved exemplars of human development, their task is to encourage others to become like them -- emotionally, intellectually and spiritually developed and empowered with Sun Energy. Instead, we judge the distance between them and us and find ourselves wanting. We persist in denying ourselves the confidence to grow to their level. Only Disciples of Light have completed all the tasks of empowerment. They have balanced selfishness-selflessness, triumphed over fear and neediness, and demonstrated the strength to reach out to others in truth and love. They beckon us to follow them. Will we take up their challenge, or will we disempower ourselves with the belief we're not capable of being like them?

(4) How Discernment Is A Tool for Growth

After we see and understand the different developmental levels, we can use this information to facilitate our own growth to higher levels of being. Seeing those at lower developmental levels (Disciples of Darkness, Power Mongers, and Disempowered Dependents), alerts us to their games. We no longer get snared by our own fear and neediness, nor do we empower them with our blindness, naiveté, and silence. We see them as second graders playing at being adult and powerful. The illusion that they hold power over us loses credibility and we no longer fear their strength.

Yet the lesson of discernment is greater than seeing and disempowering all the illusions that hold us captive in fear. Discernment enables us see the lessons we must master if we are to move toward and join the Armored Awake and Disciples of Light. With discernment we are ready to begin tackling our

252

lessons. We can look honestly and objectively at the significant people who have affected the way we see ourselves and the world around us. We can see their emotional, intellectual and spiritual maturity levels. Who was instrumental in shaping your life, your thoughts, feelings, beliefs? What were their essences and levels of development? What challenges did they present to you? Have you been privileged to be near a Disciple of Light, and if so, how did you react? Did (do) you put him or her on a pedestal with adulation and awe, or did you strive to become more like him or her?

Epilogue: Mark had two Disempowered Dependent parents who looked very different on the surface. His alcoholic father was a hard-working martyr when sober but reverted to a selfish, poor me child without discipline or self-love when he started drinking. In his alcoholic state, he showed the destructive side of a Disciple of Darkness, heaping physical and verbal abuse on defenseless family members. Mark internalized his father's negative messages and grew up seeing himself unlovable, inadequate, and a nuisance to others. Mark's mother was a Disempowered Dependent. She tried to smooth things over when her husband fell into one of his drunken tirades. Ironically, her selfless martyrdom served only to enable her husband's alcoholism. Had she been empowered, she would have warned him to get help and heal, or she and the children would leave. If she'd been able to do this, Mark might have internalized a new message of dignity, integrity and strength. He would have known he deserved better in life than the abusive treatment handed him by his father. His father's poor me, victim stance and his mother's role as disempowered martyr left him indelibly imprinted as unworthy, weary, and shameful.

Today Mark is in a marriage with a Power Monger wife who manipulates him and their children, in a job that's overdemanding and underpaying, and in friendships that are shallow. Mark's lesson is to transcend the Disempowered Dependent trap that held his parents captive. He must expunge the ingrained messages of helplessness and hopelessness. Fortunately, Mark has several beneficial qualities that will aid in overcoming the crippling legacy handed down by his parents. He is both intellectually and spiritually advanced, giving him the curiosity to learn and grow and the faith to persevere. His major deficit is in the emotional sphere. Primarily numbed to emotional nuances, he is only in touch with anger -- and then only when he's pushed into a corner and feels he must come out swinging just to survive.

So Mark needs to challenge himself to grow emotionally and heal his childhood wounds. He needs to understand that his parents, not he, are responsible for his family's problems. He must stop blaming himself for being inadequate and unlovable. He must confront his Power Monger wife and leave if she refuses to grow. He needs to assess his strengths and look for work that's affirming and respectful of his talents and his worth. He needs to look for Armored Awake and Disciple of Light friends who will help guide him on his journey.

Each of us has been handed disempowering messages throughout our lives from parents, teachers, friends, and others. We need to remember those messages. We need to accurately assess the essences of those who delivered them. If they were motivated by fear or control, we need to see them clearly for what they are. We need to go through the grief process and let go of all the disempowering messages that have held us back. We must take up the challenge of growing to a higher level of being.

The next few pages summarize the qualities of differing levels of emotional, intellectual, and spiritual maturity and the developmental types (Disciples of Darkness, Power Mongers, Disempowered Dependents, Armored Awake, and Disciples of Light). Rate yourself and significant people in your life according to their levels of development. The task of growing toward empowerment should become clearer. Your job is to recognize and grow past the emotional, intellectual, or spiritual traps that kept the other significant people in your life arrested in an undeveloped state. You are to become greater than the sum of your pre-programmed, conditioned, and unhealed parts. Don't worry. You will not destroy the love you feel for your parents (or any other significant person) by acknowledging their flaws. Instead, you will find that you can gratefully acknowledge the positive lessons they did provide through *both* the strengths and weaknesses they displayed. It is time to discern and see the truth, to love and to let go. It is time to move to a higher place of wisdom, strength, and peace.

Disciples of Darkness

Emotional Development

- not aware of own emotions; numbed out
- not sensitive to others' feeling or rights
- impenetrable ego boundaries
- no meaningful connection with others
- don't understand unconscious motivations
- no fear/no conscience
- present cardboard image - no real self

Intellectual Development

- keen and accurate observers of others
- use knowledge of others to manipulate
- understand power dynamics between people
- seek absolute control over others through fear
- anticipate likely outcomes of behavior
- concrete thinker - materialistic
- competent to achieve goals

Spiritual Development

- ego centered, not able to love
- committed to only serving self
- no moral values
- life goal - greed, power, lust
- negative empowerment
- destructive force
- steal power from others

Power Mongers

Emotional Development

- not aware of own emotions; numbed out
- not sensitive to others' feelings or rights
- impenetrable ego boundaries
- no meaningful connection with others
- don't understand unconscious motivations
- present cardboard image - no real self
- lots of fear/no conscience

Intellectual Development

- not adept at understanding others
- blindly follow those with power
- crude understanding of power dynamics
- seek external approval and rewards
- do not anticipate likely outcomes
- concrete thinker - materialistic
- awkward and generally incompetent
- life goal: greed, power, lust

Spiritual Development

- ego centered, not able to love others
- committed to only serving self
- conventional moral values (do what others say is right)
- not truly empowered
- guided by own self interest
- steal power from others

Disempowered Dependents

Emotional Development

- not aware of own emotions; numbed out
- somewhat sensitive to others' feelings
- self-protective ego boundaries
- co-dependent interpersonal relationships
- lack of psychological knowledge of unconscious motivations
- present cardboard image (victim, caretaker)
- lots of fear
- some conscience, but primarily ruled by insecurity

Intellectual Development

- do not understand others or self
- deny knowledge of power dynamics
- naive, manipulative and manipulated
- can be controlled by others or controlling of others
- unwilling to anticipate likely outcomes
- concrete thinkers - materialistic
- incompetent, insecure and needy
- life goal: please others, be loved

Spiritual Development

- may appear other-centered
- committed to being dependent
- conventional moral values (externally- oriented, please others, be accepted)
- give power away to others
- guided by own ego-interest
- don't want to control self or others

258

Armored Awake

Emotional Development

- aware of own emotions
- sensitive to others' feelings and rights
- self-protective ego boundaries
- can meaningfully connect with others
- understand unconscious motivations
- armored - only let a few see real self
- fear-oriented; self-defensive

Intellectual Development

- keen and accurate observers of others
- use knowledge of others to help them
- understand power dynamics between people
- seek to empower others
- anticipate likely outcomes of behavior
- abstract thinkers - principle-centered
- fear prevents achievement of goals

Spiritual Development

- balanced self- and other-centered
- unconditional love blocked by fear
- transition between conventional and post-conventional moral
  values
- empowerment blocked by fear
- transition between world and spiritual orientation
- fearful that others will steal power
- life goal: avoid being burned

259

Disciples of Light

Emotional Development

- very aware and expressive of own emotions
- very sensitive to others' feelings and rights
- penetrable ego boundaries
- deeply and meaningfully connect with others
- acute understanding of unconscious motivations
- present real self
- no fear
- ruled by highest morals and love principle

Intellectual Development

- keen and accurate observers of others
- use knowledge of others to help them
- understand power dynamics between people
- seek to empower others
- anticipate likely outcomes of behavior
- abstract thinkers - principle-centered
- fully achieve goals

Spiritual Development

- balanced self- and other-centered
- gives unconditional love
- internally-oriented and post-conventional moral values
- have conquered fear
- spiritual orientation
- guided by mission and higher power
- life goal: fulfill mission, love completely, spread empowerment

DIMENSIONS OF HUMAN MATURITY

Characteristics of the Mature Person

Emotional sensitive to and considerate of own emotions and feelings of others; permeable ego boundaries; connects genuinely with others; scrutinizes own motives and intents; understands others' motives; appropriately expresses own emotions; supports emotional honesty of others;understands the unconscious motivations of behavior; owns emotional maturity which leads to understanding of self and others; presents real self and is vulnerable; not consumed with self-protection, more trusting; capable of high level motivations - love, fairness, justice, etc.; values integrity and high moral convictions; committed to growing emotionally and psychologically.

Intellectual able to think in abstract terms; embraces post-conventional moral values; able to understand psychological dynamics of human behavior; understands the multidimensional nature of human problems; introspective thinkers who see complexity within issues; inquisitive and curious; visionary andcreative; independent and internally-oriented; has wisdom as well as knowledge; spreads wisdom to others; asks questions about life's meaning; acutely aware of meaning and interconnectedness of life events.

DIMENSIONS OF HUMAN MATURITY

Characteristics of the Mature Person

Spiritual   seeks a personal relationship with divine and universal power; respects the truth that transcends and permeates all religions; adheres to principles of love and service to others; inclusive of all religious beliefs that are loving and empowering; spiritual beliefs based on unity and love of God; internally-oriented spiritual beliefs and experiences; finds the Truth of God within; empowered to model love, truth and courage; sees and avoids the snares and illusions of the world; high moral orientation based on love of God and others; continuous self-scrutiny of own motives and intents; values personal integrity, pleases God and self.

DIMENSIONS OF HUMAN MATURITY

Characteristics of the Immature Person

Emotional numbed out feelings; unable to connect with others' feelings; impermeable ego boundaries; no genuine or deep connections with others; no self-scrutiny; committed to using others for self-gratification; no genuine expression of emotions; is not supportive of others' needs; blind to unconscious motivations of own or others behaviors; emotional immaturity leads to judgment and manipulation of others; wears mask of acceptability and is not truly vulnerable to others; obsessive self-absorption, selfishness, and self-protection; no trust of others; ruled by base animal instincts - not capable of true love, fairness, justice; see life as a win-loose war game; downward spiral into self-destruction and despair

Intellectual able to think only in concrete, materialistic terms; not able to truly understand or integrate abstract moral principles; views problems in dichotomous, black-white, right wrong perspectives; simplistic thinkers with mundane, elemental views on issues; follows the lead of others, doesn't question; shallow, dependent and parasitic relationships; externally-oriented; may have knowledge but no wisdom; accept token answers about life's meaning from others; in a fog, aren't aware of interconnected meaning in life events

DIMENSIONS OF HUMAN MATURITY

Characteristics of the Immature Person

Spiritual   ascribes to certain religious doctrines and church dogma; arrogantly defends religious beliefs as the only one truth; imposes beliefs upon others; seeks control over others; seeks to disempower others; beliefs based on fear of God; externally-oriented beliefs based on rules and doctrines; rely on others to decipher Truth of God; fearful, childish dependence; entrapped by world's snares and illusions; ego-centered orientation without adherence to moral principles; lack of conscience; no self-examination of motives and intents; wants to be acceptable to others; has external orientation of power and prestige

Chapter Nine

*Interdependency: Reaching Out in Power
and Love*

Interdependency:
Reaching Out in Power and Love

I had two dreams, one after the other. I'm sure they go together, but I don't have a clue what they mean. In the first dream, I'm washing my car. It's a summer night and the car doors are open as I clean out the back seat. Suddenly a small child rushes in the front passenger's door and crawls over the seat to the back. I try to steady him so he won't fall. His tiny, sharp fingernails pierce the skin of my forearm and I begin to bleed. Large hands reach through the door and grab the child. In the darkness, I see white teeth and flashing eyes. "You shouldn't leave your doors open," booms a man's voice. I don't notice the man and child leaving because I'm looking at my bleeding arm and wondering why these crazy things happen to me.

I'm also in my car in the second dream. I'm driving slowly because it's very foggy. I come to a stop light and glance up to see a large, bald-headed man approaching the door. He raps on the window in a slow, deliberate and menacing way. I know he's sinister -- a grim reaper type who wants to kill me. I want to drive away, but I freeze in fear. He knocks harder on the window and the glass cracks in a spider web of broken lines. He knocks harder on the broken window and as his hand breaks through the flimsy barrier, my life flashes before my eyes. I've squandered my life, my gifts, and now it's over.

- Janet, age 35

Permeable Boundaries: Open Enough to Connect, Closed Enough to Protect

Janet's dreams showed her two sides -- one side too open, naive, impulsive, and feeling; the other side too closed, fearful, slow, and analytical. Janet has a problem balancing *ego boundaries* -- the self protective walls we have that preserve our identity, time and energy. Janet is primarily selfless -- an other-focused, feeling female who puts her heart on the line and her head in the sand. Janet has been emotionally scratched and left bleeding many times

267

by others who used her but gave nothing back. When this happens, her inner voice warns her to close her doors and put up her defenses. Then Janet swings to the other extreme, fearful to the point of paranoia and unwilling to let anyone in. Her fear freezes her in inaction. She's afraid to claim her power and she's afraid to live. During her closed periods, she's too paralyzed to fight for herself and break through her self-imposed barrier. Janet needs to balance her openness to love with her discernment of others. She needs to know with whom to be open and with whom she should close up and self-protect. If Janet continues to swing between the two extremes -- so open and selfless that she allows herself to be hurt and so closed that she disallows association with anyone else -- she will indeed squander her life and her gifts. She'll consume her life energy salving her wounds or protecting herself from further harm.

The Need for Emotional and Intellectual Integration

Janet's dreams also warned of her need for emotional and intellectual *integration*. When Janet's heart dominated, she was open and frequently got hurt by others who were still undeveloped children. When her head was in command, she froze in fear and cautiously scrutinized others for signs of their ill-intent. Janet's head and heart need to work in concert so she's open with those who enhance her growth and well-being and closed with those who want to use and abuse her. We need to balance and fully integrate our emotions and our minds if we seek full empowerment.

When we're not fully integrated, we come either from our emotional side or our rational side, but not from a balanced head/heart perspective. The world does a better job educating and rewarding our rational side, so the mental side predominates. This is particularly true for males, who have been actively discouraged from developing and maturing emotionally. From early childhood, boys are taught not to cry, not to show vulnerability, and not to

268

connect deeply with other males, lest they be labeled gay. Girls don't face the same inhibiting expectations. With best friends, they freely share their most intimate thoughts and feelings and openly express vulnerability.

In adulthood, we rarely have the opportunity to identify emotions and understand what triggers them. Few of us are taught how to safely and effectively vent pent up feelings. Since the educational and business sectors lean so heavily toward intellectual development, therapy is probably the only place people find a safe haven to nurture and explore their emotional selves. There are two primary impediments to emotional maturity: failure to complete grief work and repression of emotions through the defense mechanisms of intellectualization or rationalization.

Completing Grief Work: Janet's dream indicated that her tunnel work of emotional purification was unfinished. Unresolved fear was keeping her unbalanced. Her need to be loved and accepted competed with her need for safety and security. Janet has talked about her childhood trauma of being sexually abused by a neighbor. Still she hasn't reached emotional resolution of this experience that continues to unconsciously rule her. She must push through the stages of grief -- anger, depression, bargaining and acceptance. Until she fully owns the pain of her trauma, and until she is emotionally and mentally integrated, she'll swing between her need to be loved and her need to self-protect.

Janet's emotional-mental integration will begin only when she fully expresses her rage at the selfish man who ruthlessly used her. This man, a Disciple of Darkness, focused on his own needs and wants and ignored the needs of a child. He didn't care about the destruction his selfishness caused. As a child, Janet didn't possess the power to confront and stop her abuser. As an adult, she can now own the power of her repressed rage. She is no longer a child and is now fully able to defend herself. She can write the man a letter and confront him about his injustice and cruelty. She may even decide to turn a report into the police in his community, and thereby protect other children from a vicious pedophile. As she allows herself to feel and to express her anger, Janet will also feel depression and sorrow about the losses she's sustained. She was betrayed by an adult who should have protected her. Consequently, she lost her trust in other people. She lost her innocence and she lost her freedom to live without fear. Most of all, Janet lost her self-esteem. All this she must acknowledge, feel, and move through, for it was this abuse that caused her to feel soiled and imperfect. She blamed herself for the sexual acts and labeled herself bad. Janet had a dark secret and she feared others would find out and condemn her.

Janet lived in fear and shame from age eleven. She needs to grieve the loss of the happy and carefree child she was before the molestation took place. Janet was a Sun Child, but a Black Hole adult dimmed her brilliance. Now it's time for Janet to grieve the lost years of creativity and joy that would have been her destiny had the Black Hole adult not crossed her path. She needs to get angry enough to defy the Black Hole's attempt to destroy her. Instead of playing and replaying the old tapes telling her she's unworthy and of little importance, she now needs to cast away the lies that have contaminated her energy and her self-love. She must acknowledge that the Black Hole adult was the soiled and bad one -- not she.

While Janet is needy for others' love and acceptance, she has not learned to love or accept herself. No one can give her what she refuses to give herself. When her need for love is most urgent, Janet becomes a selfless giver, hoping to earn love by giving herself away. More often than not, she attracts users who aren't developed enough to love and who are too selfish to give back. With the childhood molestation, Janet's definition of love was warped. The molester convinced young Janet that she was being loved. Now Janet has to untangle being used from her understanding of love.

When Janet has fully exhausted the anger and depression stage of her grief, she can move forward into the bargaining stage. It is during bargaining that her mind searches for answers to the question, "Why?" Why did this terrible thing happen to me? Why did the pedophile choose me? How could this man appear to be warm and caring when he was sinister and calculating? Why did her parents trust him? Why was she never able to tell her parents, or anyone else, what happened? Janet already knows the answers to some of the questions. For example, Janet understands she was a needy child -- wanting affection and attention and getting little of either from her parents. She was easy prey for the pedophile who lived next door.

Janet also understands that her abuser is capable of vile acts because he's a different type of person than she is. Janet is a Disempowered Dependent who selflessly gives and naively trusts. Her abuser is a Disciple of Darkness -- emotionally immature, spiritually dark, extremely selfish, and predatory in nature. Janet has stopped asking how the pedophile could have done what he did. She no longer projects her own moral standards onto others. She now sees the darkness and immaturity in others. Clearly seeing the Disciple of Darkness enables her to see others who are undeveloped and who prey on guileless victims. Her's was a horrible lesson in discernment.

The last stage in the grief process is acceptance. Acceptance is a state of peace that comes when one has thoroughly exhausted anger and sorrow. Acceptance does not mean forgiveness, although forgiveness may be a part of acceptance. Forgiveness assumes a one-up, parent or judge position. Because we generally are unable to thoroughly understand the reasons for others' transgressions, we aren't in a position to judge them.

Acceptance, in contrast, does not call for an objective judgment of the offender's culpability. Acceptance doesn't wipe

271

the slate clean and pretend that nothing harmful happened. There is still room within the concept of acceptance for cosmic justice. The offender is still held accountable for his transgressions. He is still expected to repent and grow beyond his base level of emotional and spiritual development. The value of acceptance for the victim is his release from vengeance and self-destructive fury.

Now that Janet has committed to her own emotional and spiritual development, she can see how underdeveloped her transgressor was. She is indeed in high school while the pedophile languishes in kindergarten. She no longer has to give power to her abuser by fearing him or hating him. She no longer has to distrust everyone else and project the pedophile's sickness onto them. She can see the differences between people at different levels of development.

Repression of Emotions through Intellectualization and Rationalization:
While some people run from emotions because of unresolved pain, others have never developed emotionally. Like a kindergarten student who has not been exposed to reading and, therefore, doesn't know how to read, some people have little exposure to their emotional side or to the emotional sides of others. John is a person who never developed emotionally because he lived in the sterile world of intellectual robots. His mother was a psychologist whose counseling style was to be the "one-up expert." She understood why others behaved as they did but she didn't have to get down in the mud and feel what they felt. She was above emotions. John's father was a lawyer who was ever busy fixing the problems of others. He focused outwardly and seldom looked at his own feelings. When John was around twelve, he remembers his parents talking about an open marriage. While still living together, they went their separate ways and lived parallel, but estranged lives. When John was fifteen, his parents legally separated and divorced. They remained friends and equally participated in raising him and his sister. John doesn't remember

272

any fights between his parents. He doesn't remember grieving the divorce because it all seemed so civil and rational. Now in adulthood, John doesn't understand his wife's emotions and is unable to share his emotions with her. John doesn't see the need for emotional venting. Instead of feeling, he comes up with a rational solution for any obstacle. If his wife, Sandy, gets angry, he keeps his distance until 'she gets herself under control.' Sandy is tired of living in this emotional desert and she's now demanding a vibrant, growing, and honest connection with John.

"I just want John to understand me -- and to give himself to me. I love his fairness, his non-judgmental attitude, and his ambition. What he loves about me is my passion, my caring, and my enthusiasm. So I love his 'head stuff' and he loves my 'heart stuff.' I'm trying to teach him more about emotions, but sometimes I get tired and irritated. It's like teaching an adult about sex. At thirty, John should be competent in expressing and feeling his emotions, but he's like a little kid who doesn't know how to feel. I understand why he's this way, but it's about time he changed!" Sandy sighed and looked downward in despair.

John certainly has some grief work to do about his parents' divorce, but in addition to venting the hurt and anger he feels, he desperately needs to emote and learn how to read others' emotions. What's sad is that society applauds homes like John's -- professional, rational, and cold. John is now paying the price of non-connection because feelings were never allowed to surface in his home environment. He's in kindergarten in his emotional development and has a long way to go to be emotionally aware and mature.

Choosing Other Graduate Students to Connect With

After completing grief work and learning to integrate emotions and intellect, we are ready to tackle interdependence -- the stage of joining honestly and deeply with others who are also ready for mature, growth-enhancing relationships. Those who have moved through their grief and codependency emerge into a new sense of adequacy and wholeness. Incorporating the lessons of discernment make us ready for connecting with other graduate students in interdependent relationships.

A prerequisite for interdependent connecting is owning one's power and truth and offering this gift of self to other empowered beings. Interdependent partners share equal responsibility for the furtherance of their relationship. The unequal power and controlling manipulations found in codependent relationships don't exist in interdependent relationships. Interdependent partners encourage each other's continuous growth and confront their weaknesses. Their connections are based in truth, love and want rather than need and fear. The characteristics of interdependent relationships are very different from codependent relationships.

Characteristics of Interdependent Relationships

1. Interdependent relationships teach us to share our truth with safe, non-judging peers

Individuals who are ready to connect in Interdependent Relationships have grown beyond the neediness and control of codependency. They have challenged and resolved their own internal fears and hurts. They are not above their lower emotions, they simply are no longer held captive by them. They scrutinize their own motives and behaviors. No longer defensive or fearful of revealing who they are, they freely share with those who are safe and non-judging. They have reached the state where their thoughts, feelings, and actions stem from a mature awareness of *why* they think, feel, and act as they do in any given situation. This awareness makes them open to constructive feedback from others who are, like themselves, open and committed to self-growth. Connections based in truth and candor allow them

274

to share both their healthy and mature sides and their immature and unhealed sides. With equals who desire mutual support and understanding, the depth of connection and the significance of personal interactions increase.

Committed therapy clients reach a point where they understand the origins of their dysfunctional thoughts and behavior. They learn to take the risks and challenges to change self-defeating patterns. They reach a point where they are ready to fill up with positive experiences and affirming connections. We often recommend they join a therapy group that provides positive interactions with other growing and aware people. The therapy group provides a safe, loving, and accepting environment to vent emotions, show unhealed wounds, and receive affirmation for progress. The therapy group is at the high level of maturation and ready for interdependent connecting when they show candor in sharing embarrassing secrets and courage in giving their perceptions to others even when their observations might be offensive.

Donna's Wednesday night group had been meeting for about a year when they reached a plateau and seemed ready to terminate group counseling. Donna had worked individually with group members and knew they had not shared some of their dark secrets with each other. She warned that unless they developed trust in each other and individual courage to stand in their total truth, they would fail to connect on a deep, interdependent level. The next week several secrets were shared during the group meeting. One member, Susan, was quiet during the session and didn't talk. Another group member, Jane, was committed to total truth and felt compelled to bring out her feelings about Susan's non-sharing behavior.

"Susan, you seem to be outside the house looking in the window. Why don't you come in and join us?" Jane said.

Susan replied that she really didn't want to talk.

Jane shot back. "This is making me very uncomfortable to say this, but your response is not acceptable to me. I want to honor your free will, but it's your pattern to distance yourself from the group. It's not fair to the rest of us. We take risks telling our truths and revealing our innermost secrets, thoughts, and feelings. You safely retreat into silence. You have no right to be a voyeur. If you don't participate and share who you are, you have no right to watch us. I'll trust you and feel safe with you only when you dare to take the same risks I'm taking. Only when you show me who you really are will I know you and trust you."

Susan was silent for a long moment while the other group members held their breaths waiting for her reply. Finally, Susan's body relaxed into the chair and she let out a sigh, as if relieving herself of a burden.

"You're right. I'm still too scared to take risks and show you who I really am. I'm scared to share my truth lest you judge or ridicule me. Intellectually I know that none of you will judge me, but the emotional scars from a ridiculing and shaming family freeze me in inaction. I know you all love me. I need to understand it emotionally and take the risks to reach out and trust. Thank you for helping me see myself and being courageous enough to speak what you saw. I know it was hard to say something that could provoke my anger. You obviously love me enough to take the risk of sharing your truth. I guess that's what real love and real connection are."

Interdependent connections are with equals who are committed to truth and mutual growth. Often, after the emotional catharsis of individual psychotherapy, group therapy is needed to practice new ways of acting and new ways of relating with others. Interdependence is rare, stimulating, and nurturing. It helps us move from codependent silence and control to a free and open way of being with others.

2. *Interdependent connections are Adult/Adult connections*

Interdependent partners accept full responsibility for their interactions and are willing to join with equals in mature adult/adult relationships. These are starkly different from codependent relationships. There are no power games or control maneuvers between Interdependent partners. There is freedom, acceptance, honoring of each others' free will, and focusing on being and becoming. Doing and spreading goodwill are natural by-products of being in this elevated state, but these relationships are not based on doing.

When people are open to self-scrutiny and willing to correct deficits that impede genuine connecting, then they're ready for an adult/adult connection. They must first remove defenses that impede their growth and blind them to learning new ways of perceiving and acting. They must look at the naked truth about themselves and the emotional forces that shape how they think and what they do.

Couples who have moved through codependency have the job of scrutinizing their partnership roles as well as scrutinizing their individual motives. They must forge a balanced adult/adult relationship from the ashes of parent/child codependency. Carl and Charlotte assumed the task of moving from codependency to interdependency. During a joint counseling session, they described a typical fight. Charlotte, more organized and structured, had approached Carl with a list of things she wanted to do over the weekend. She asked Carl to add his wants to the list so they could plan their weekend. Carl glanced at the list and grunted, "It's OK with me." The weekend came and Carl decided it was more important to go look at houses than to complete Charlotte's task list. She reluctantly acquiesced because she knew Carl would pout if she didn't. Her irritation showed through, however, and Carl angrily accused her of not wanting to plan for the future with him. He then shocked her by saying that they should spend time planning their separation. Charlotte spent the next few hours soothing his ruffled feelings.

In counseling, Donna told them they were pandering to each other's weaknesses rather than demanding empowered adult behavior.   Instead of accepting Carl's cursory review and acceptance of the list, Donna advised Charlotte to demand that Carl be an equal adult and participate in planning joint weekend activities. She explained that people can easily slither out of responsibility if they don't take ownership of a plan through participation. Donna also advised more open communication of their feelings with one another. If Charlotte had explained her need for focus and discipline, and Carl had explained his need for spontaneity and flexibility, compromise may have prevented the escalation of ill-feelings.   Donna then confronted Carl's threat to separate.   She told him the flight response was linked to a learned pattern of running away from life problems and fears. Instead of apologizing or absorbing blame, she instructed Charlotte to place responsibility back on Carl. Carl's fears of rejection and abandonment caused him to swing to an extreme conclusion that was not warranted. Carl needed to look at the immaturity of his flee response and commit to complete healing of his fears.

Without defensively blocking Donna's advice and her analysis of the reasons for their dysfunctional transaction, Carl and Charlotte absorbed the lessons needed for their growth into full adulthood. They scrutinized themselves and were appreciative of advice that would lead them to a more empowered adult/adult union. They committed to making each other aware of their emotions, to speaking their truth openly and pushing each other to their highest level of maturity and connection.   They committed to an empowered adult/adult relationship.

3. *Interdependent partners expect equality and reciprocity in their relationships*

Instead of relying on someone else to do the things they would rather avoid, interdependent partners assume the responsibility of becoming fully sufficient. They don't lean on others to take care of their basic needs. They don't buy into gender roles that limit their growth and independence. Parasitic, one-up/one-down relationships are seen for what they are -- growth inhibiting and destructive to both the leader and follower.

Whenever one person in a relationship fails to clear himself or herself of emotional impediments, the potential of their bond is lessened. Whenever people accept less than wholly self-sufficient they are falling short of interdependent connecting. Angela is one person who came face-to-face with death and decided she could no longer accept inequality in her thirty-year marriage. Angela had always been the able caretaker of the family. While their children were young, Angela toed the line of discipline, while Hugh, her husband, chose to be more permissive and laid back. When their youngest reached high school, Angela joined the land development firm that Hugh managed. From the beginning, she took over the responsibility for daily operations leaving Hugh free to chase speculative ventures. Ultimately the ventures failed, largely because Hugh was obsessed with selfless caretaking of damaged, selfish people. Now Angela is fifty-five and a survivor of breast cancer. She's tired of taking all the responsibility. Therapy taught her that she was the hero child in an alcoholic family, an experience that imprinted her with the codependent message "love is earned." Angela worked hard to free herself from codependency. She's now pushing Hugh to look at his own abusive family and the emotional havoc it's caused him. Angela is tired of being the responsible mother of an undeveloped husband. She's now demanding he become her equal.

When Hugh started seeing Donna, he complained about

Angela's demands on him to change and grow. One day he told Donna about a problem his daughter, Maria, was having in her marriage. His son-in-law, Al, was raised in a military family where everyone's energy concentrated on the father. Now a father himself, Al arrogantly pursues his career aspirations without regard for Maria's wants and needs. Maria was ready to give Al an ultimatum -- either he grow past his selfishness or she would leave him. Hugh asked if Al were likely to recognize that his selfishness and immaturity were destroying the relationship. Donna replied that two conditions would probably determine if the strained relationship would improve. The first condition was the depth of Al's commitment to Maria and their child. The second was Maria's strength and perseverance in pushing Al to becoming an equal partner. Suddenly Hugh got it.

"I'll stop complaining about Angela from now on. What she's doing is pushing me to be her equal. She's waited for me to grow up for thirty years. I couldn't talk to her about my feelings. I told myself that I was protecting her when I didn't share my fears and insecurities. What I was really doing was shutting her out. We lived out our roles, but we didn't really connect. She deserves better. Maria deserves better with Al. It's time I become strong enough to be Angela's equal." Breaking through denial and looking at his deficits were Hugh's first steps out of codependency and into the equality of an interdependent relationship.

4. *Interdependent relationships empower rather than enable*

People who have gone through tunnel work seldom turn back toward codependency. Their commitment to growth and empowerment leads them to seek others who are also willing to scrutinize themselves and stand in truth. Those who are ready for interdependent relationships aren't interested in "playing down" with those less developed. That's not to say they are unwilling to help others who earnestly want to grow. Those committed to

280

enlightenment and truth are welcomed as colleagues, no matter where they may be along their journey toward empowerment. However, those ready for interdependent relationships generally separate from those choosing to stay asleep in codependent denial and weaknesses. The separation may be intellectual and emotional rather than physical. When one refuses to grow, those more enlightened accept their decision with sadness. Old codependent relationships fade as awakened people move onward where they find others who hear the same call. Again, graduate students need other graduate students to stimulate and support their mutual growth.

5. *Their Friendship and Love is Freeing*

Interdependent relationships differ from codependent relationships in their absence of power manipulations or control tactics. Each person in the relationship is free to decide what is right and true for him or her. The autonomy found in interdependent relationships contrasts with obligatory codependent associations. Instead of spending time and energy because of external expectations, people spend time with each other because they want to and because their connections are meaningful and rewarding. They don't spend idle time acting out roles. Rather, they spend time together learning, growing, and enjoying life.

Using the analogy of energy exchange, a codependent relationship with one less developed person will pull energy from the more developed person. With interdependent relationships, the energy transfer is equal. Instead of feeling drained of energy, interdependent partners are charged up by their intellectual, emotional and spiritual equals. This equality frees them from caretaking so they're able to grow continually upward.

6. *They Connect in Truth, Love, and Want -- Not Need*

Individuals at this level connect in truth, love, and want rather than fear and need. There is no obligatory association in interdependence. People choose to be with others because they gain by doing so. Each interdependent partner has progressed or is in the process of progressing past growth-inhibiting fears. Because the partners are wholly self-sufficient, their purpose for connecting with others is mutual growth and enjoyment rather than codependent neediness.

The urge to connect interdependently was reported in a client's dream. Janice was unhappy in her codependent marriage where she was the stronger partner. She took the bulk of responsibility for mundane tasks, emotional support, and creative planning within her family. When her children were teen-agers, Janice met Mark, a new colleague who was every bit her equal. She denied and repressed her attraction to Mark because of her marriage and family obligations. She never knew if Mark felt the same for they never acknowledged the attraction.

Ten years after first meeting Mark, Janice was in a different job and had "settled" for the level of connection in her marriage. She felt vaguely depressed and listless. She was surprised when she dreamed of Mark one night. In the dream she had an exciting new idea and picked up the phone to tell him about it. But, at the point she was dialing Mark's number, her husband walked into the room. She felt embarrassed and quickly hung up. Later she tried to call Mark again, only to remember that he had moved from his old residence. As she spoke with the directory assistance operator, her husband walked into the room again. She hung up without asking for Mark's number. And so the dream continued, with Janice trying to reach Mark, but being continually blocked by her husband's entrance into the room.

When Janice told Donna the dream, Donna commented that the bond between her and Mark was obviously strong,

282

extending five years since she had last seen him. She wanted an equal partner to relate to and to share her excitement over a new idea. She obviously felt that her husband was not her equal, and she had no desire to share this information with him. But her obligations to her husband blocked her communication with Mark. The codependent marriage was based on need. Janice had probably reached a point in life where she wanted to connect with an equal in love, want, and truth.

7. *Relationships are based on being and becoming -- not doing*

The focus of these relationships is on *being and becoming* rather than *doing*. One of the most difficult obstacles in couples' counseling is to help people move past their finger pointing. Blaming another person for what they did or did not do creates an impasse that many couples can't or won't surmount. Blaming the other person and seeing oneself as guilt-free creates a defensive blindness that is lethal to true connecting.

In our counseling and workshops, we urge people to look past what their partners have *done* and instead concentrate on *who they are*. The emphasis switches to the essence of the person. Is the person loving, courageous, and curious? Does he or she engage in objective self-scrutiny and accept constructive feedback? Does he accept his human-ness and dark side while ever growing toward the light? Is he uplifting and inspiring? Do we feel better after spending time with him? These questions focus on the true essence of the person, and are more important than the minutiae of day-to-day *doing*. One cannot achieve interdependent relationships by doing. Readiness for interdependence depends on one's ability to be his true self and his willingness to offer this gift of self to another empowered being.

Another aspect of doing that is contrary to interdependence is that doing constitutes an act of commission -- an overt act is committed. But what about acts of omission --

283

when someone is expected to do something and doesn't. For example, a husband is expected to be sensitive to his wife's emotional needs (and vice versa). But suppose she is upset and crying and he does nothing. What's impeding the intimate bond between husband and wife? Not what he does, but what he fails to do. The invisibility of acts of omission makes it difficult to see the root of a connection problem. However, if judged by the level of being, the problem (the husband's lack of emotional development) is easy to see. In this case, the husband simply was not emotionally mature enough to connect with his wife's needs. Therefore, intimacy was obstructed.

Donna and Michael experienced the difference between *codependent doing* and *interdependent being* early in their marriage. It was late at night and they were working on an important project. Michael made a comment that Donna disagreed with. When Donna voiced her disagreement, Michael asked what was wrong with her (implying that she was in a bad mood). Donna told him that she had a right to disagree without his blaming and shaming her. Michael realized her hurt and anger, and quickly responded by asking Donna for a kiss. When she told him she wasn't ready to kiss and bury her irritation, he looked genuinely concerned. She then told him to relax because her love for him was based on who he was and not on what he said or did. She knew him fully and loved him because of his essence of goodness, love, and courage. Disagreements will come and go between couples, but when the relationship is based on the inner cores or essences of the partners, the bond is securely anchored.

Steps for Achieving Interdependent Relationships

Interdependence is defined as a relationship based in truth and love in which partners facilitate their mutual growth to wholeness. In interdependence, friends and intimate partners join in total truth and openness with one another. How do people achieve the readiness to connect interdependently? The major steps in achieving readiness for Interdependence are (1) balancing the mind and emotions; (2) moving from externalized needs to internalized needs; (3) trusting spiritual guidance; (4) recognizing our mirrors; and (5) learning to attach and detach.

(1) *Balancing Mind and Emotions*

Emotional clearing is the key to achieving alignment between mind and emotion. Those ready for the depth of interdependent relationships have cleared themselves of major fears in the basement cleaning of tunnel work. With a keen ability to scrutinize themselves, they are no longer tossed about by unconscious motivations. They understand their own emotions and are sensitive to the emotions of others. They are able to respond genuinely from their hearts. While discernment is more mental and intuitive, catharsis and healing are more emotional. To do both simultaneously is difficult but imperative. Sandy found out how difficult mental/emotional balance was after six months in therapy.

Sandy shuffled into Donna's office and collapsed on the sofa with a sigh.

"Are you tired or depressed today, Sandy?" asked Donna.

Sandy threw a sofa pillow in Donna's direction. "Damn it, how do you know how I'm feeling before I know it? I've been depressed all week, hardly working at all, but I didn't realize it until this morning. Why should I be depressed? Christmas was always a happy time -- in fact, the only happy time in our family. Dad would make a special effort to stop drinking. Mom was busy with Christmas and wasn't as depressed as she usually was. But here I am at Christmas time and I'm totally depressed. I really don't want to go home this year."

"Sandy, you've been in therapy for six months now. Your eyes are opened. While your parents gave you what they could, they didn't give all you needed. You now see that Christmas was just a time to put on a happy mask and play at connecting. There was no deep connection between your parents. There's no intimate bond between you and your parents. Now you want that depth and truth in your adult relationships," Donna explained.

Sandy nodded her agreement. "Yes, I'm just so tired of being Miss Entertainment, smiling and acting happy for others. I want to be me, and if me is sullen, I want to be accepted for being sullen. I want others to love me for who I am. I want to know how to bond genuinely with others, but damn, it's like being expected to pass a physics exam and no one has taught me physics. I'm angry that no one taught me to love myself and to connect with others. They still don't love themselves enough to be open and fearless. Deep down, they fear that they are inadequate -- and they fear being rejected. Dad will drink to drown out his fears and Mom will simply avoid anything that's touchy or too deep. I understand why they are that way, but I want them to be different. I want them to know me and allow me to know them."

Sandy had learned a lot during her six months of therapy. Her ability to discern the motives and levels of development of others had increased dramatically. She learned how to appropriately vent her feelings. And she learned that it hurts when you see the stunted maturation of loved ones., but don't have the power to change them. For now, Sandy continues to balance her mind and emotions and she looks for others who do the same.

(2) *Moving from Externalized Needs to Internalized Needs*

Just as people become more internally oriented as they progress to higher levels of understanding, they also focus on different life needs. The psychotherapist, Abraham Maslow, outlined five different levels of human need. The needs are hierarchical in nature: that is, a person must satisfy lower level needs before advancing to higher level needs.   In our experience, we've found people working on multiple need levels at the same time. From the most basic to the most advanced, human needs are (1) physiological; (2) safety and security; (3) love and belongingness; (4) self-esteem; and (5) self-actualization.

Physiological needs: Physiological needs include the things we need to survive physically: air, food, shelter, etc. Those focused on physiological survival operate as if they are living in a war zone: all's fair to ensure their survival. There is little focus on the rights or needs of other people. It is a "survival of the fittest world" for those fixated on their physiological needs. People fixed at this level hesitate to step on or hurt others to ensure their own survival. They win at other people's expense. Those overly concerned with money, status, or position are fixated on their physiological needs. They often come from emotionally and/or physically deprived or abusive homes. Parents only care about themselves, and their children grow up to model this self-absorption. Disciples of Darkness and Power Mongers are stuck on physiological needs.

Safety and security needs: Safety and security needs are based on a person's perception that self protection is essential for his survival in a hostile world. People raised in unstable, abusive, or alcoholic households often exhibit unmet safety and security needs. Because they were neglected or abused, they never learned to trust others. They generally don't strike out at others. Like turtles, they retreat into their shells for survival.   Their predominant attribute is fear. They look out after number one; it matters little if others are being hurt as long as their security isn't jeopardized. Disciples of Darkness and Power Mongers are also stuck trying to meet these needs.

Love and belongingness needs: Most people live day-to-day without having their need for love and belongingness satisfied. They grow into adulthood believing that the only way to be loved is to meet the expectations and needs of others. Always externally focused on other people, they spend little time learning to love themselves. Most people base love and belongingness on superficial connecting and unspoken *doing contracts*: "I'm loved if this person spends time with me or that person buys me a gift."

As long as we haven't done our internal work and learned to love ourselves fully, our need for love and belongingness is met only on a surface level. This need is satisfied only when we connect on a deeper level -- at the core of our being. Only when we truly touch the heart and soul of another do we find the need for love and belongingness satisfied. Disempowered Dependents are stuck at this level, trying to meet love and belongingness needs by appeasing others. Armored Awakes and Disciples of Light have learned to meet their love and belongingness needs by first focusing on and loving themselves.

Self-esteem needs: True self-esteem is realized by few of us, and only when we know ourselves and our abilities well enough to let go of all fear of inadequacy. Our security is not based in the ungrounded arrogance of ego, but in the confidence and self-knowledge that we are sufficient. We believe in our creative abilities and find fulfillment following the inner voice that guides us to pursue our true life work. The world doesn't define us, nor does it define our purpose. This we do for ourselves. People with high esteem are independent of the world's judgment. We know who we are and don't need external adulation to feel worthy and important. Armored Awakes and Disciples of Light are capable of satisfying self-esteem needs. The other three maturational types (Disciples of Darkness, Power Mongers, Disempowered Dependents) are not ready to claim true self-esteem.

Self-actualization needs: The need for self-actualization refers to our innate drive to reach our full human potential. Although we all have this need to fulfill our highest purpose and meaning, few among us do the work or take the risks to achieve

288

self-actualization. Maslow estimated that fewer than 1% of the population ever reaches self-actualization. He included Abraham Lincoln, Thomas Jefferson, Albert Einstein, and Eleanor Roosevelt among the handful who were self-actualized.

It's basic human nature to attend to lower needs before recognizing and meeting higher needs. A person who has not adequately met his safety and security needs is unlikely to be working on his self-esteem needs. The hierarchy of needs loosely relates to age and level of development. In childhood, the emphasis is on physiological and safety/security needs. During adolescence, the focus switches to love and belongingness needs. By extension, those who reach true maturity should be focused on self-esteem and self-actualization. Few reach empowered adulthood. The majority come from codependent homes that teach fear, weakness, and control. As a result, they will be developmentally delayed and fixated on lower needs.

The lower needs (physiological and safety/security) are externally-oriented and environmentally-dependent. During peace time, those living in a prosperous society take physiological and safety/security needs for granted. When the environment is hostile (in wartime or in poverty-stricken nations) the lower physiological and safety/security needs dominate. Whether these first two needs are met depends largely on the environment around a person. The higher needs are more internally-focused. For example, self-esteem and self-actualization are generally specific to the individual and independent of external conditions. Mother Teresa, a nun living in a severely poverty-stricken area, is an example of one who rises above the external circumstances and functions on the self-esteem and self-actualization levels. We've read about prisoners of war who maintain high spirits and serve as inspirations of hope for others. These are people operating at higher need levels. They rise above the fears attached to physicality and function on a spiritual level.

The transition point between the lower, externally-oriented needs and the higher, internally-oriented needs falls at love and belongingness. Codependents define love and belongingness externally. If they are loved and accepted by others, then they believe this need is met. Those who have completed tunnel work are more emotionally, intellectually and spiritually mature and define love and belongingness internally. Love and belongingness is met when they learn to accept and love themselves. The progression of human growth toward wholeness is the movement from lower, externally-focused needs to higher, internally-focused needs. As we progress on the road to empowerment, we become less focused on outer circumstance and more focused on inner truth.

(3) *Trusting Spiritual Guidance*

The processes of internal referencing and intuitive awareness we have outlined in this book almost automatically open a person to spiritual development. Spiritual development focuses on the abstract rather than the concrete, the whole instead of the part, the pattern instead of the isolated piece. When we commit to spiritual maturity, we commit to rise above the mundane worries of the world and to view our lives from an elevated vantage point. Questions such as "How do the experiences and events in my life fit together to form a pattern?" become important. "What is the meaning of my life experiences?" "What is my life purpose?" "Why are certain people a part of my life and what are they teaching me?" All of these gain significance as inner fear and doubt are released and we claim our importance as integral parts of the Universal plan. We experience life from an elevated vantage point and we become open to spiritual guidance. Spiritual guidance comes in many forms: meditation and prayer, dreams, visions, peak experiences, near death experiences, implausible synchronicities, and knowings. Regardless of the form it takes, all spiritual guidance seems to lead toward one goal: to reunite people with their core beliefs and principles. Donna tells about a dream that signified her own commitment to spiritual awakening and development:

I was riding a magnificent white horse along the edge of an ocean. A dispassionate observer, I watched myself in the dream as if watching a movie screen. Yet I felt all the emotions of the actress within the drama.

My horse was running at full speed. I bent forward, hanging onto his neck to avoid falling. At first I thought it was excitement and exhilaration I felt. Then I realized I was terrified. I was looking desperately for a place to hide. I glanced upward to the top of the cliff bordering the beach. There was an old farmhouse and a barn behind it. My horse gingerly climbed the steep path upward. The farmhouse appeared abandoned. We traveled around the house to the barn. Once inside, I secured the doors. I washed the perspiration from my horse and lovingly brushed his long flowing mane. This was truly a beautiful animal, but he was more than an animal to me. I loved him with an intensity reserved for special relationships.

Tired from the long ride, I lay down on a pile of hay and drifted to sleep. Suddenly a loud noise awakened me. In the semi-darkness of the barn, the light streaming from the opened doors blinded me. The silhouetted shapes of four men were approaching. My heart beat quickened and fear strangled my voice
"Give us the horse!" the lead man demanded.

"No!" squeaked out of me, barely audible.

"We don't want to harm you. Give us that horse, and you won't be harmed."

The battle in my mind was rapid and fierce. If I gave up my horse, I might escape with my life. If I didn't, I would surely die. There was no escape. I had to make an immediate and irreversible decision. I knew they'd kill my beloved horse. I was his only chance. He had been with me all my life. How could I go on living without him? But he was a horse. Wasn't a human life more important?

291

Something inside me took over.   It was a force so great it conquered fear. It was a determination so strong it was immovable. The next voice I heard was steady and sure. I could hardly believe the voice came from me .... "You'll have to kill me first before you get my horse!"

-*Donna's dream*

"I awoke immediately after speaking this final conviction, so the dream didn't play out to a conclusion. Some days after this vivid dream I asked another psychoanalyst to help me interpret the meaning. Claiming competency in Jungian dream analysis, he said the white horse symbol had something to do with repressed sexuality. This didn't ring true with me, so I discarded his idea. Some years later, embroiled in a stressful battle against the unfair tactics of corrupt university administration, I turned to the Bible for guidance."   The Bible opened to Revelation 19:11-14:

Then I saw heaven opened, and behold, a white horse. And He who sat on him   was called Faithful and True, and in righteousness He judges and makes war . . . And the armies in heaven, clothed in fine linen, white and clean, followed Him on white horses.

The Bible verse pointed to the true meaning of my dream. I was committed to truth and righteousness and the white horse carried Christ who was also committed to stand for these principles. The dream occurred during a tumultuous period when administrators lied about me to keep me from winning tenure. This experience would sorely test my commitment to self-love and self-esteem. Would I be destroyed by their slanderous words and inhumane treatment toward me -- or would I cling to the truth and to my faith?   My belief in universal justice and love was unshakable. As represented in my dream, the fear of death (and death of my beloved career) wouldn't dissuade me from my commitment to love and truth.

I looked around at my colleagues at the university. One by one, they all capitulated to the dictatorial power of a malignant force that ruled with fear and attracted other dark-spirited people to the university. The manipulations of the KGB or the ruthless power tactics of the Mafia were the same energies that infused the university. Faculty and students became more and more despondent and hopeless. The light of truth and love were almost completely destroyed.

Only one person, Michael, stood with me against the evil power of Disciples of Darkness. Michael and I had a force within us that didn't allow us to surrender to man's evil. They couldn't steal our white horses. Love and truth were the foundation of our being. Our experience opened our eyes and we saw how undeveloped and cowardly others were. We learned that we genuinely connected only with those who shared our conviction to stand for truth and love. We also learned that these people are few.

Many claim to stand on principle, but when confronted with the possibility of personal loss, they choose the safe path and conform to the wishes of those who hold power. Too much of what we call reality is unprincipled, ego-centered "me-ism." The risks in being truly principled and standing on truth and love are just too great. It's easier and safer to talk about principles but hypocritically hide when adherence to principles exacts a price. Hypocrites disregard the inner voice urging them to grow to full empowerment. They numb out their feelings and stay imprisoned in fear. When choosing to get along with the unprincipled majority, they actually surrender a most precious inner gift -- truth and righteousness. Only empowered people stand for principle. Only developed people will stand for truth and love. Only Disciples of Light will sacrifice themselves to move mankind to a higher place. These few are capable of interdependent connecting and true friendship. We can choose to become empowered and connect interdependently with other evolved souls, but first we need to shed the world's false security and follow our inner core of truth and love.

(4)   _Recognizing Our Mirrors_

Our *mirrors* are the people who are like us. Their commitment to self-empowerment reflects our own commitment to wholeness. They are the people who are capable of really connecting with us. We need to recognize our mirrors because we need them for support and for modeling. Like actual mirrors, they reflect back to us the lessons we need to learn -- the directions we need to follow to grow. They are our guides who help us find and unlock our inner truth. At the stage of interdependence, our mirrors exhibit sterling qualities of true friendship -- a deep and mutual trust, similar levels of development, openness and vulnerability in sharing inner truths and feelings, and a commitment to earning an A+ in the school of life.

Connecting with those who serve as our mirrors is the exact opposite of what is found in *codependent* relationships. Our mirror connections are deeply truthful and are based in mutual respect, shared responsibility, and joint caring and commitment. They are not judging, manipulative, or controlling. These are the people we can count on to tell us when they believe we are wrong, and to praise us when we succeed. They will stand by us when the chips are down. They are strong enough to join us in a true heart connection.

In the foyer of our home hangs a small calligraphic inscription. It depicts an open doorway with the saying "A friend is one who comes in when the whole world has gone out."   How sad but true. Many of us go through life not knowing who our real friends are.   The illusion of true connection and friendship surrounds us. We all have acquaintances we consider friends: co-workers, neighbors, and family members. When we hit one of those rough spots in life, our friends are put to the test of true friendship.

294

The sad truth is many of the people we feel closest to are really nothing more than acquaintances. What makes the difference? What are the qualities of a deep and meaningful relationship? The answer lies in the degree to which we connect interdependently in truth, love, and courage. Interdependent connection is largely determined by our own commitment to living our deepest internal principles and finding those with the same commitment.

(5) *Learning to Attach and Detach*

Readiness for interdependent relationships brings with it changes. We need to attach to those like us who have committed to growth and empowerment and detach from those who languish in codependent fear, stagnancy, and neediness. While attachment is exciting, detachment is painful. Art learned that readiness for interdependency was the bittersweet mixture of attachment and detachment.

From infancy on, Art was different from other boys. He silently observed the human dramas occurring around him. As he grew up, his introspective nature separated him from the rough and tumble world of male competitiveness. An inner gauge signaled the misfit between the world's exploits and his inner truth. In most cases, he decided to detach from the games others engaged in without conscious awareness or examination -- he simply followed his unconscious knowings. For example, he saw little use in Catholic ritual and masses said in Latin. For him, religion was a hollow and impersonal game, so he simply abandoned religion.

Art clearly saw that his parents didn't have a truly loving and bonded relationship. Although he didn't understand codependency during his youth, he knew that his parents stayed together because they believed there was no other choice. The relationship between them was controlling and fearful. Art hated their arguments and the household tension. His parents' dysfunctional relationship made Art fearful of romantic connections. He saw male-female relationships as hollow and ritualized game playing. Relationships held interest only until the inevitable power and control games of codependency emerged. He wanted truth, challenge and freedom in his relationships. Not finding the right ingredients in male-female relationships of the '70s, he sought interdependence in communal living. The group of men and women he lived with sought honesty and self-growth in their connections. They were after the true connections that were lacking in their families. The communal family became a family substitute with the members trying to teach each other how to attach.

Art did attach to several group members, but as the years passed the tolls of living eroded their energy and strained their bonds with each other. Group members ministered to the physical and emotional needs of a man within their surrogate family who slowly died of a brain tumor. Art and others accepted the responsibility of caring for this dying loved one. The physical price was great -- increased stress, loss of sleep, and frazzled nerves. The emotional price was greater -- loss of the attachment they so cherished. The attachment was pushed aside by the emptiness of loss and fear of pain. When you attach deeply and then lose that attachment, it hurts. So Art and the others began numbing out. After the man's death, the surrogate family started to scatter.

One by one, family members left the house and chose codependent relationships to retreat to. Equality, challenge, and truth were not major ingredients of their new relationships. Donna saw Art years after he left the communal group home. His eyes sparkled and an easy smile widened as he talked about his days living in the group home. He had found attachment for a brief time, only to lose it. He was now in an unhappy marriage with an emotionally abusive wife. He was back to his original state of detaching from the controlling games of others. His wife tried to steal his self-esteem and his power. His only means of protecting himself was to emotionally detach.

In a counseling session, Donna told Art about her personal attachment and detachment lesson. She was given a Siamese kitten, Muffet, soon after graduating from college. This cat was her baby for the six years before her first child was born. She diligently guarded Muffet's well-being by keeping her inside the townhouse apartment at all times. The busy street outside was dangerous for roaming animals. But the more anxious Donna became to keep Muffet inside, the more determined the cat became to get outside. As soon as the door cracked, Muffet darted outside with lightning-fast speed. One night Muffet darted out the door and hid in the woods behind the apartments. She was frantic with worry, but her search was futile. For over an hour Donna searched for her. Finally she just gave up and sat on a stump and cried. Anger, fear, and sorrow poured out until her emotions were exhausted. Then Donna regained her mental clarity and realized her foolishness. She was so intent on protecting herself from the pain of losing Muffet that she failed to act in a loving way -- concerned about her cat's needs and rights. Muffet was imprisoned by Donna's fear. No wonder she tried to escape at each possible chance.

Donna resolved to love Muffet as much as she could without worrying about losing her. If Muffet returned, Donna decided she would let her outside the apartment for frequent walks. Donna believed she was strong enough to endure the grief if Muffet died in traffic during one of her visits outside. She resolved to let go of her fear and control and cherish the time she had with Muffet. Love and fear are opposite forces. By holding onto fear, Donna was strangling love. As if waiting for Donna's inner transformation from fear to love, Muffet appeared shortly thereafter. Muffet lived nineteen and a half years. She went outside and enjoyed her freedom for the rest of her life and died a natural death of old age.

Muffet's story was parallel to Art's fear of attachment. Art was afraid to attach because when he had tried it, he was hurt. The close attachments he had at the communal home had disintegrated. After the loss of friendships, Art built a protective wall around himself and he married a woman incapable of attaching. In choosing a detached relationship, Art was giving in to his fear. He feared the pain of loss. He ultimately faced the same decision as Donna had with her cat: Would he stay safe by catering to his fears or would he risk the possible pain of loss for the joy of knowing love and attachment? The choice is ours also -- will we attach to love or will we attach to fear. We can't attach to them both -- for one repels the other.

Interdependency allows true attachment. Connections are deep, honest and real. It hurts when you lose an interdependent attachment. It hurts even more when people don't risk true heart connections, but rather hide behind their fears and numb their feelings. Interdependent relationships are the exact opposite of relationships based in fear and dependency. Interdependent connections demand truth and commitment to growth. It's the ability to connect deeply, to give without barriers, and to receive in total honesty that prepares us for total empowerment and intimate love.

Chapter Ten

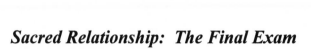

Sacred Relationship: The Final Exam

Sacred Relationship: The Final Exam

I'm walking down the narrow streets of Charleston, South Carolina. I'm wearing a long, dark dress that looks like Civil War era fashion. I enjoy the sight of pastel-colored townhouses and huge shade trees lining the pebble-stone streets. I come to a familiar townhouse and pull the brass door knocker on the massive mahogany door. An older woman opens the door. She's also wearing old-fashioned clothes: a dark dress with flowing skirt skimming the floor, a high-neck collar edged with lace, and a tight bodice that makes her slim figure appear taut and erect. She has an air of authority and integrity. Her long, light-colored hair is neatly tied up in a bun, reminding me of a proper English school marm. She's very attractive, with soft eyes and relaxed smile.

"What do you want, my dear?" she asks as I wait outside her door.

"I want you to arrange this marriage," I answer.

"You're much too young, you're not ready yet," she replies to my request.

I'm aware that I'm about twenty years old -- certainly old enough to decide if I want to marry. Behind me stands a shadowy figure -- a young man I believe, but I can't see him clearly. He's probably the one I want to marry, but I can't see his face so his identity is muted in the dream.

"I'm old enough to marry, and I want you to arrange this marriage," I insist in a louder voice.

"You don't know what you're asking. This will be very difficult. You don't know how hard this will be. Give this more time. You'll be ready someday, but not now." Her caring and concern are evident in the kind tone of her voice.

I simply will not be dissuaded. "Look here. I have earned all this gold from my acting. I am very accomplished. I'll give it all to you if you arrange this marriage." I pull a cloth pouch from a pocket in my skirt. Untying the drawstrings and loosening the top, I grab several large gold coins from the pouch.

301

She looks amazed at my display of wealth. She then nods her head and holds out her hand for the bulging pouch. She quickly turns to grab a cloak hanging on a nearby nail. After swirling the cloak around her shoulders and securely tying her bonnet, she rustles by me and heads down the narrow street.

Not until I see her figure fading in the distance do I realize that she is me. I'm both the young woman and the older woman. The older me is wiser, but the younger me is more determined and enthusiastic.

dreamed by Debra, age 43

The meaning of this dream was not clear for several years. Debra wasn't contemplating marriage at the time -- in fact just the opposite. Her marriage of twenty years was more a business contract than a vibrant, growing marriage. She and her husband had long neglected passion and romance. Debra was struggling with the decision to leave a comfortable, but dead, relationship. Soon after the dream, Debra decided to separate from her husband. During a therapy session, Debra told Donna of her dream and her confusion about its meaning. Donna suggested the two views of herself portrayed in the dream -- the older, wiser woman and the young, determined woman -- may indicate a conflict between her desire to grow and face new life challenges and her fear of risk-taking and change. Her higher, more spiritual self was represented by the older woman who urged patience. Her younger self was more worldly and didn't fully comprehend the difficulty involved in a commitment. Marriage is a commitment, and Donna believed that Debra was ready to commit to a personal transformation. Debra had been ensnared in codependency for forty-three years and now it was time for her to commit to taking risks and leaving her fears behind.

Except for her marriage relationship, Debra was already advanced. She had a doctorate and was successful in her career. She was in individual counseling and also went to a therapy group

302

twice a month. The women in Debra's group were very open and honest. On the emotional and intellectual levels, Debra was indeed head and shoulders above others. Debra was well on her way to becoming self-actualized until George entered the picture. Debra had been separated for only three months when George expressed interest in dating her. At first Debra declined, saying that she wasn't ready to date. But George persisted and Debra decided to go out "as friends." What she learned during the friendship phase was that George was so much like her that he could complete her sentences. He knew what she was thinking and he was particularly sensitive to what she was feeling. What could have been her greatest blessing turned into Debra's worst nightmare. As her attraction turned into love, the darkest corners of Debra's emotional basement pushed upward. Debra became jealous of George's business relationships with women. She looked for any signs that he was leading her on or ready to abandon her. She picked unnecessary fights when he didn't show her undivided attention. Debra's hard won independence and emotional maturity were sliding down the drain. Instead of progressing toward self-actualization, she was retreating into codependent control and fear.

Debra felt she was going crazy. She'd rather push George away than deal with the fears and volatile emotions sweeping over her. During a counseling session, she asked Donna to help her make sense of her roller coaster feelings.

"Some days are fine. But then I find myself getting angry because George hasn't called and then I feel used -- like I'm there for him when he wants me, but he's not there for me. I know he needs some time alone, and so do I, but when we are away from each other I get suspicious of him. I'm not really sure he loves me. Neither of us talks about the future. I don't know if it would make any difference if we were planning marriage. My head says that a deep, committed relationship isn't contingent on a legal contract. I was married to Tom and we never connected so I know that legal formality isn't the answer. I feel deeply connected on all levels -- intellectual, emotional, and spiritual -- with George. It's as if we are one soul in two bodies. I've never loved anyone like I love George. My heart is afraid of the tremendous vulnerability I feel. A marriage commitment would help assure me, but both of us are afraid to bring the subject up. I know he's afraid of rejection, and I guess I'm still afraid of abandonment." Debra looked to Donna for understanding and empathy.

"Debra, I know what you're going through because it's exactly what I went through when Michael and I were going together but were not committed to a long-term relationship. Other sacred relationship partners go through this anguishing phase. Remember your dream about the older, wiser you and the younger you? The older woman told you to reconsider your resolve to get married. She told you that marriage was too hard and you weren't ready. But the younger you insisted you were ready and freely gave your hard-earned acting money to pay for the marriage. I think you've been acting your entire lifetime -- playing the codependent game by marrying an emotionally unavailable partner, earning educational degrees, and being successful in your career. Your acting has taught you much and you're willing to trade in your rich lessons for the chance to truly connect in love. But a true marriage is difficult to achieve. First of all, you'll be taking the greatest risk in your life. If you truly connect on a deep level with another, what happens to you if that person leaves?

I remember when my two children, Dana and David, were born. I looked at them and they were so tiny, so sweet and perfect. Both times, I felt a love so powerful it floored me. I especially remember the fear I felt with my first born. When I first looked at her, I surprised myself by saying, 'Donna, you have really gone and done it now. If anything happens to this baby you'll be devastated!' Prior to her birth, I kept a safe distance between myself and others. Now my defenses were all gone. There was no distance, only complete union of emotion and soul.

That's what you're risking with George. Your connection with him has the potential of being so deep that you'll be destroyed if he leaves. That's why part of you keeps trying to push him away. If he leaves now, you'll still be safe and numb. If you give your heart fully and he leaves, you'll collapse under the pain. George is your mirror. He is so like you that the boundaries between the two of you are blurred. The greatest risk in life is to love fully and without boundaries. Debra, you know this, because this is your greatest fear. Your father left when he divorced your mother, and you haven't seen him since you were thirteen. You thought you had finished your grief work, but George has brought up your deep hurt and fear of being abandoned. Your higher self told you that a true marriage was difficult and you weren't ready, but you insisted. Now George is in your path -- and you either heal completely and grow to wholeness or you live out your life wearing a false mask and acting a role."

Donna's words were sharp but true, and Debra appreciated the honesty. It took several more months, but Debra regained her security and self-esteem. She trusted her own sufficiency to handle the ups and downs of life either with or without George. She resolved to move beyond fear and connect fully if and when George was also ready for a sacred relationship.

When people connect on a deep level of emotional and intellectual understanding, they often assume that the road they travel in building and strengthening their relationship will be smooth. Our experience is that the opposite occurs. When people have the greatest likelihood of joining with a soul mate, they encounter the greatest obstacles. Yet, the brave of heart persevere and learn the lessons that lead to the deepest and most complete of all human connections.

The Purposes of Sacred Relationships

We can choose to see the world as a place that victimizes us or we can choose to see the world as a classroom offering continuing opportunities and lessons for personal growth and empowerment. Unfortunately, most of us grow into old age without ever knowing or being exposed to a truly empowered person. We have few, if any, models to pattern after. There are plenty who claim to be teachers and who offer to help us along our paths. But, on closer inspection, we find these "teachers" as out-of-balance as we are.

The answer to empowerment cannot be found outside, in a book, a dogma, or in the wisdom of a *guru*. It can only be found within each one of us. We must claim our power -- and to do that, we must release those things that hold us back. In this book, we have led you through the process of tunnel work during which you develop a deep intimacy with your feelings, your anger, your hurts, your fears, and your need to control. We've emphasized the need to embrace each of your hurts and fears so they no longer control you. This 's the process of owning our power.

We each hold the keys to our own happiness. But to claim it, we have to give up our claim as victims. We must stop seeing life, and the world, as a contest which we must control and win -- or we must lose. Life is not a negative experience unless we choose to see it so. For us, life is about *becoming* and *being* empowered. Empowerment is that place described by Carl Rogers where, no matter what the circumstance or difficulty confronting us, we know we are *sufficient*. In that place, joy lies in the day-to-day experiences of living. Each heartache or triumph provides us with repeated opportunities to experience and grow through the full gamut of human emotion, creativity, and courage.

The exciting good news is that we do get some help along our journey into full empowerment. We certainly receive help from others who have matured and who can join with us in interdependent connections. If we are open to it, help may come in the form of the love of our life. This is the sacred relationship Debra described and it can be the most invigorating and intense experience we ever know. By the time we are ready for a sacred relationship, we have released many of the hurts and fears that previously blocked or impeded us from reaching deep, intimate love. The sacred relationship cleanses us of any negativity or fear which remains.

A sacred relationship is the final exam that tests us in the ultimate love and empowerment lesson. We see at least five purposes of sacred relationships: (1) they teach us to connect fully on *all* levels -- physical, emotional, intellectual and spiritual; (2) they cleanse us of any residual fears or unhealed wounds; (3) they mirror the "Divine Feminine" and "Divine Masculine" and help us incorporate and balance both within us; (4) they test our empowerment -- our attainment of self-actualization; and (5) they teach us about Divine Love.

1. Sacred Relationships teach us to connect fully on all levels -- physical, emotional, intellectual and spiritual.

One of the primary difficulties in achieving *Sacred Relationships* is that people are expected to pass the ultimate test of finding and maintaining true love without being able to observe models of how to do this. How many long-married couples do you know who are happy, in love, energetic, vital, and growing toward self-actualization? At the beginning of a romantic relationship, there is excitement and joy as each partner tries to please the other. But time tempers the love and excitement, and

307

eventually one or both partners tire of putting their best foot forward. The day arrives when romance dies and the couple settles into a codependent ritual. Eventually they grow bored or irritable with one another. They begin to engage in power plays and the mutual massaging of each other's weaknesses and neediness. Hope and commitment are replaced by acceptance and quiet desperation. Encouragement to explore, to strive, to grow, if ever present in the relationship, either becomes a battle or comes to an end.

The *sacred relationship* involves two whole individuals who are ready to connect fully on *all* levels: emotional, physical, intellectual, and spiritual. It's the all inclusive and complete nature of the connection that makes the sacred relationship so powerful. With no walls or barriers, there simply is no place left for each partner's fears and weaknesses to hide. Opportunities for and expectations of vulnerability, truth, and intimacy exist in this relationship at an intense level not experienced outside a sacred relationship.

Here are two people, totally open and vulnerable to each other, who insist there be no hidden recesses, fears, or hurts, to create barriers. There is only complete honesty, acceptance and belongingness. It is this total honesty and openness that serves up the ultimate test of one's empowerment. Having committed to move beyond the control of ego, fear, and lower emotions, these partners must forcefully confront and work through any remaining obstacles to a full and complete connection. In codependence, fear and control rob empowerment from both partners. In the sacred relationship, both are already empowered and sufficient. As each mirrors and supports the growth of the partner, the union becomes exponentially more powerful until it models the essence of Divine Love.

When people are ready for a sacred relationship,

308

neediness is not the glue of their attraction. Readiness for a sacred relationship often arises after a person has given up hope of finding the right partner. Carl, a friend of ours, says he had concluded that all his relationships with women would continue to be shallow and temporary. "When I started feeling comfortable about being a bachelor, Rebecca showed up in my life," Carl laughed. From the first day, Carl knew Rebecca was different from the other women he had dated. She was just like him -- searching for truth, dedicated to self-growth, and comfortable living the single life. They didn't engage in the silly male-female games that aimed at trapping and controlling. Their's was an attraction of equals. Only equals can connect fully on the emotional, intellectual, spiritual, and sexual levels as true marriage partners.

Rebecca and Carl married within a year of meeting. In their mid-thirties when they met, they forged their relationship in the strength of maturity. The unresolved issues of young adulthood were behind them, so there were few barriers to their intimacy. During one of our weekend retreats, Carl asked us if there were a secret club for sacred relationships. The interdependent connections he had discovered during those few days had surprised him. He hadn't believed that people, and strangers at that, could be so open, truthful, and connected with each other. Carl was also excited that what he and Rebecca experienced in their relationship was not an illusion -- that it was real and there was a name for it. In a sense, the club Carl asked about is real. It exists automatically whenever those developed enough to join heart, mind, body and soul meet. The sacred relationship is the reward for living in truth and following our inner urge to grow into full empowerment.

2. Sacred relationships cleanse us of residual fears and unhealed wounds.

Sacred relationships bring with them a paradox: the greatest love and brightest light attract the greatest fear and darkest parts of our being. Empowered love is a sacred love -- one that stretches people to grow past any remaining fears and insecurities. As Debra found when George entered her life, her residual fears and wounds surfaced. As Michael likes to put it, "a sacred relationship reveals any neglected cobwebs in our emotional basement."

When the reward is high, the risks and effort required are often rigorous. The reward of a sacred relationship is the achievement of ideal human unity. We only get this reward when we're strong enough to stand in pure love and pure truth without the contaminating influence of fear.

A sacred relationship often comes after we have gone through a series of failed or unsatisfying relationships. We learn by our mistakes that something is wrong with relationships built on neediness and control. Donna learned on Valentine's Day that her relationship with Michael was still anchored in neediness and control. Her soul's message was, "Stand on your own two feet first and don't try to complete yourself in a relationship. Then and only then will you be ready for the deepest and most connected of all loves." When she found completeness within herself, she was able to cut the strings of neediness and codependency. Each partner in a sacred relationship must be self-sufficient and motivated to grow to his or her ultimate potential. Through the mirroring of issues and lessons, sacred relationship partners are purged of any unresolved fears and unhealed emotional wounds.

3. Sacred Relationships mirror, integrate, and balance the Divine Feminine and Divine Masculine within us.

Carl Jung, the psychoanalyst, borrowed from Greek mythology and Eastern philosophy when he described the masculine (animus) and feminine (anima) aspects of the person. On reflection, it is easy to see the more developed a person is, the more balanced is the anima and animus within his or her personality make-up. The sacred relationship provides a mechanism for facilitating and achieving this balance. Those in codependent relationship are too consumed playing the roles of the one-down, needy child and the one-up, big parent to be open to new learning opportunities. It is different for the partners in a sacred relationship. Having progressed past fear and need to control, sacred relationship partners are open to learning from each other and from the opportunities presented to them in life. Their ultimate goal is to reach unity -- a perfect heart and soul connection. They are like one soul that has taken up residence in two bodies -- there is no resistance to joining and becoming One. It is expected.

The anima and animus are also called the Divine Feminine and the Divine Masculine. While the characteristics of each type are not gender-specific, men generally display more Divine Masculine qualities and women generally display more Divine Feminine qualities. The qualities typically attributed to each are listed below:

Divine Masculine	Divine Feminine
* assertive	* receptive
* goal oriented	* other oriented
* forceful	* passive
* closed boundaries	* open boundaries
* rational	* emotional
* selfish	* selfless
* ego-centered	* nurturing

* competitive	* connecting
* logical	* intuitive
* power-oriented	* people-oriented
* responsible	* dependent
* focused	* flexible
*autonomous	* joining

It is obvious from this list that some of the imbalances we've discussed in this book (e.g., selfishness vs. selflessness, emotional vs. intellectual, open vs. closed boundaries, etc.) can be found firmly rooted in the feminine and masculine archetypes. What would it be like if the two were balanced? That seems to be an important part of our evolution as human beings -- and a major goal for each of us as we live out our lives.

What would a person, male or female, look like who had achieved a healthy balancing of their masculine and feminine energies? Such a person would:

* maintain appropriately open *or* closed boundaries, depending on the persons or situations they encounter;

* be sensitive to his or her own needs and feelings, as well as to the needs and feelings of others;

* own responsibility when appropriate and allow others to own responsibility that is rightfully theirs;

* maintain a disciplined and focused, yet spontaneous and whimsical approach to life;

* stay grounded in the rational, but uplifted by the intuitive;

* balance selflessness and selfishness;

* focus on accomplishments while remaining receptive to guidance and opportunities;

* be assertive in standing for righteousness and justice, while maintaining a humbleness associated with service;

* integrate mind and heart; standing self-sufficient yet able to connect deeply.

These balanced Divine Masculine/Divine Feminine traits are rarely found except in the most advanced humans. They are our goals. Acknowledging and overcoming the fears that keep us from becoming these traits are our work. It is the Sacred Relationship that offers us both the opportunities and the support we need to smoothly integrate the two sides of a wholly developed person.

4. Sacred Relationships test our attainment of self- actualization.

In Chapter Nine, we explained that people growing in empowerment become increasingly more internally oriented. Empowerment means releasing and letting go of the external rules and shoulds imposed on us by the world. Empowerment is the journey inward to find our own truth. As we move along the inward path toward empowerment, we find ourselves increasingly guided by our own inner truths, inner knowings, and steadfast moral principles. We become less and less influenced by outside forces. People and circumstances lose their power to define our perspective on life.

Maslow calls the most empowered people *self-actualized*. Self-actualized people have struggled on that difficult path inward and have completed the process of full empowerment outlined in previous chapters. They are able to connect fully with those who have at least matured to the level of interdependence.

313

Self-actualized people display the following characteristics:

* they are able to discern the developmental levels motives of others;

* they understand their own motivations, biases and defense mechanisms;

* they embrace both the positive and negative qualities in themselves and others without judgment or guilt;

* they have conquered most, if not all, of their inhibiting fears;

* they react to others in an authentic and spontaneous manner;

* they are emotionally developed and understand their own and others' feelings;

* they focus on service and growth rather than ego satisfaction;

* they are internally oriented and are not heavily influenced by external expectations or forces;

* they are independent and self-reflective;

* they are intrigued by life's complexities;

* they have high moral values of justice, fairness, compassion, and love;

* they connect deeply and truthfully with others who are

capable of interdependent relationships;

* they decide for themselves what is right and wrong and ascribe to a higher power for guidance;

* they find humor and joy in life, yet take life seriously;

* they have a need to create and have the capacity to be visionary leaders;

* they avoid simple and judgmental thinking and would rather see the many sides of complex issues;

* they value spiritual maturity and place value in their personal life mission.

Sacred relationship partners will exhibit many, if not most, of these qualities and will be working on those they have yet to master.

5. *Sacred Relationships Challenge Partners to Learn about Divine Love.*

During the course of completing their tunnel work, most people come to a point where they feel compelled to offer up their fears to something higher than themselves. For us, letting go of fears and control meant an increased faith in God and a growing faith in the existence of a divine plan for our lives. Indeed, a successful transit through one's emotional basement, using truth as a scouring pad to cleanse and polish one's deepest and most troubling dark spots, requires faith. We are not necessarily talking about religious faith, for many religions subject the person to a one-down relationship with their God. The differential between God and any human being is totally obvious, using any scale or criterion you care to choose. So when we say the individual must meet God as an adult, we are not saying as equals. We are simply

315

saying that it does not serve one well to play victim and poor-me for anyone, even God. Confidence in one's self, even before the Creator of All Things is not the same thing as arrogance. Self-respect and self-love are quite compatible with humility. If we are serious about growing and becoming fully empowered, we must own our own power.

It is our belief that God expects us to grow so that we fully manifest the God-part that lies within each one of us. Certainly, God expects us to own and proudly display our inner divinity so that it shines brightly outward, healing and reassuring all whom we meet along the path of life. The faith that is required for tunnel work is the unflinching faith that we are part of the Divine, and that regardless of what mistakes we make, we are and always will be loved by our Creator. Mistakes are how we learn and it is through our intent that we are ultimately measured. We must go forward in faith, and trust that all that we need to make the transit through our deepest fears and self-imposed limitations will be provided.

It's this foundation in faith that allows us to give ourselves completely to a Sacred Partner. We know even though we become one with our partner, we have lost nothing of our own identity. We have only gained. We are no longer alone. For the first time in our lives, we know and we feel real love. Couples connected in this manner form the only true marriage, and such marriages are rare upon the face of the Earth.

With such a joining, comes yet another reason for happiness and joy -- the revealing of the couples' life work and divine purpose. Because they are attuned to divine inner guidance, Sacred Partners are mutually aware of their joint purpose In humbleness, twin-flame partners do not boast of achievement, for they know they did not earn this love. Divine Love is a *gift* offered only when two are ready to receive the gift

316

and use it to accomplish their life mission -- to serve as emissaries of Love.

Epilogue

Susan had been quiet during the group therapy session. Cathy observed for awhile and then decided to ask Susan if something were wrong. "Susan, you seem to be sad. Am I right? Is something bothering you?"

Donna knew that Susan was disturbed because she had called earlier in the week and said that she was having anxiety attacks, was waking every night at 3:00 a.m., and was then unable to fall back to sleep.

I'm disturbed, but I don't know why. There's nothing specific. It's just that my life seems to be slipping away from me. I seem to be always on the outside looking in. I don't know how to talk with people. I feel much more comfortable listening to others than I do sharing my own thoughts and feelings. People tell me I stand back and analyze them and that makes them uncomfortable. Why can't I be more like you, Cathy? You're open and comfortable with people." Susan dabbed at the tears that seemed more a response to self-frustration than sadness.

"Don't use me as a model for connecting with others," Cathy responded. "I've been trained to be the consummate caretaker. I know how to be in the one-up, nurturing parent role. But I'm having stress attacks about committing to Danny. I really love him. He's willing to look at himself and do the work to learn to connect with me. He's the first man I've met who has the potential to connect with me on a deep level -- and I'm scared to death of him. Because the potential for love is so great, the potential for hurt is great. I keep thinking about my parents and how unhappy they were with each other -- even though they stayed together for a lifetime. Suppose Danny and I end up that way. Maybe we'll stop working at connecting and loving each other. Connecting and committing to another person petrifies

319

me."

Susan and Cathy are on the psychospiritual path to love, intimacy and happiness. They're at different points in their journeys to sacred relationships. Susan grew up in a child-centered environment with the parents passing their unfulfilled hopes and dreams on to their four children. Susan knew that something wasn't right in her family, but she didn't know to label the dysfunction as codependency. Her parents needed the security of control over their children. Their importance was secured by doling out affection and attention to the children in small doses. The children's reward for conforming and achieving was the distinction of being mother's or father's favorite child. The children came to see love as an expendable commodity. If one child got a parent's love and attention, the others were ignored.

Susan's siblings were compared and pitted against each other. There was much ridicule and judgment coming from both parents and children. Of course, the comparisons resulted in jealousy and competitiveness among the siblings. As adults, they still compete and often find themselves estranged from each other. Susan's way of surviving in this competitive and critical family was to be perfect. High achievement in school and church earned her parental praise. Her academic prowess was unchallenged by her brother and sisters. But now in adulthood, Susan doesn't have school success to buffer her ego. She feels like a failure because she hasn't done anything extraordinary with her life. She had learned early in life that she secured love by "doing." Now that she isn't earning accolades for achievement, she feels unimportant and unlovable.

Susan has a grown son from her one marriage which soured early. She was involved with a succession of men after her divorce, but none of them measured up to Susan's standards. Now she feels alone, unhappy and unable to affect much positive change in her life.

Donna saw Susan as aloof and believed she was ready for honest feedback about her habit of pushing others away. "Susan, you do stand back and analyze people. Your parents taught you not to trust others. After all, other people are likely to judge and criticize you the way your family members did each other. Your fear is keeping you from connecting with others."

Susan had a scowl on her face when she faced Donna with her reply. "But my parents were good people. They did as well as they knew how to do. I feel defensive when you criticize them."

Donna's response was soft and understanding. "I know they were very good people and I know they loved you a lot. But they weren't developed enough to teach you a most important life skill -- how to connect in love and truth with other people. They taught you about control and self-protection. Your family isolated themselves from others. You were dependent on them for social and financial support well into your forties. Your siblings have gone through multiple divorces each, and they're still not happy. Susan, your family isn't unusual - they're the norm. Very few people are taught to trust and talk and feel. They don't really know how to love and they are unable to connect. But most people are unaware of their deficits in loving and connecting. Most are only vaguely aware of their dissatisfaction with near-miss connections. They believe what they have is about as good as it gets. You, however, are smart enough and hopeful enough to know that something better is possible."

"Well, I did know that my relationships in the past were superficial. I only fell into one codependent marriage and I've forgiven myself for that because I was just a kid at the time. I couldn't lie to myself about my feelings about those other men I dated. Several asked me to marry them, and I just couldn't bring myself to do it. I guess my intuition kept me from falling into dependent and needy relationship traps. But when will I finally be ready to join with an equal partner?" Susan had spent years in therapy before she came to Donna for counseling. She now believes she didn't get anywhere with her former counselor, but she's paid her dues and now she wants a pay-off.

Donna encouraged Susan to give herself credit for the progress she'd made thus far. "Susan, I see you at the stage of Interdependency. You've already recognized your selflessness and have done a lot to balance it with doses of self-love. You've tackled your codependent caretaker role and you now know how to take care of yourself. You've stepped away from the demeaning and controlling games that your family members still play. You've demanded honesty and openness with your siblings and with your son. You've gone through the pain and anger of being left by your husband. And you've learned to open up and share your feelings with group members. I believe you're now working on trusting yourself. When you can trust yourself to accurately discern the motives and developmental levels of others, you'll be ready for true and deep connections with other mature people. You've learned to trust your group members because you see them clearly and know that they are loving people. Your ability to judge those who are ready to join with you in mature relationships will increase. You seem to be on the brink of readiness for true connecting."

"She's right, Susan. You've grown tremendously in your ability to be open and share with us in the group," added Cathy. "I also learned who I could trust and who was ready for a relationship -- and who wasn't ready. I made friends with some wonderful people. Then Danny came along. My fear of intimacy rose up and I tried to push him away. But we're still together after two years and we're both working hard on an intimate and lasting relationship. I believe the right man is around the corner and you're just polishing your readiness for a deep and intimate relationship."

Susan reflected on the progress she had made during the last few months. She was able to talk openly with group members. Previously, she kept her thoughts and feelings locked inside. She had taken risks to tell them the secret and embarrassing things that once froze her in fear and humiliation. They responded in love. She had even lost twenty pounds and felt younger and more attractive than she had in years. A smile affirmed her satisfaction with herself.

Sacred Relationships: The Psychospiritual Path to Love, Intimacy and Happiness gives us a blueprint for ridding ourselves of the impediments to true love connections. We need to scrutinize our selfless/selfish imbalance, consider our codependent patterns, and free ourselves of the repressed emotions and fears that hold us captive. We must learn to see ourselves clearly and to discern the maturational levels of others. Then -- we're ready for interdependent connecting with others who are also committed to emotional, intellectual, and spiritual self-actualization. When we're ready, a sacred relationship will present itself to us. Any residual fears and neediness will surface as we face the possibility of true connection and deep love.

Some people may be able to travel the psychospiritual path by themselves, but for most people companions are not only welcome -- they're essential. Group therapy is one way to meet and gain support from others who are traveling the path to self-actualization and true heart connections. *Sacred Relationship Seminars and Retreats* are also available for those who would like to meet others on the psychospiritual path to true human unity.

References

Beattie, Melody. *Codependent No More.* New York: Harper & Row Publishers, Inc., 1987.

Beattie, Melody. *Beyond Codependency.* New York: Harper & Row Publishers, Inc., 1989.

Carlson, Richard and Benjamin Shield. *Healers on Healing.* Los Angeles, California: Jeremy P. Tarcher, Inc., 1989.

Cloud, Henry and John Townsend. *Boundaries: When to Say Yes, When to Say No to Take Control of Your Life.* Grand Rapids, Michigan: Zondervan Publishing House, 1992.

Desteian, John. *Coming Together - Coming Apart: The Union of Opposites in Love Relationships.* Boston, Massachusetts: SIGO Press, 1989.

Forward, Susan. *Toxic Parents: Overcoming Their Hurtful Legacy and Reclaiming Your Life.* New York: Bantam Books, 1989.

Fromm, Erich. *The Art of Loving.* New York: Harper & Row Publisher, 1956.

Gorman, Margaret. Psychology and Religion: A Reader. New York: Paulist Press, 1985.

Hendricks, Gay and Kathlyn Hendricks. *Conscious Loving.* New York: Bantam Books, 1990.

Kubler-Ross, Elisabeth. *On Death and Dying.* New York: Macmillan Publishing Co., Inc., 1969.

Maslow, Abraham. *Toward a Psychology of Being.* New York: Van Nostrand Reinhold Company, 1968.

Mellody, Pia. *Facing Codependence.* New York: Harper & Row Publishers, 1989.

Moore, Thomas. *Care of the Soul.* New York: HarperCollins Publishers, 1994.

Redfield, James. *The Celestine Prophecy.* New York: Warner Books, Inc., 1993.

Rubin, Lillian. *Intimate Strangers: Men and Women Together.* New York: Harper Colophon Books, 1983.

Satir, Virginia. *Peoplemaking.* Palo Alto, California: Science and Behavior Books, Inc., 1972.

Satir, Virginia. *The New Peoplemaking.* Mountain View, California: Science and Behavior Books, Inc., 1988.

Schaef, Anne Wilson. *Beyond Therapy, Beyond Science: A New Model for Healing the Whole Person.* New York: HarperCollins Publishers, 1992.

Sylvest, Vernon. *The Formula: Who Gets Sick, Who Gets Well, Who is Unhappy, Who is Happy and Why.* Fairfield, Iowa: Sunstar Publishing, Ltd., 1996.

Wegscheider, Sharon. *Another Chance: Hope & Health for the Alcoholic Family.* Palo Alto, California: Science and Behavior Books, Inc., 1981.

Wegscheider-Cruse, Sharon. *Choice-Making.* Pompano Beach, Florida: Health Communications, Inc., 1985.

Weiss, Brian. *Only Love is Real.* New York: Warner Books, 1996.

Welwood, John. *Journey of the Heart.* New York: Harper Collins Publishers, 1996.

Williamson, Marianne. *A Return to Love.* New York: HarperCollins Publishers, 1992.

Woititz, Janet. *Marriage on the Rocks.* Pompano Beach, Florida: Health Communications, Inc., 1979.

Woititz, Janet and Alan Garner. *Lifeskills for Adult Children.* Deerfield Beach, Florida: Health Communications, Inc., 1990.

About the Authors

Dr. Donna Boone and **Dr. Michael McDonald** are a husband-wife team who have combined their many years of psychotherapy and university experience to form **Psychotherapy and Educational Services**, whose goal is to promote healthy interpersonal relationships among individuals in the home and workplace.

With over 20 years each as a psychotherapist and professor, both believed that psychotherapy and organizational training lacked an essential ingredient -- attention to the spiritual impetus of growth and self-actualization. Having experienced the powerful experience of their own spiritual transformations, they incorporated theirs and their clients experiences in writing **Sacred Relationships: The Psychospiritual Path to Love, Intimacy and Happiness.**

They conduct Sacred Relationship seminars in major U.S. cities and retreats at Healing Waters Center in the Shenandoah mountains of Virginia. The **Sacred Relationships Workbook** was developed for use in the retreats and includes many self and partner psychotherapeutic assessment instruments that help guide individuals, couples and families in their emotional and spiritual growth.

You may contact Drs. Boone and McDonald at the following mail, phone, fax, and internet addresses:

Psychotherapy & Educational Services
10507 Mountainbrook Court
Richmond, Virginia 23233

1-800-811-2341   fax: 804-282-5946
e-mail: sacred@mindspring.com

Readers may also be interested in related P&ES products and services:

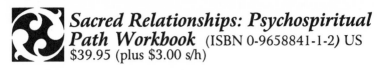

Sacred Relationships: Psychospiritual Path Workbook (ISBN 0-9658841-1-2) US $39.95 (plus $3.00 s/h)

This practical guide was developed by Dr. Boone and Dr. McDonald for use in their *Sacred Relationship Weekend Retreat Workshops*. It has been compared to six months of intense psychotherapy.

The self and partner assessment instruments and introspective exercises lend insight and objectivity to your search for personal growth and human unity. Scoring services and psychotherapeutic reports are included in the price of the workbook. An economical way to obtain professional therapeutic information about your psychospiritual development and needs.

Sacred Relationships Seminars and Weekend Retreats

Sacred Relationships Seminars and *Sacred Relationship Retreat Workshops* are held in major U.S. cities for singles, couples, and families. Call for a schedule of the seminars planned for your region. Special sessions can be arranged for church or other groups.

Seminar fees: singles $200/couples $365. Weekend retreats are priced separately. Retreats are held at Healing Waters Center in the beautiful Shenandoah mountains of Virginia. Call for space availability for residential mountain retreat workshops.

To order books or request workshop registration or information:

Psychotherapy & Educational Services
10507 Mountainbrook Court
Richmond, Virginia 23233

1-800-811-2341   *fax: 804-282-5946*
e-mail: sacred@mindspring.com   *website: empowerlink.com*

VISA & MASTERCARD WELCOMED